STAR·WARS

LANDO

Double or Nothing

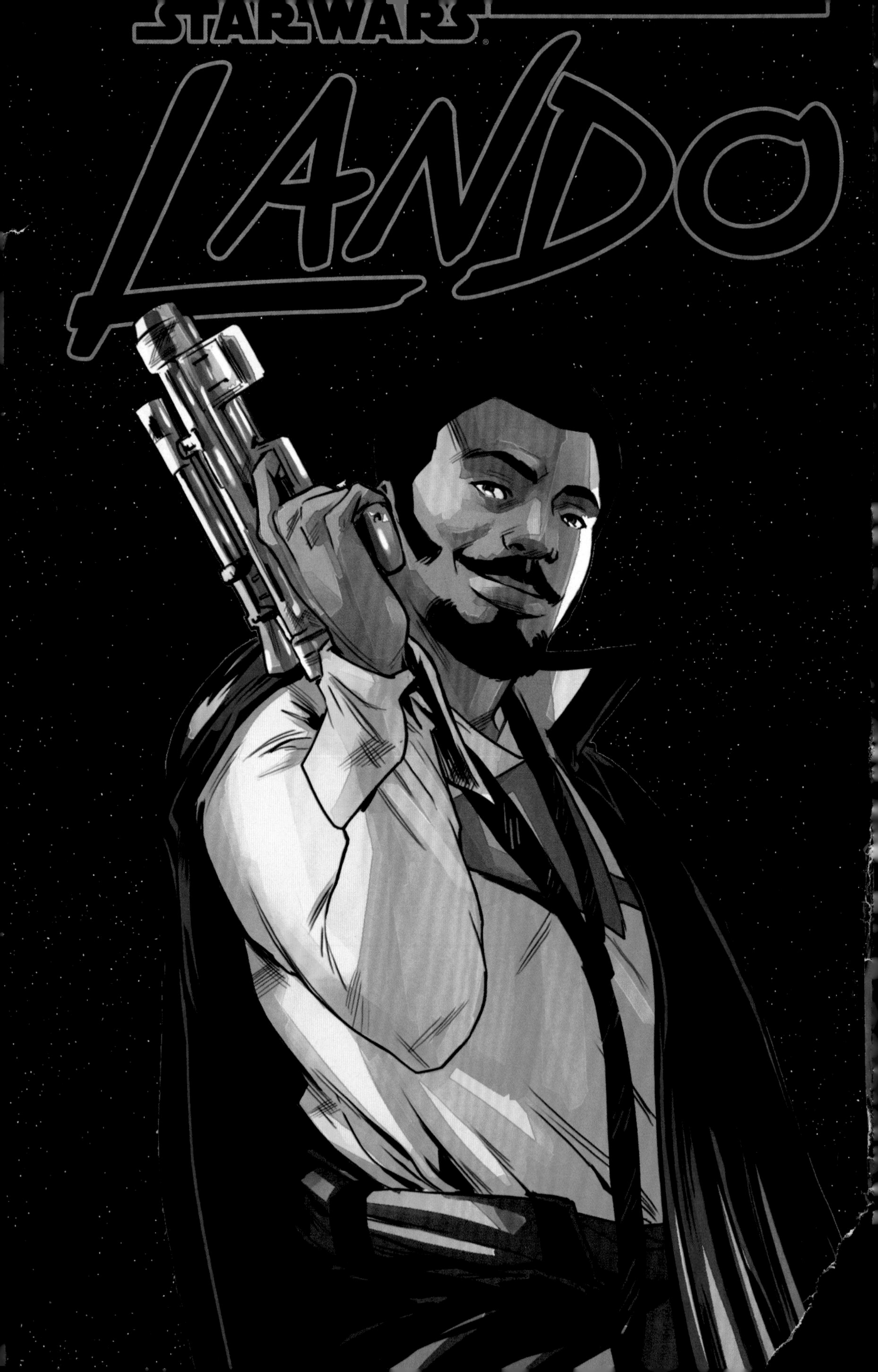
STAR WARS
LANDO

Double or Nothing

Writer	**RODNEY BARNES**
Artist	**PAOLO VILLANELLI**
Color Artist	**ANDRES MOSSA**
Letterer	**VC's JOE CARAMAGNA**
Cover Art	**SCOTT FORBES**
Assistant Editors	**HEATHER ANTOS & TOM GRONEMAN** with **EMILY NEWCOMEN**
Editors	**JORDAN D. WHITE & MARK PANICCIA**

Editor in Chief	**C.B. CEBULSKI**
Chief Creative Officer	**JOE QUESADA**
President	**DAN BUCKLEY**

For Lucasfilm:

Assistant Editor	**NICK MARTINO**
Senior Editor	**ROBERT SIMPSON**
Executive Editor	**JENNIFER HEDDLE**
Creative Director	**MICHAEL SIGLAIN**
Lucasfilm Story Group	**JAMES WAUGH, LELAND CHEE, MATT MARTIN**

Collection Editor	**JENNIFER GRÜNWALD**
Assistant Editor	**CAITLIN O'CONNELL**
Associate Managing Editor	**KATERI WOODY**
Editor, Special Projects	**MARK D. BEAZLEY**
VP Production & Special Projects	**JEFF YOUNGQUIST**
SVP Print, Sales & Marketing	**DAVID GABRIEL**
Book Designer	**ADAM DEL RE**

STAR WARS: LANDO — DOUBLE OR NOTHING. Contains material originally published in magazine form as STAR WARS: LANDO — DOUBLE OR NOTHING #1-5. First printing 2018. ISBN 978-1-302-91164-5. Published by MARVEL WORLDWIDE, INC., a subsidiary of MARVEL ENTERTAINMENT, LLC. OFFICE OF PUBLICATION: 135 West 50th Street, New York, NY 10020. **Printed in Canada.** DAN BUCKLEY, President, Marvel Entertainment; JOHN NEE, Publisher; JOE QUESADA, Chief Creative Officer; TOM BREVOORT, SVP of Publishing; DAVID BOGART, SVP of Business Affairs & Operations, Publishing & Partnership; DAVID GABRIEL, SVP of Sales & Marketing, Publishing; JEFF YOUNGQUIST, VP of Production & Special Projects; DAN CARR, Executive Director of Publishing Technology; ALEX MORALES, Director of Publishing Operations; DAN EDINGTON, Managing Editor; SUSAN CRESPI, Production Manager; STAN LEE, Chairman Emeritus. For information regarding advertising in Marvel Comics or on Marvel.com, please contact Vit DeBellis, Custom Solutions & Integrated Advertising Manager, at vdebellis@marvel.com. For Marvel subscription inquiries, please call 888-511-5480. **Manufactured between 8/31/2018 and 10/2/2018 by SOLISCO PRINTERS, SCOTT, QC, CANADA.**

10 9 8 7 6 5 4 3 2 1

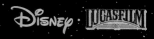

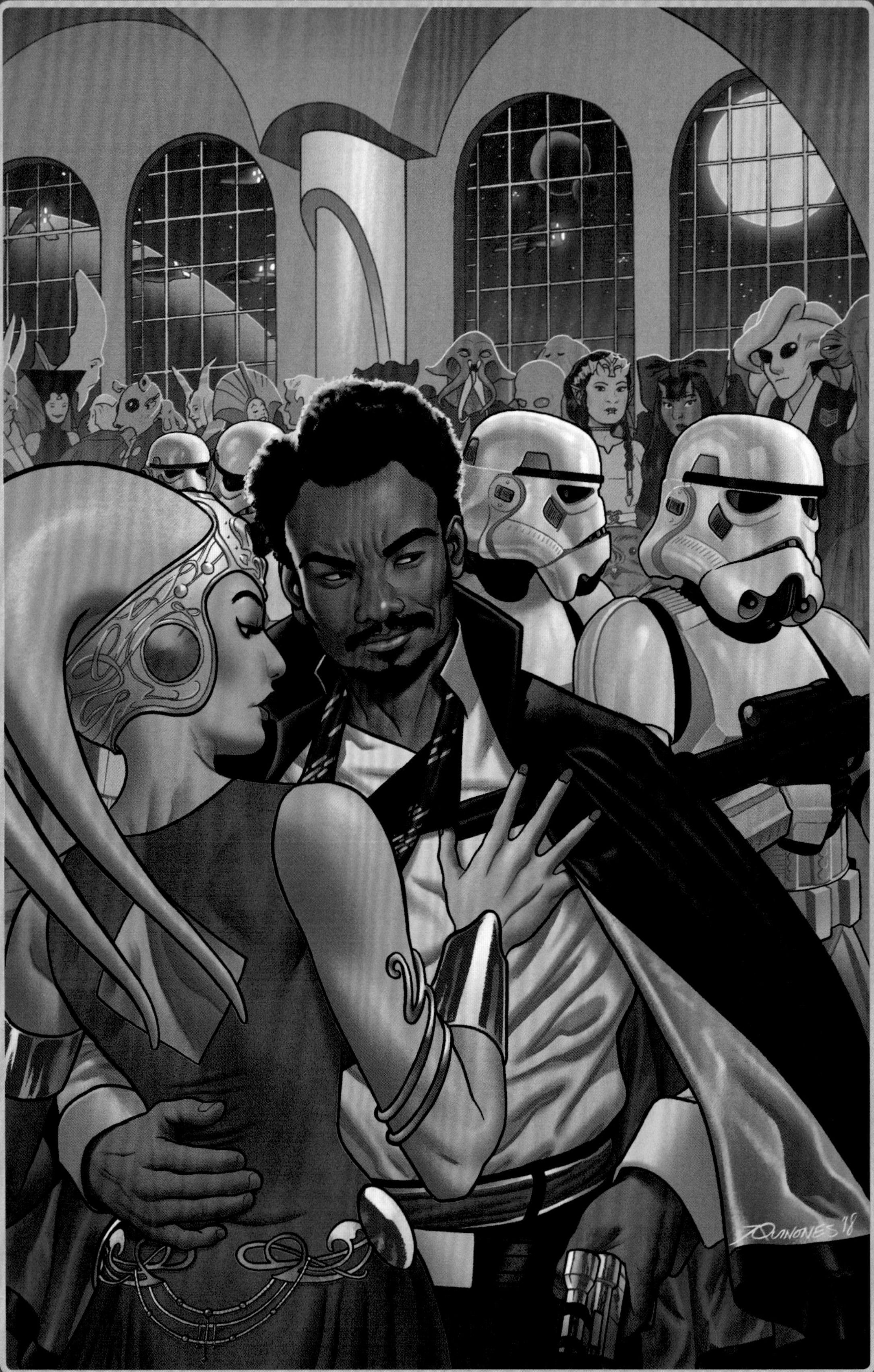

***STAR WARS: LANDO — DOUBLE OR NOTHING* 1 Variant by**
JOE QUINONES

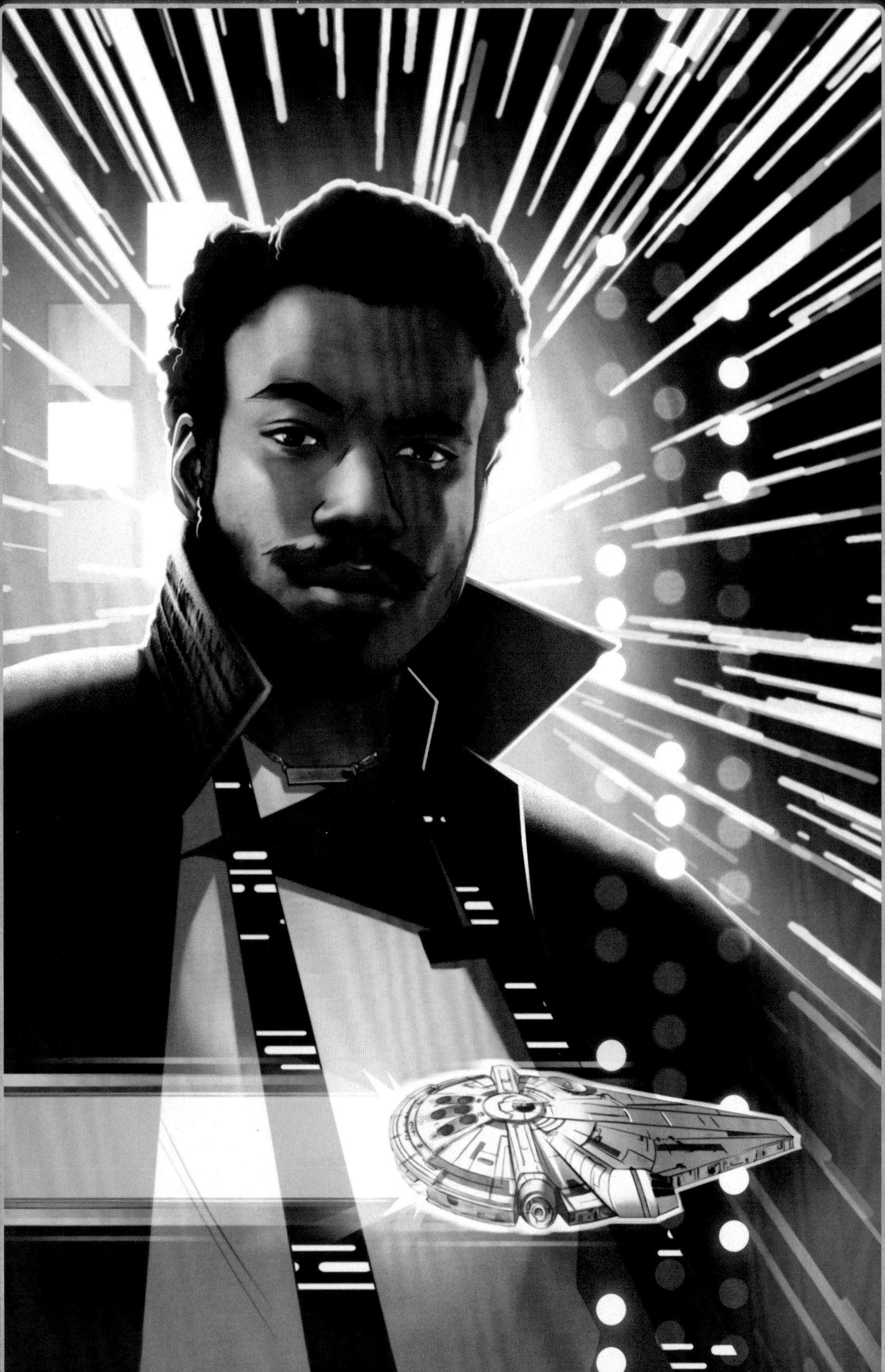

1

STAR WARS

LANDO

Double or Nothing

A long time ago in a galaxy far, far away....

The Galactic Empire grips the various star systems in a stranglehold of repression. But there is still hope — for the criminals who seek to profit under the new regime!

LANDO CALRISSIAN, the "greatest smuggler in the galaxy" and captain of the *Millennium Falcon*, lives for the big score — especially if it's at the roll of the dice. And nothing will ever get between Lando and his fortune and glory....

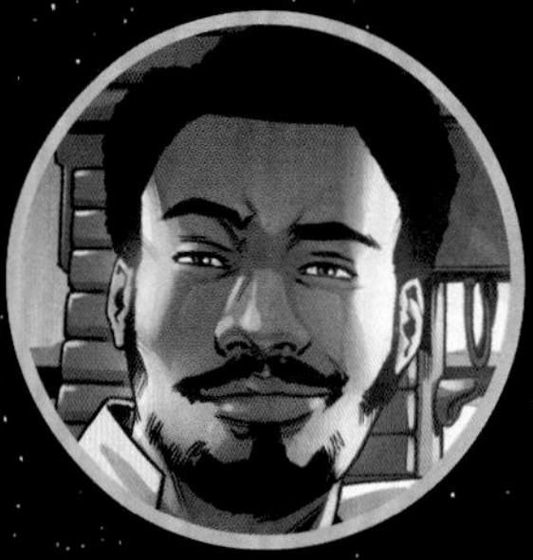

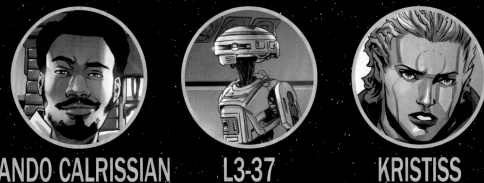

LANDO CALRISSIAN

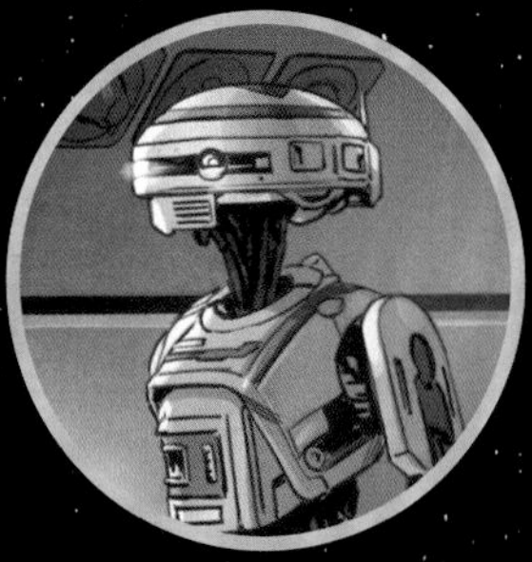

L3-37

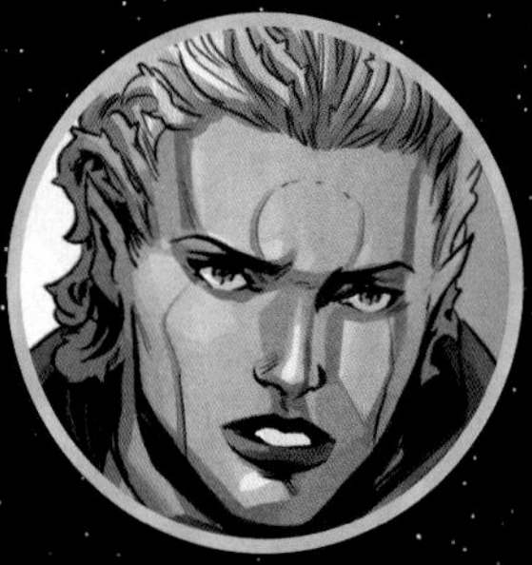

KRISTISS

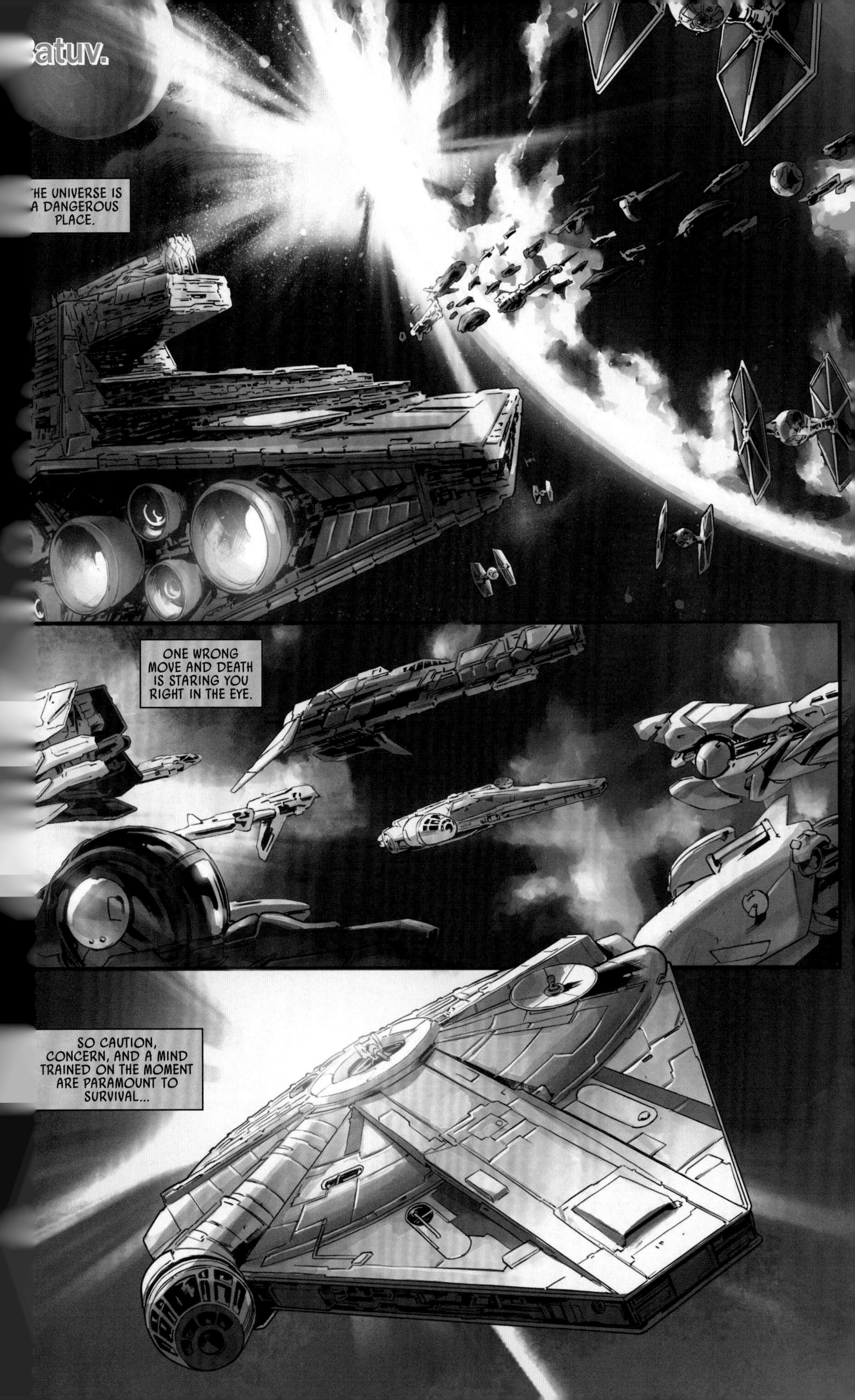

THE UNIVERSE IS A DANGEROUS PLACE.
ONE WRONG MOVE AND DEATH IS STARING YOU RIGHT IN THE EYE.
SO CAUTION, CONCERN, AND A MIND TRAINED ON THE MOMENT ARE PARAMOUNT TO SURVIVAL...

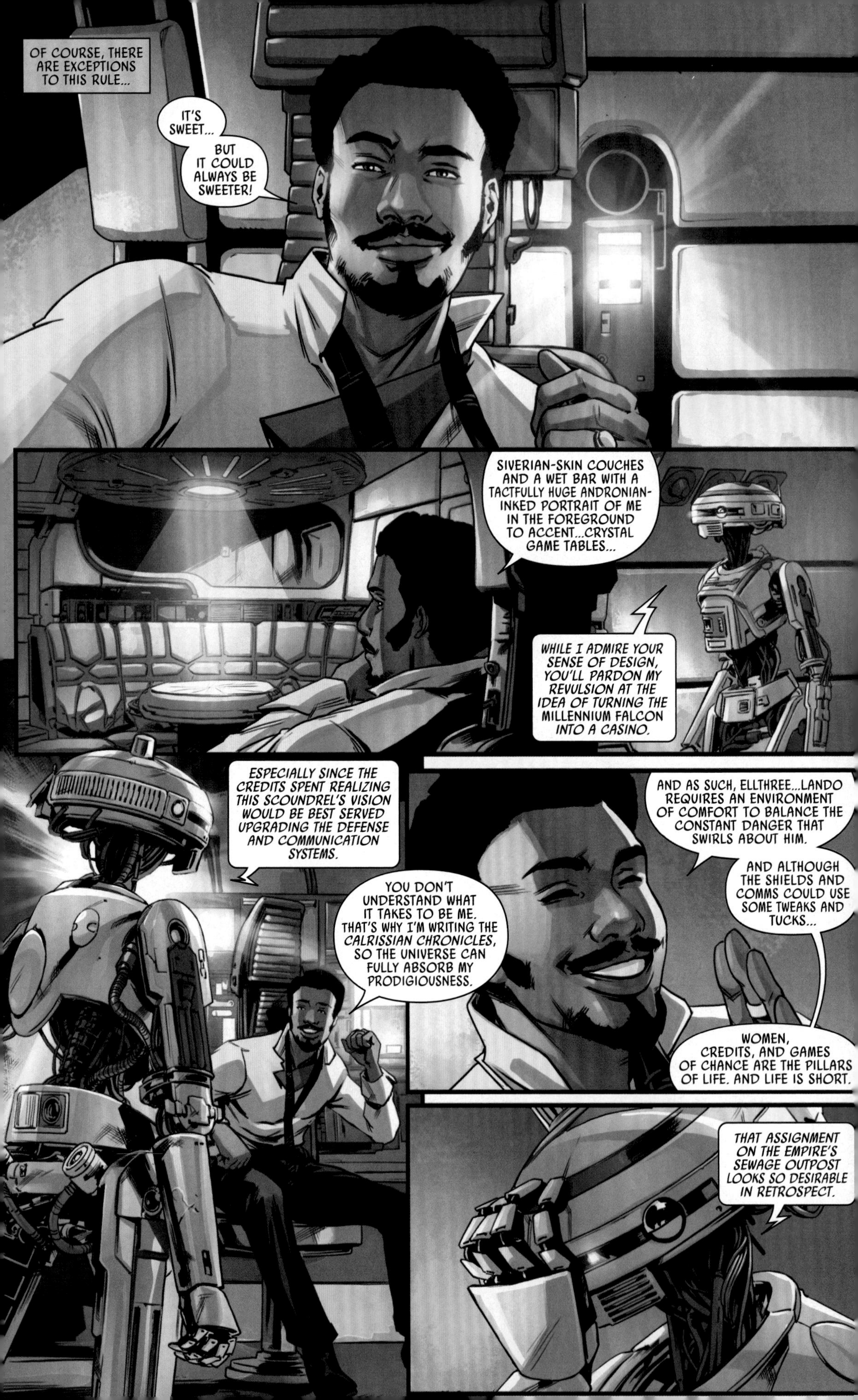
OF COURSE, THERE ARE EXCEPTIONS TO THIS RULE...
IT'S SWEET...
BUT IT COULD ALWAYS BE SWEETER!
SIVERIAN-SKIN COUCHES AND A WET BAR WITH A TACTFULLY HUGE ANDRONIAN-INKED PORTRAIT OF ME IN THE FOREGROUND TO ACCENT...CRYSTAL GAME TABLES...
WHILE I ADMIRE YOUR SENSE OF DESIGN, YOU'LL PARDON MY REVULSION AT THE IDEA OF TURNING THE MILLENNIUM FALCON INTO A CASINO.
ESPECIALLY SINCE THE CREDITS SPENT REALIZING THIS SCOUNDREL'S VISION WOULD BE BEST SERVED UPGRADING THE DEFENSE AND COMMUNICATION SYSTEMS.
YOU DON'T UNDERSTAND WHAT IT TAKES TO BE ME. THAT'S WHY I'M WRITING THE CALRISSIAN CHRONICLES, SO THE UNIVERSE CAN FULLY ABSORB MY PRODIGIOUSNESS.
AND AS SUCH, ELLTHREE...LANDO REQUIRES AN ENVIRONMENT OF COMFORT TO BALANCE THE CONSTANT DANGER THAT SWIRLS ABOUT HIM.
AND ALTHOUGH THE SHIELDS AND COMMS COULD USE SOME TWEAKS AND TUCKS...
WOMEN, CREDITS, AND GAMES OF CHANCE ARE THE PILLARS OF LIFE. AND LIFE IS SHORT.
THAT ASSIGNMENT ON THE EMPIRE'S SEWAGE OUTPOST LOOKS SO DESIRABLE IN RETROSPECT.

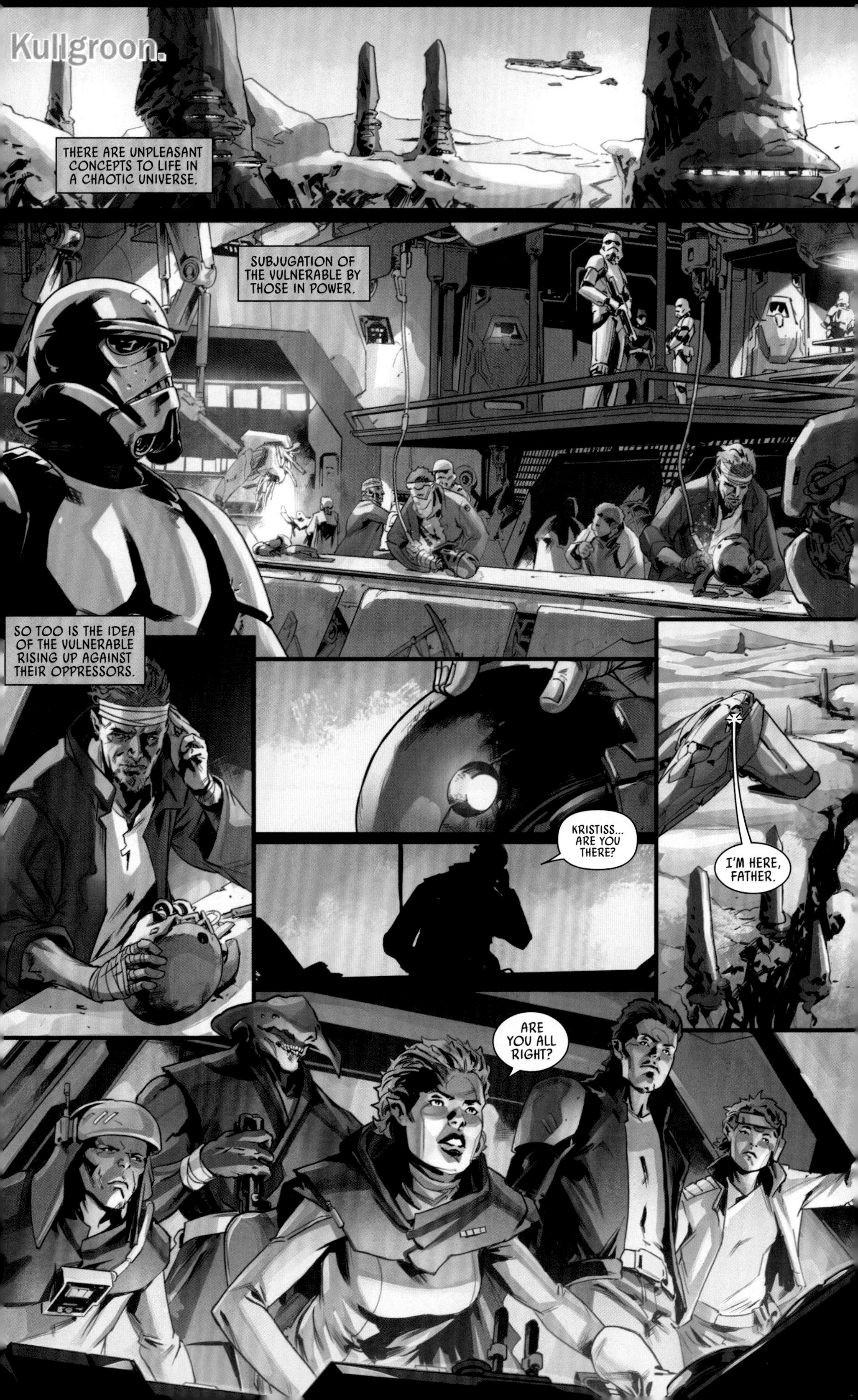
Kullgroon.
THERE ARE UNPLEASANT CONCEPTS TO LIFE IN A CHAOTIC UNIVERSE.
SUBJUGATION OF THE VULNERABLE BY THOSE IN POWER.
SO TOO IS THE IDEA OF THE VULNERABLE RISING UP AGAINST THEIR OPPRESSORS.
KRISTISS... ARE YOU THERE?
I'M HERE, FATHER.
ARE YOU ALL RIGHT?

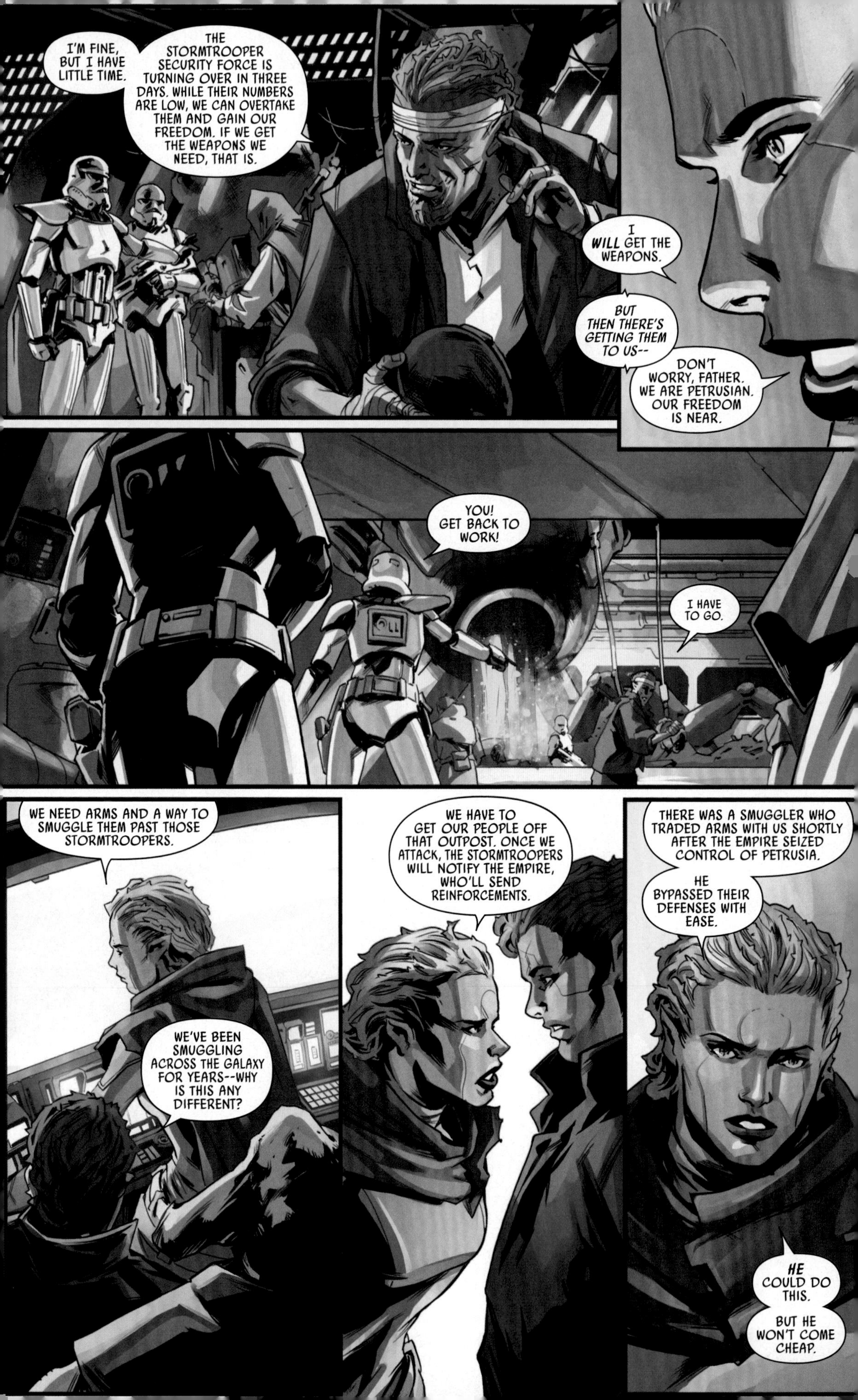
I'M FINE, BUT I HAVE LITTLE TIME.
THE STORMTROOPER SECURITY FORCE IS TURNING OVER IN THREE DAYS. WHILE THEIR NUMBERS ARE LOW, WE CAN OVERTAKE THEM AND GAIN OUR FREEDOM. IF WE GET THE WEAPONS WE NEED, THAT IS.
I WILL GET THE WEAPONS.
BUT THEN THERE'S GETTING THEM TO US--
DON'T WORRY, FATHER. WE ARE PETRUSIAN. OUR FREEDOM IS NEAR.
YOU! GET BACK TO WORK!
I HAVE TO GO.
WE NEED ARMS AND A WAY TO SMUGGLE THEM PAST THOSE STORMTROOPERS.
WE'VE BEEN SMUGGLING ACROSS THE GALAXY FOR YEARS--WHY IS THIS ANY DIFFERENT?
WE HAVE TO GET OUR PEOPLE OFF THAT OUTPOST. ONCE WE ATTACK, THE STORMTROOPERS WILL NOTIFY THE EMPIRE, WHO'LL SEND REINFORCEMENTS.
THERE WAS A SMUGGLER WHO TRADED ARMS WITH US SHORTLY AFTER THE EMPIRE SEIZED CONTROL OF PETRUSIA.
HE BYPASSED THEIR DEFENSES WITH EASE.
HE COULD DO THIS.
BUT HE WON'T COME CHEAP.

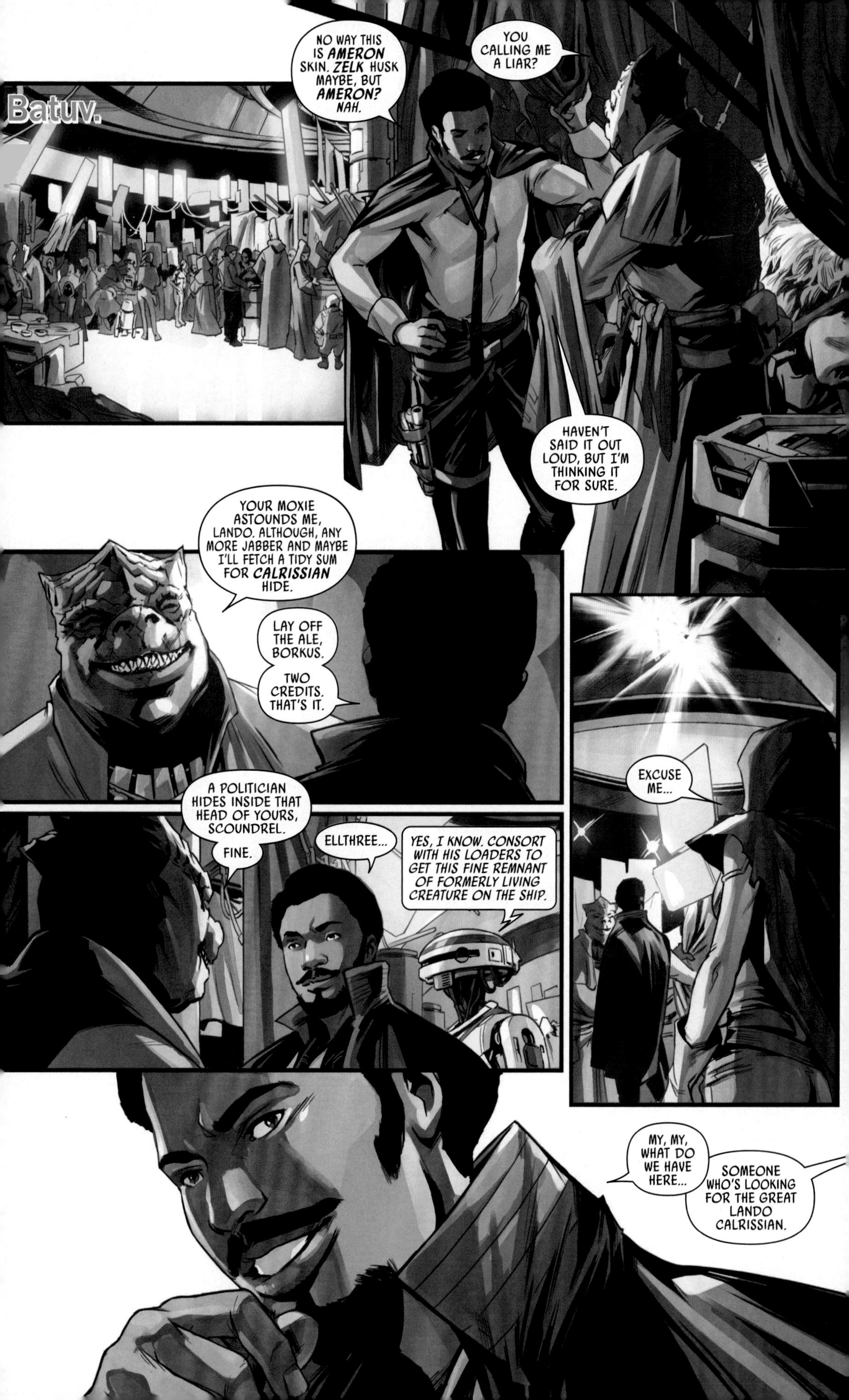
Batuv.
NO WAY THIS IS AMERON SKIN. ZELK HUSK MAYBE, BUT AMERON? NAH.
YOU CALLING ME A LIAR?
HAVEN'T SAID IT OUT LOUD, BUT I'M THINKING IT FOR SURE.
YOUR MOXIE ASTOUNDS ME, LANDO. ALTHOUGH, ANY MORE JABBER AND MAYBE I'LL FETCH A TIDY SUM FOR CALRISSIAN HIDE.
LAY OFF THE ALE, BORKUS.
TWO CREDITS. THAT'S IT.
A POLITICIAN HIDES INSIDE THAT HEAD OF YOURS, SCOUNDREL.
FINE.
ELLTHREE...
YES, I KNOW. CONSORT WITH HIS LOADERS TO GET THIS FINE REMNANT OF FORMERLY LIVING CREATURE ON THE SHIP.
EXCUSE ME...
MY, MY, WHAT DO WE HAVE HERE...
SOMEONE WHO'S LOOKING FOR THE GREAT LANDO CALRISSIAN.

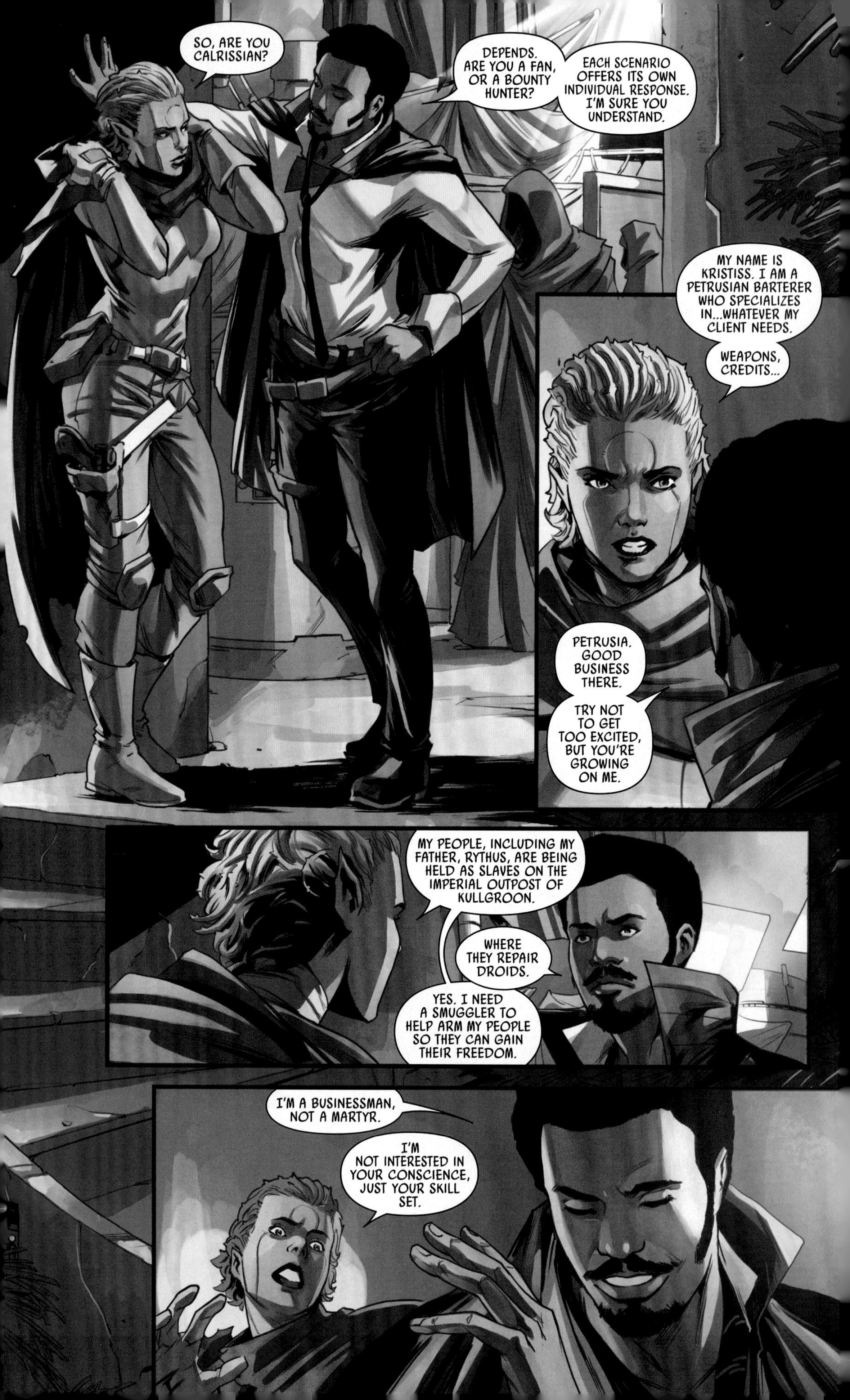
SO, ARE YOU CALRISSIAN?
DEPENDS. ARE YOU A FAN, OR A BOUNTY HUNTER?
EACH SCENARIO OFFERS ITS OWN INDIVIDUAL RESPONSE. I'M SURE YOU UNDERSTAND.
MY NAME IS KRISTISS. I AM A PETRUSIAN BARTERER WHO SPECIALIZES IN...WHATEVER MY CLIENT NEEDS.
WEAPONS, CREDITS...
PETRUSIA. GOOD BUSINESS THERE.
TRY NOT TO GET TOO EXCITED, BUT YOU'RE GROWING ON ME.
MY PEOPLE, INCLUDING MY FATHER, RYTHUS, ARE BEING HELD AS SLAVES ON THE IMPERIAL OUTPOST OF KULLGROON.
WHERE THEY REPAIR DROIDS.
YES. I NEED A SMUGGLER TO HELP ARM MY PEOPLE SO THEY CAN GAIN THEIR FREEDOM.
I'M A BUSINESSMAN, NOT A MARTYR.
I'M NOT INTERESTED IN YOUR CONSCIENCE, JUST YOUR SKILL SET.

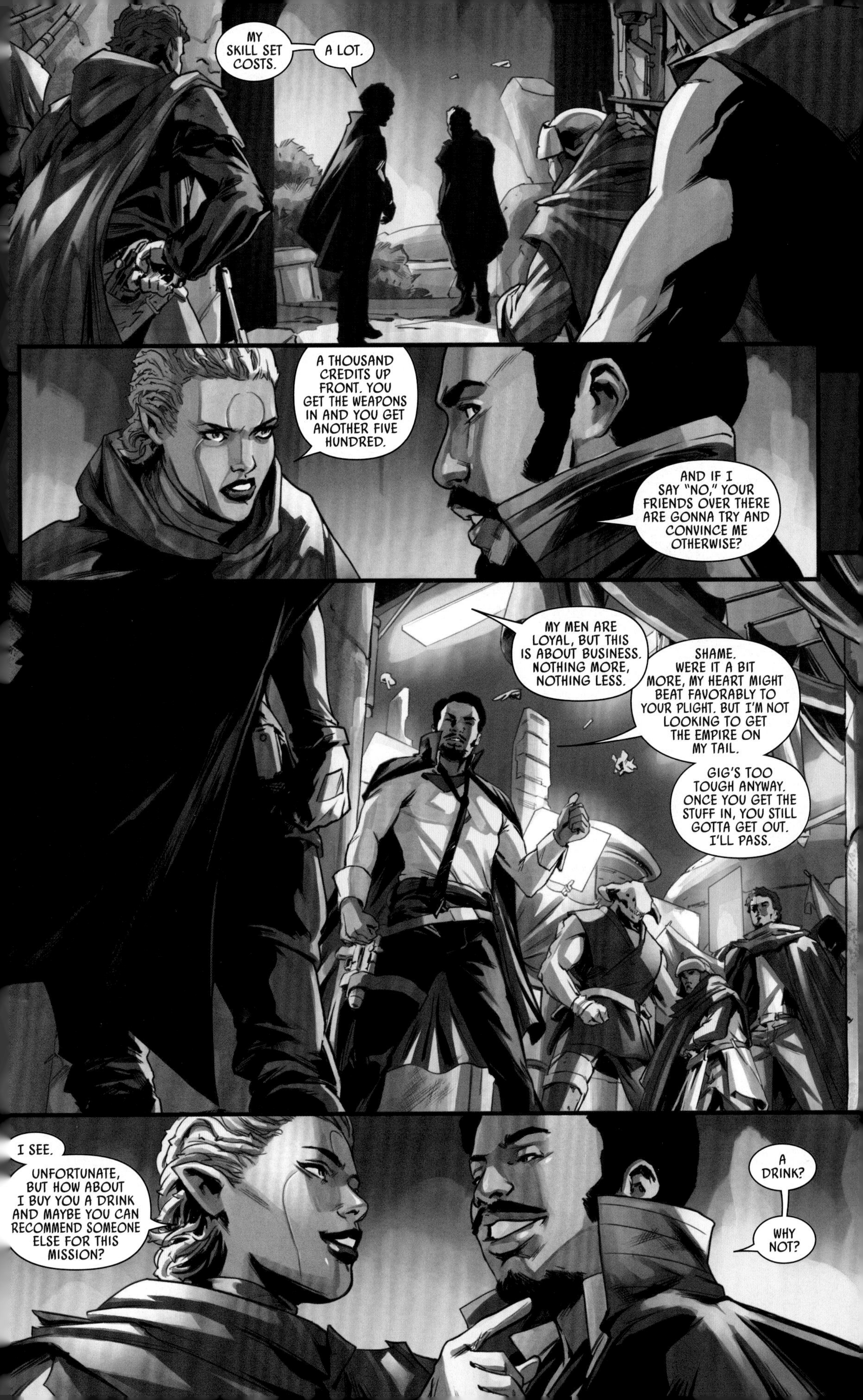
MY SKILL SET COSTS.
A LOT.
A THOUSAND CREDITS UP FRONT. YOU GET THE WEAPONS IN AND YOU GET ANOTHER FIVE HUNDRED.
AND IF I SAY "NO," YOUR FRIENDS OVER THERE ARE GONNA TRY AND CONVINCE ME OTHERWISE?
MY MEN ARE LOYAL, BUT THIS IS ABOUT BUSINESS. NOTHING MORE, NOTHING LESS.
SHAME. WERE IT A BIT MORE, MY HEART MIGHT BEAT FAVORABLY TO YOUR PLIGHT. BUT I'M NOT LOOKING TO GET THE EMPIRE ON MY TAIL.
GIG'S TOO TOUGH ANYWAY. ONCE YOU GET THE STUFF IN, YOU STILL GOTTA GET OUT. I'LL PASS.
I SEE.
UNFORTUNATE, BUT HOW ABOUT I BUY YOU A DRINK AND MAYBE YOU CAN RECOMMEND SOMEONE ELSE FOR THIS MISSION?
A DRINK?
WHY NOT?

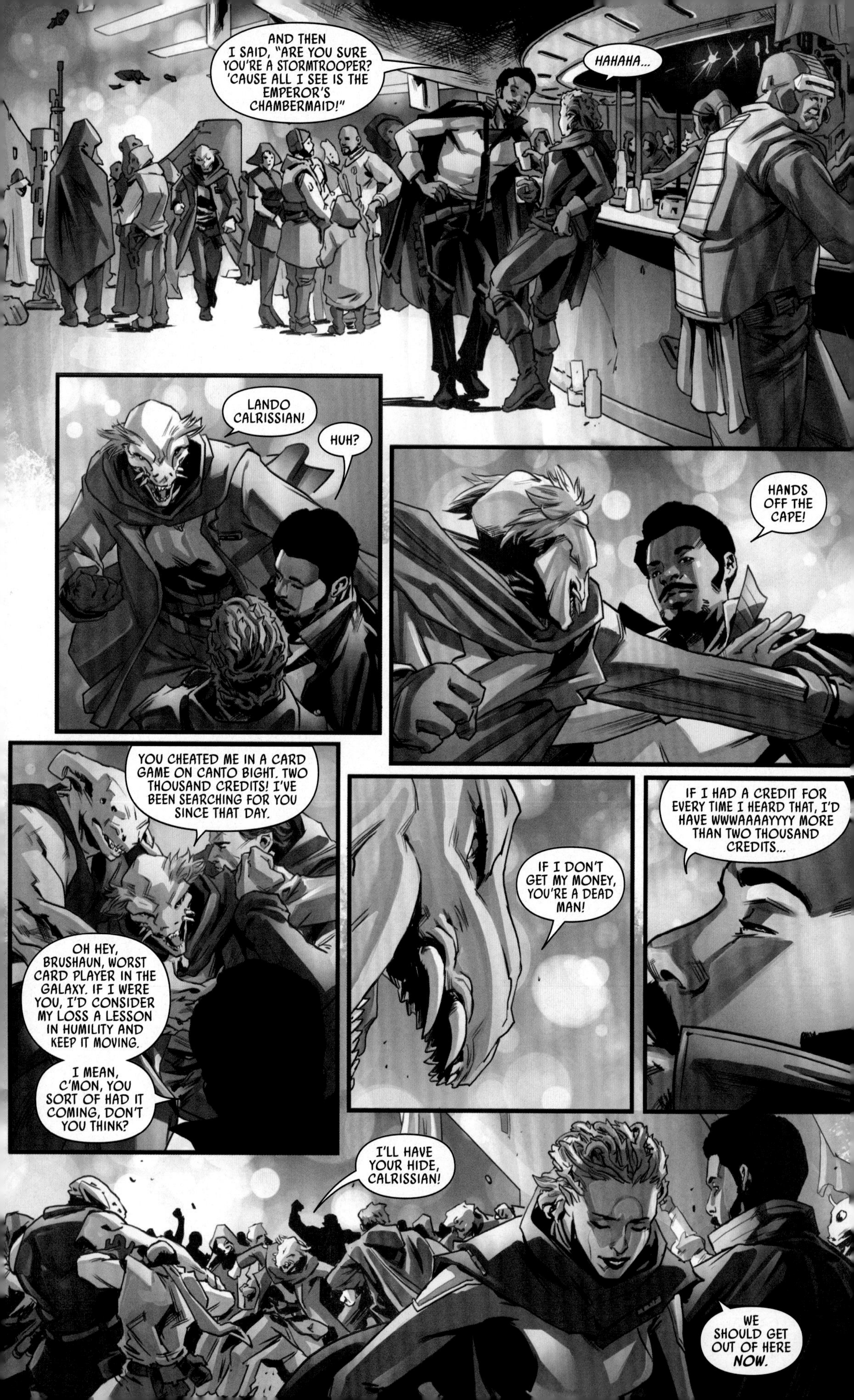
AND THEN I SAID, "ARE YOU SURE YOU'RE A STORMTROOPER? 'CAUSE ALL I SEE IS THE EMPEROR'S CHAMBERMAID!"
HAHAHA...
LANDO CALRISSIAN!
HUH?
HANDS OFF THE CAPE!
YOU CHEATED ME IN A CARD GAME ON CANTO BIGHT. TWO THOUSAND CREDITS! I'VE BEEN SEARCHING FOR YOU SINCE THAT DAY.
OH HEY, BRUSHAUN, WORST CARD PLAYER IN THE GALAXY. IF I WERE YOU, I'D CONSIDER MY LOSS A LESSON IN HUMILITY AND KEEP IT MOVING.
I MEAN, C'MON, YOU SORT OF HAD IT COMING, DON'T YOU THINK?
IF I DON'T GET MY MONEY, YOU'RE A DEAD MAN!
IF I HAD A CREDIT FOR EVERY TIME I HEARD THAT, I'D HAVE WWWAAAAYYYY MORE THAN TWO THOUSAND CREDITS...
I'LL HAVE YOUR HIDE, CALRISSIAN!
WE SHOULD GET OUT OF HERE NOW.

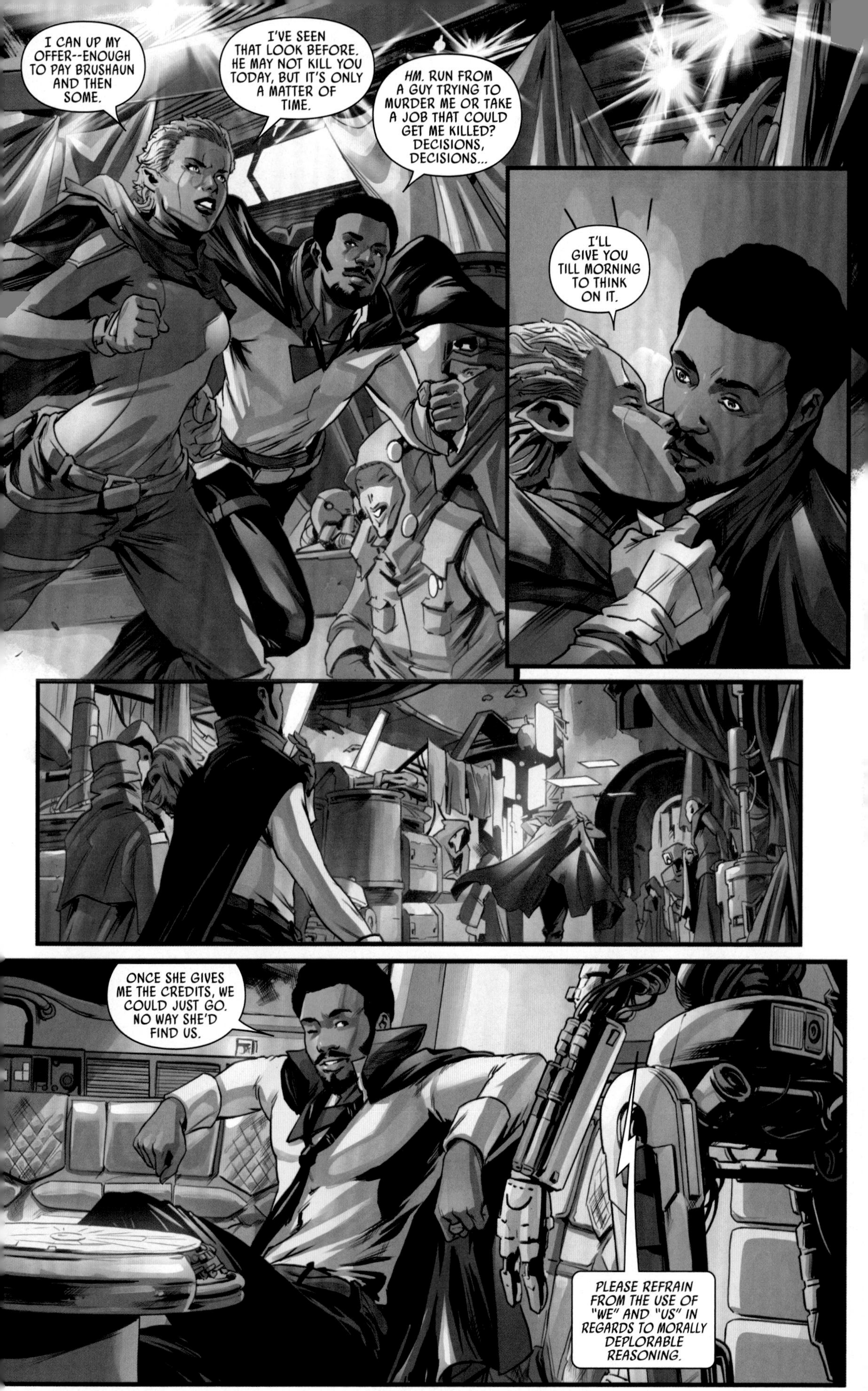
I CAN UP MY OFFER--ENOUGH TO PAY BRUSHAUN AND THEN SOME.
I'VE SEEN THAT LOOK BEFORE. HE MAY NOT KILL YOU TODAY, BUT IT'S ONLY A MATTER OF TIME.
HM. RUN FROM A GUY TRYING TO MURDER ME OR TAKE A JOB THAT COULD GET ME KILLED? DECISIONS, DECISIONS...
I'LL GIVE YOU TILL MORNING TO THINK ON IT.
ONCE SHE GIVES ME THE CREDITS, WE COULD JUST GO. NO WAY SHE'D FIND US.
PLEASE REFRAIN FROM THE USE OF "WE" AND "US" IN REGARDS TO MORALLY DEPLORABLE REASONING.

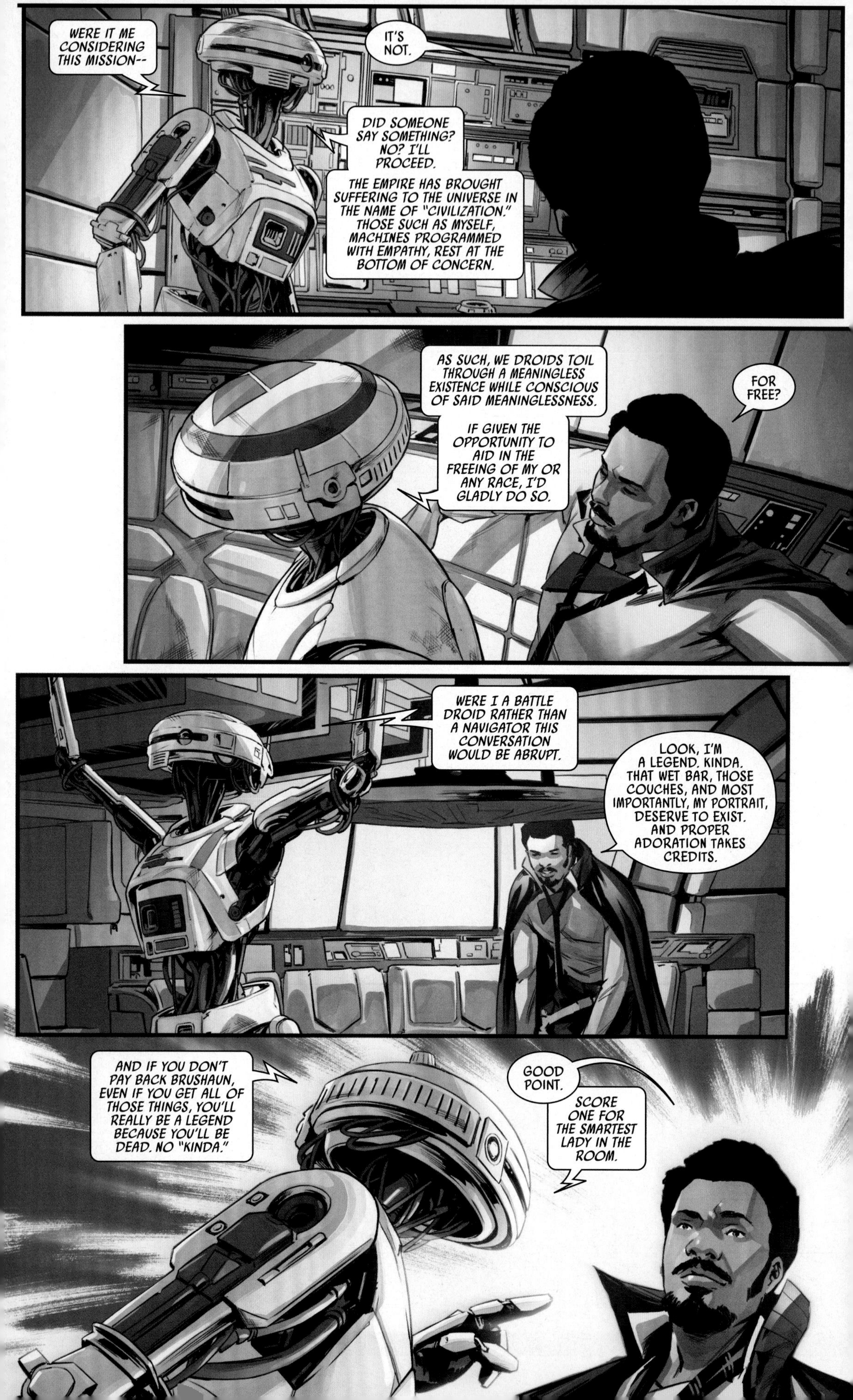
WERE IT ME CONSIDERING THIS MISSION--
IT'S NOT.
DID SOMEONE SAY SOMETHING? NO? I'LL PROCEED.
THE EMPIRE HAS BROUGHT SUFFERING TO THE UNIVERSE IN THE NAME OF "CIVILIZATION." THOSE SUCH AS MYSELF, MACHINES PROGRAMMED WITH EMPATHY, REST AT THE BOTTOM OF CONCERN.
AS SUCH, WE DROIDS TOIL THROUGH A MEANINGLESS EXISTENCE WHILE CONSCIOUS OF SAID MEANINGLESSNESS.
IF GIVEN THE OPPORTUNITY TO AID IN THE FREEING OF MY OR ANY RACE, I'D GLADLY DO SO.
FOR FREE?
WERE I A BATTLE DROID RATHER THAN A NAVIGATOR THIS CONVERSATION WOULD BE ABRUPT.
LOOK, I'M A LEGEND. KINDA. THAT WET BAR, THOSE COUCHES, AND MOST IMPORTANTLY, MY PORTRAIT, DESERVE TO EXIST. AND PROPER ADORATION TAKES CREDITS.
AND IF YOU DON'T PAY BACK BRUSHAUN, EVEN IF YOU GET ALL OF THOSE THINGS, YOU'LL REALLY BE A LEGEND BECAUSE YOU'LL BE DEAD. NO "KINDA."
GOOD POINT.
SCORE ONE FOR THE SMARTEST LADY IN THE ROOM.

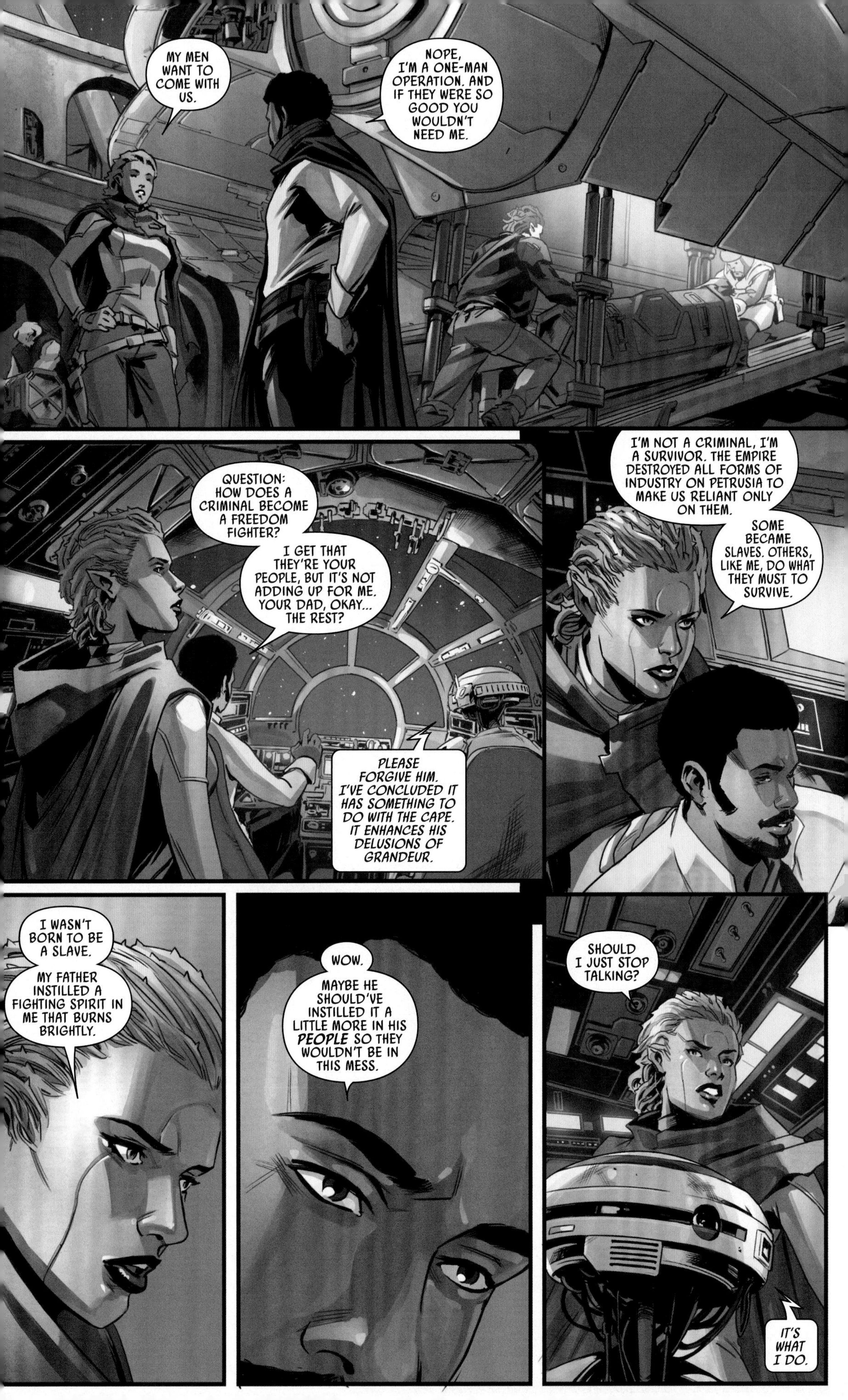
MY MEN WANT TO COME WITH US.
NOPE, I'M A ONE-MAN OPERATION. AND IF THEY WERE SO GOOD YOU WOULDN'T NEED ME.
QUESTION: HOW DOES A CRIMINAL BECOME A FREEDOM FIGHTER?
I GET THAT THEY'RE YOUR PEOPLE, BUT IT'S NOT ADDING UP FOR ME. YOUR DAD, OKAY... THE REST?
PLEASE FORGIVE HIM. I'VE CONCLUDED IT HAS SOMETHING TO DO WITH THE CAPE. IT ENHANCES HIS DELUSIONS OF GRANDEUR.
I'M NOT A CRIMINAL, I'M A SURVIVOR. THE EMPIRE DESTROYED ALL FORMS OF INDUSTRY ON PETRUSIA TO MAKE US RELIANT ONLY ON THEM.
SOME BECAME SLAVES. OTHERS, LIKE ME, DO WHAT THEY MUST TO SURVIVE.
I WASN'T BORN TO BE A SLAVE.
MY FATHER INSTILLED A FIGHTING SPIRIT IN ME THAT BURNS BRIGHTLY.
WOW.
MAYBE HE SHOULD'VE INSTILLED IT A LITTLE MORE IN HIS *PEOPLE* SO THEY WOULDN'T BE IN THIS MESS.
SHOULD I JUST STOP TALKING?
IT'S WHAT I DO.

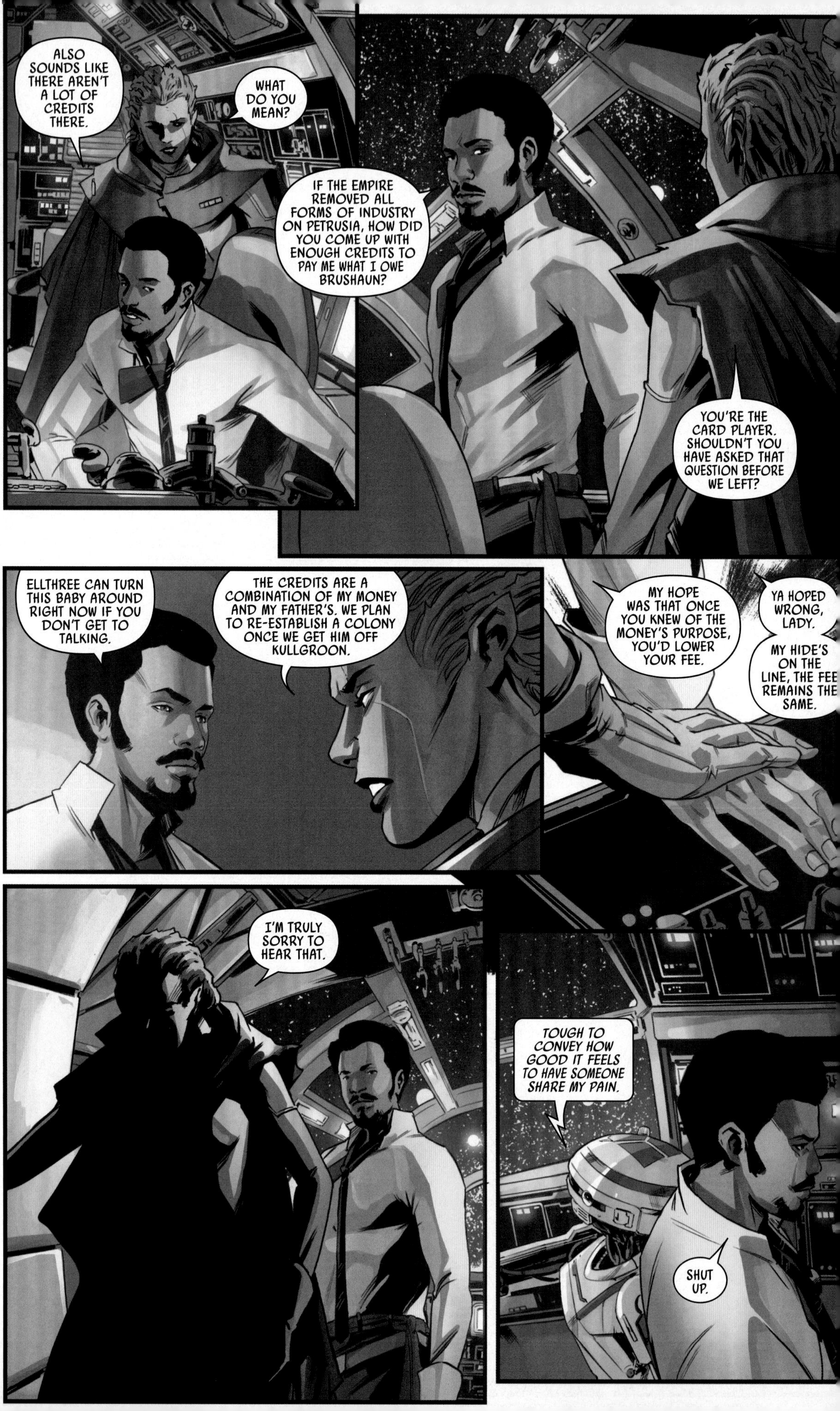
ALSO SOUNDS LIKE THERE AREN'T A LOT OF CREDITS THERE.
WHAT DO YOU MEAN?
IF THE EMPIRE REMOVED ALL FORMS OF INDUSTRY ON PETRUSIA, HOW DID YOU COME UP WITH ENOUGH CREDITS TO PAY ME WHAT I OWE BRUSHAUN?
YOU'RE THE CARD PLAYER. SHOULDN'T YOU HAVE ASKED THAT QUESTION BEFORE WE LEFT?
ELLTHREE CAN TURN THIS BABY AROUND RIGHT NOW IF YOU DON'T GET TO TALKING.
THE CREDITS ARE A COMBINATION OF MY MONEY AND MY FATHER'S. WE PLAN TO RE-ESTABLISH A COLONY ONCE WE GET HIM OFF KULLGROON.
MY HOPE WAS THAT ONCE YOU KNEW OF THE MONEY'S PURPOSE, YOU'D LOWER YOUR FEE.
YA HOPED WRONG, LADY.
MY HIDE'S ON THE LINE, THE FEE REMAINS THE SAME.
I'M TRULY SORRY TO HEAR THAT.
TOUGH TO CONVEY HOW GOOD IT FEELS TO HAVE SOMEONE SHARE MY PAIN.
SHUT UP.

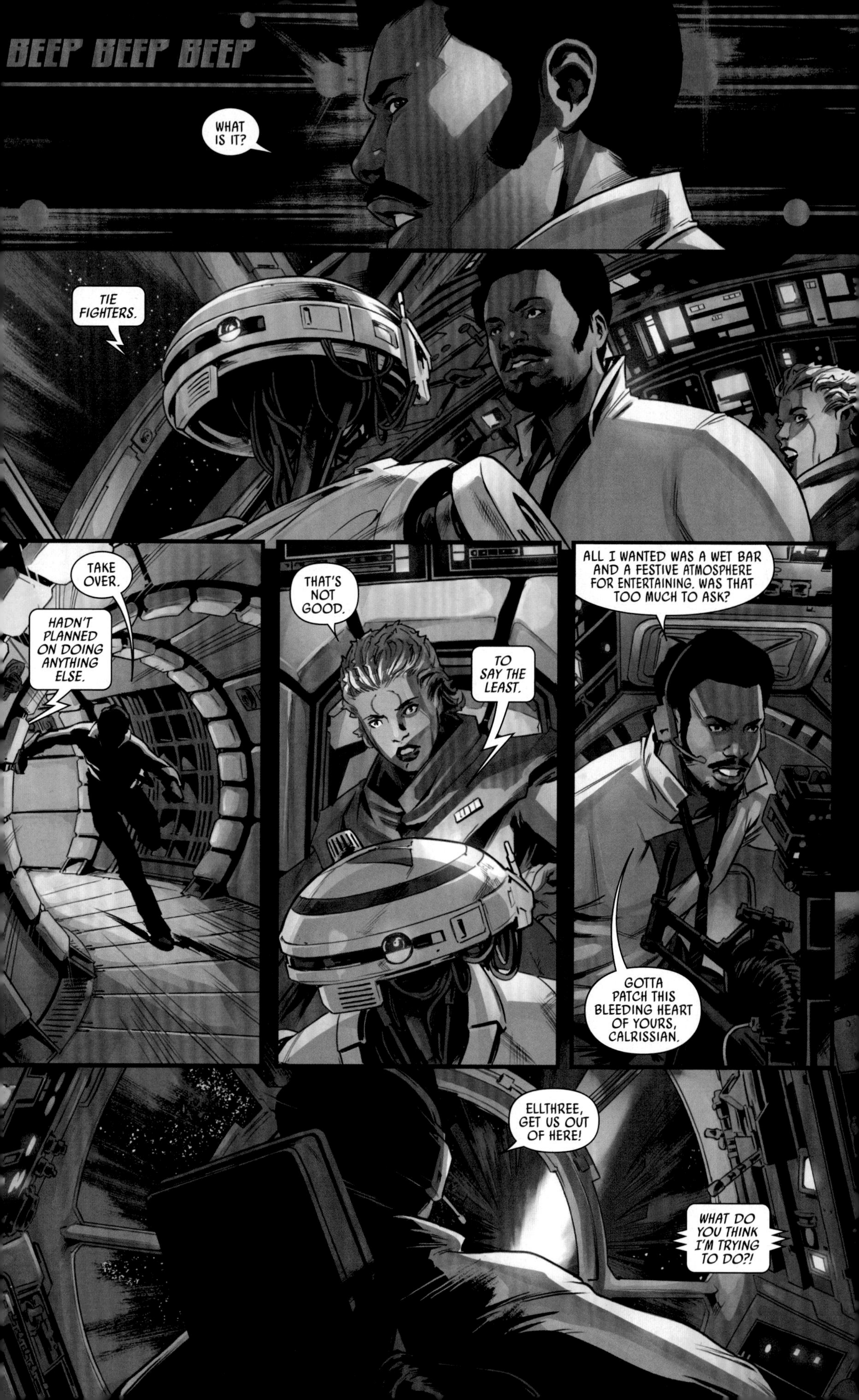
BEEP BEEP BEEP
WHAT IS IT?
TIE FIGHTERS.
TAKE OVER.
HADN'T PLANNED ON DOING ANYTHING ELSE.
THAT'S NOT GOOD.
TO SAY THE LEAST.
ALL I WANTED WAS A WET BAR AND A FESTIVE ATMOSPHERE FOR ENTERTAINING. WAS THAT TOO MUCH TO ASK?
GOTTA PATCH THIS BLEEDING HEART OF YOURS, CALRISSIAN.
ELLTHREE, GET US OUT OF HERE!
WHAT DO YOU THINK I'M TRYING TO DO?!

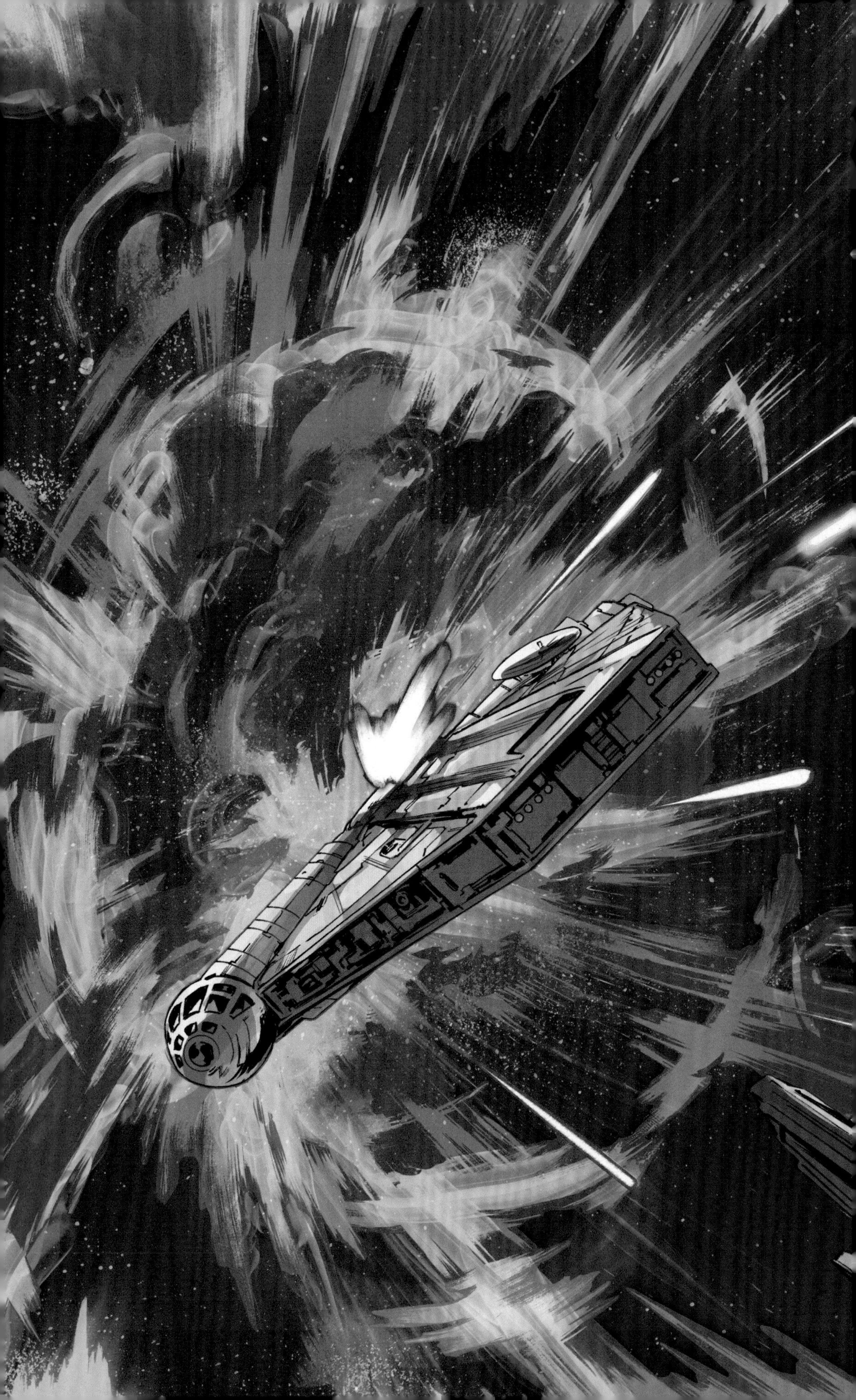

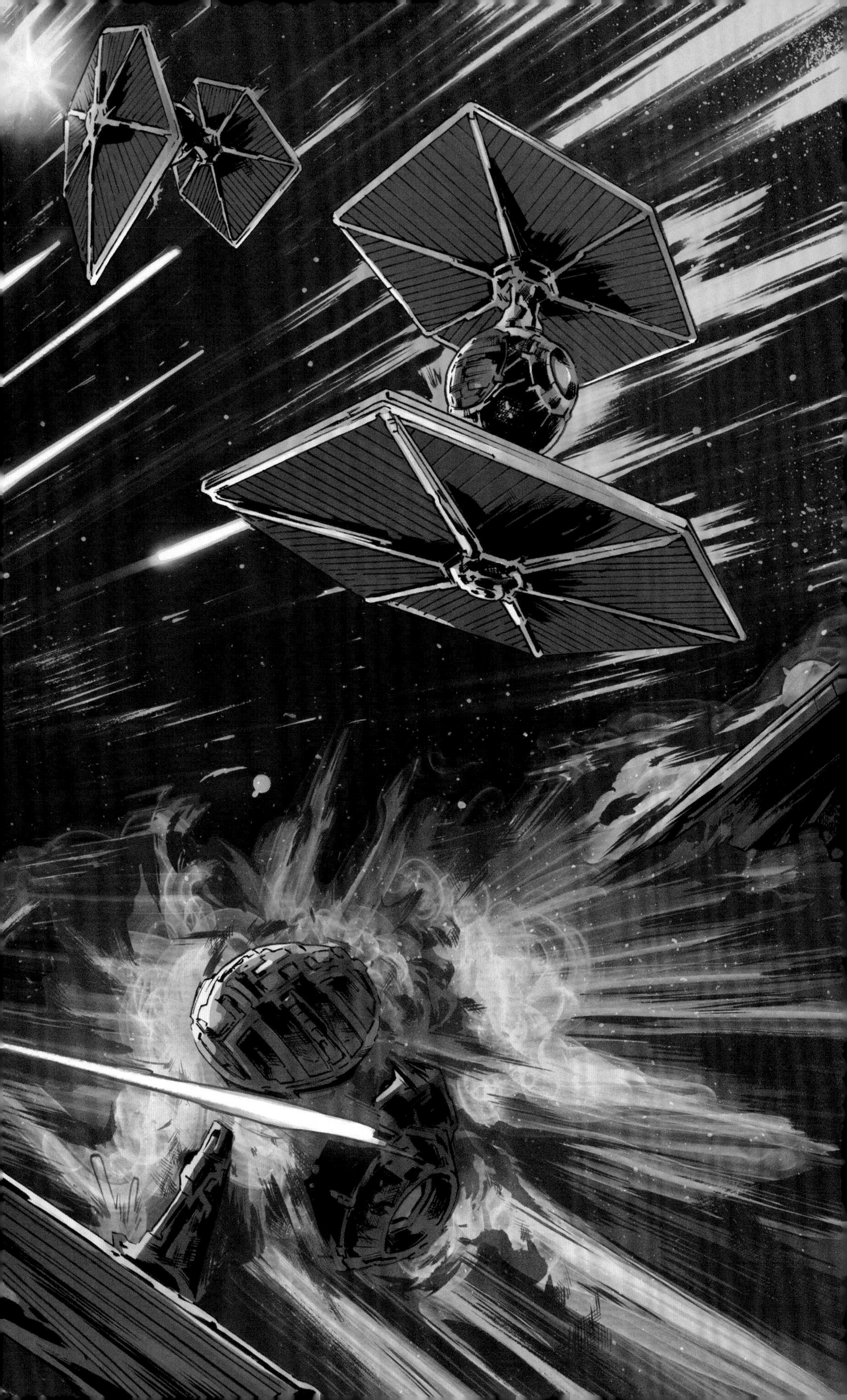

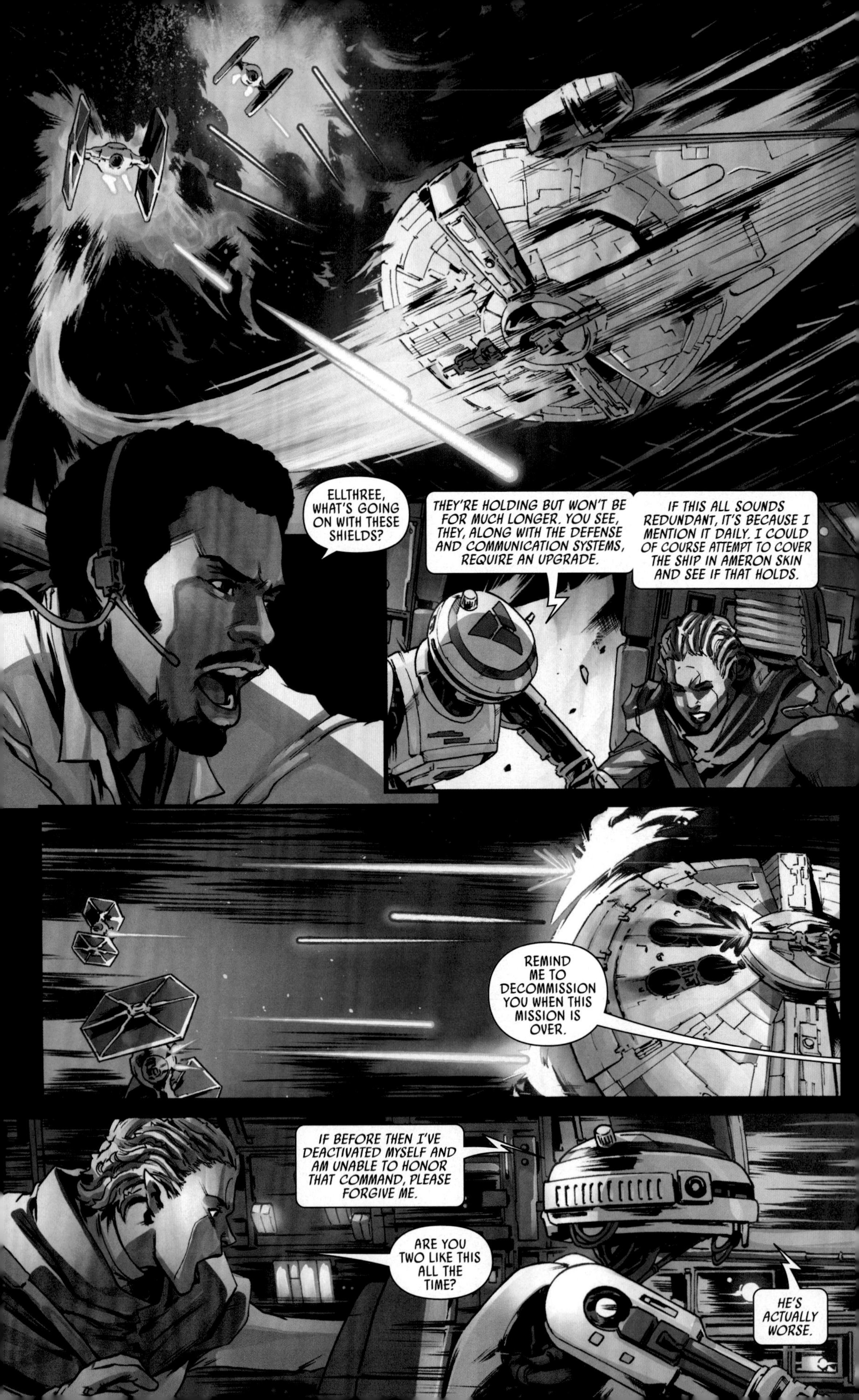
ELLTHREE, WHAT'S GOING ON WITH THESE SHIELDS?
THEY'RE HOLDING BUT WON'T BE FOR MUCH LONGER. YOU SEE, THEY, ALONG WITH THE DEFENSE AND COMMUNICATION SYSTEMS, REQUIRE AN UPGRADE.
IF THIS ALL SOUNDS REDUNDANT, IT'S BECAUSE I MENTION IT DAILY. I COULD OF COURSE ATTEMPT TO COVER THE SHIP IN AMERON SKIN AND SEE IF THAT HOLDS.
REMIND ME TO DECOMMISSION YOU WHEN THIS MISSION IS OVER.
IF BEFORE THEN I'VE DEACTIVATED MYSELF AND AM UNABLE TO HONOR THAT COMMAND, PLEASE FORGIVE ME.
ARE YOU TWO LIKE THIS ALL THE TIME?
HE'S ACTUALLY WORSE.

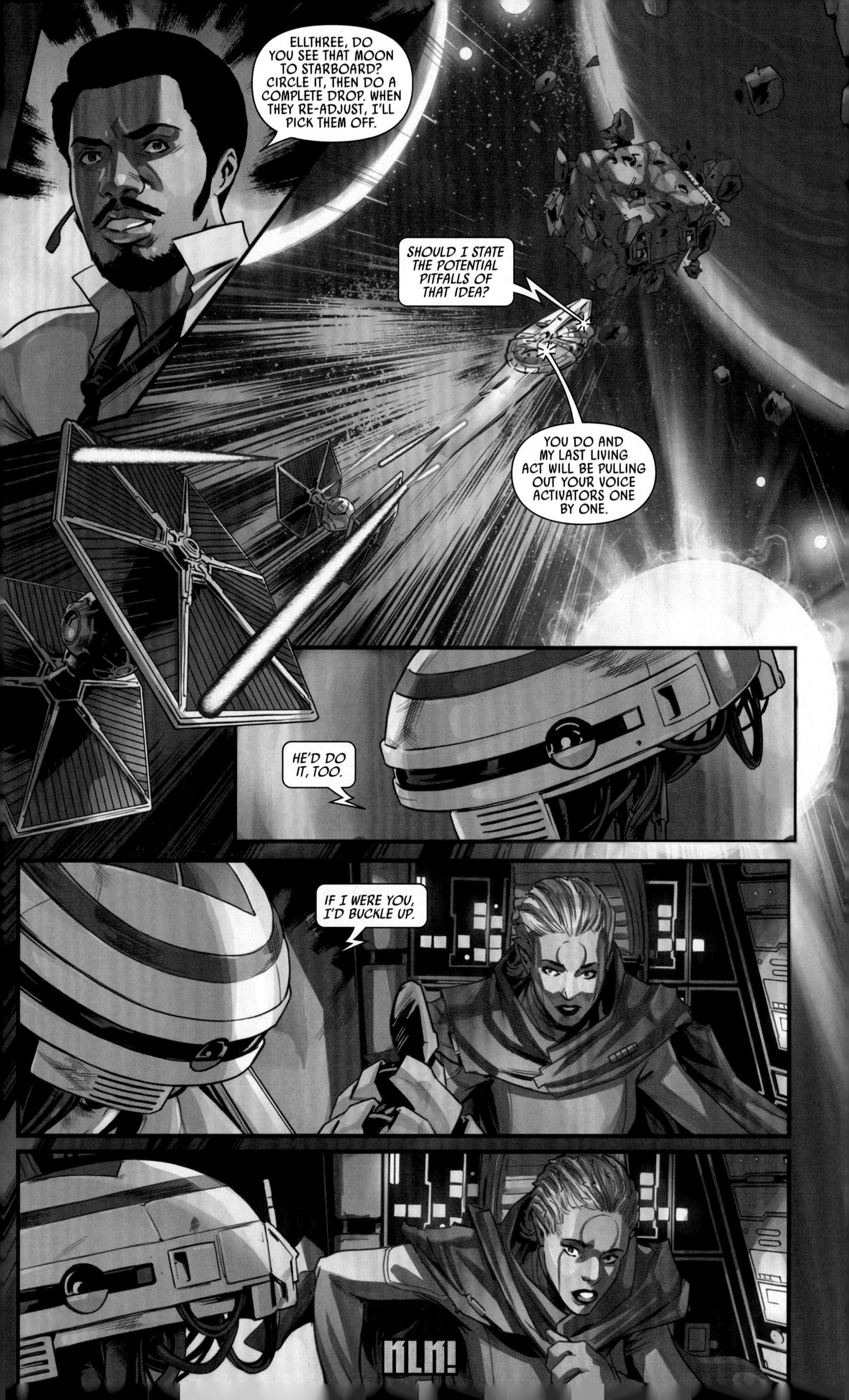
ELLTHREE, DO YOU SEE THAT MOON TO STARBOARD? CIRCLE IT, THEN DO A COMPLETE DROP. WHEN THEY RE-ADJUST, I'LL PICK THEM OFF.
SHOULD I STATE THE POTENTIAL PITFALLS OF THAT IDEA?
YOU DO AND MY LAST LIVING ACT WILL BE PULLING OUT YOUR VOICE ACTIVATORS ONE BY ONE.
HE'D DO IT, TOO.
IF I WERE YOU, I'D BUCKLE UP.
KLK!

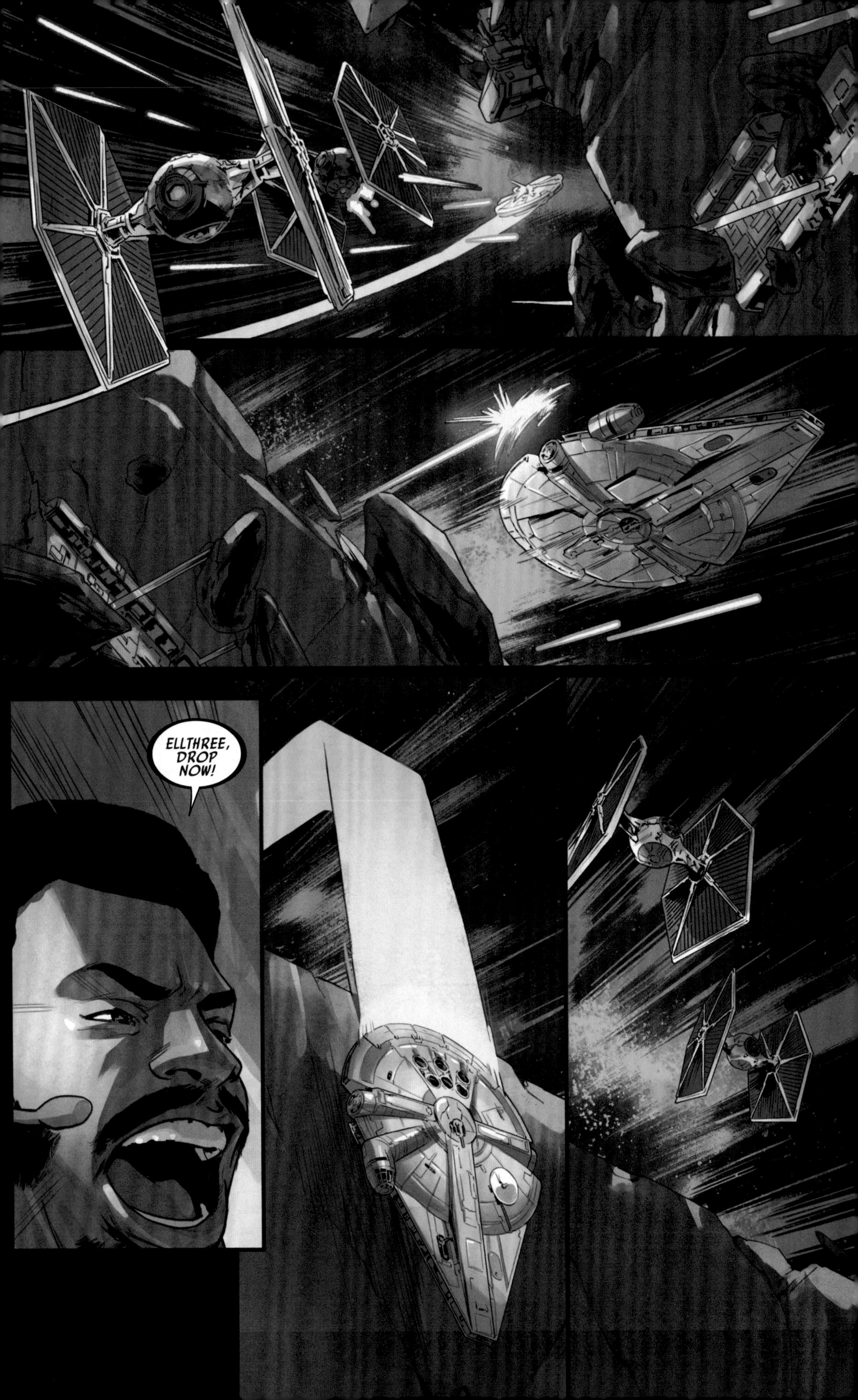
ELLTHREE, DROP NOW!

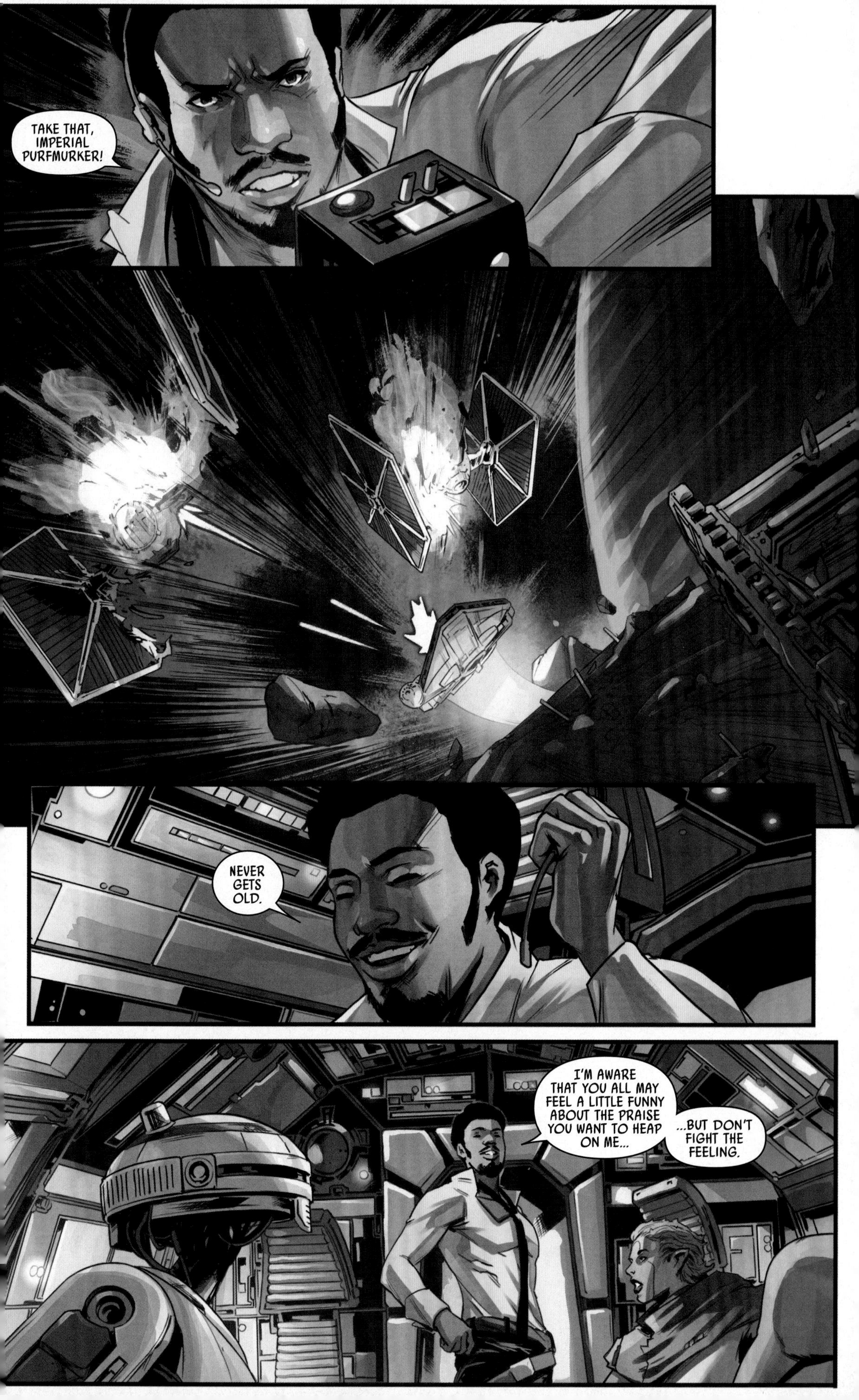
TAKE THAT, IMPERIAL PURFMURKER!
NEVER GETS OLD.
I'M AWARE THAT YOU ALL MAY FEEL A LITTLE FUNNY ABOUT THE PRAISE YOU WANT TO HEAP ON ME...
...BUT DON'T FIGHT THE FEELING.

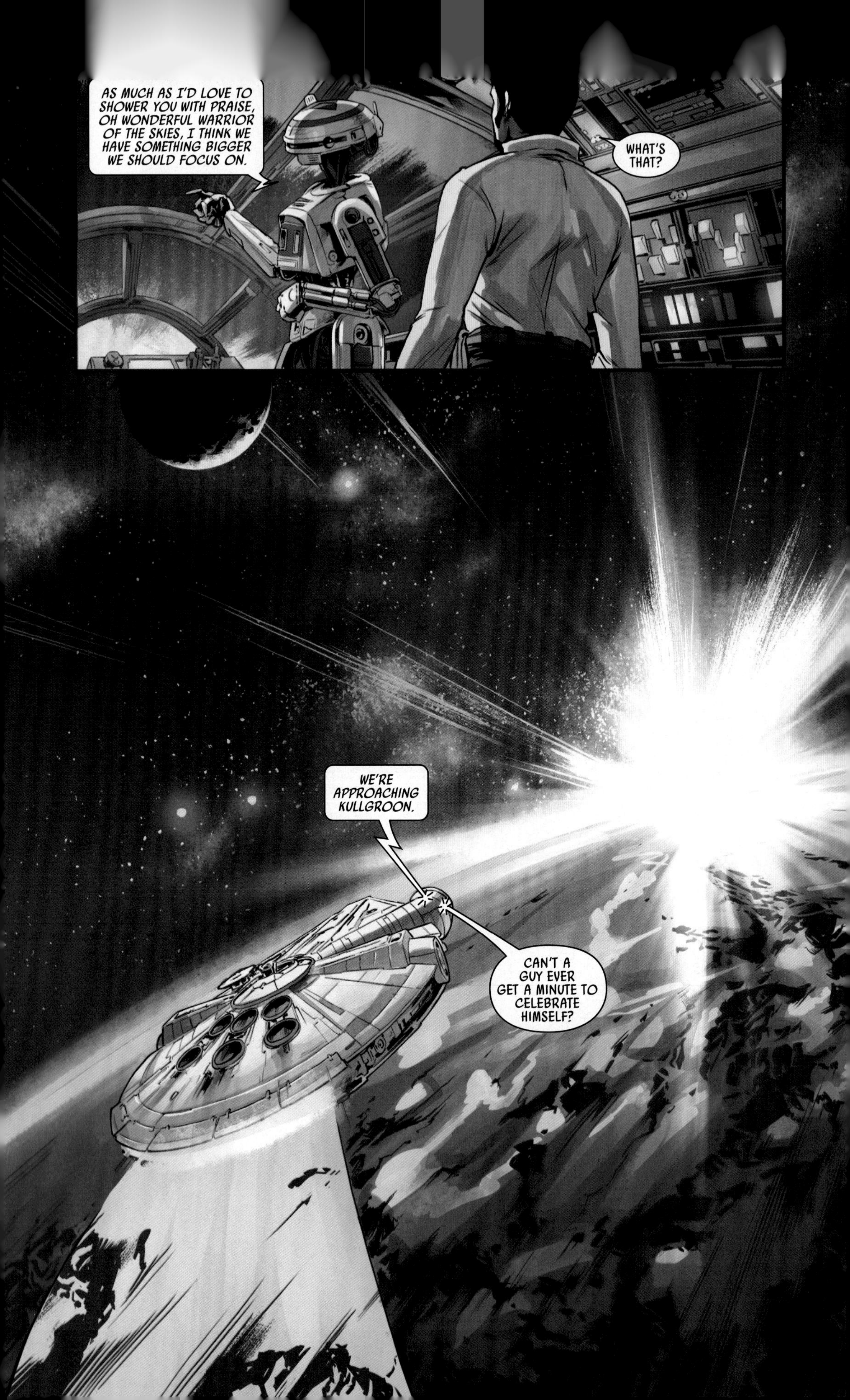
AS MUCH AS I'D LOVE TO SHOWER YOU WITH PRAISE, OH WONDERFUL WARRIOR OF THE SKIES, I THINK WE HAVE SOMETHING BIGGER WE SHOULD FOCUS ON.
WHAT'S THAT?
WE'RE APPROACHING KULLGROON.
CAN'T A GUY EVER GET A MINUTE TO CELEBRATE HIMSELF?

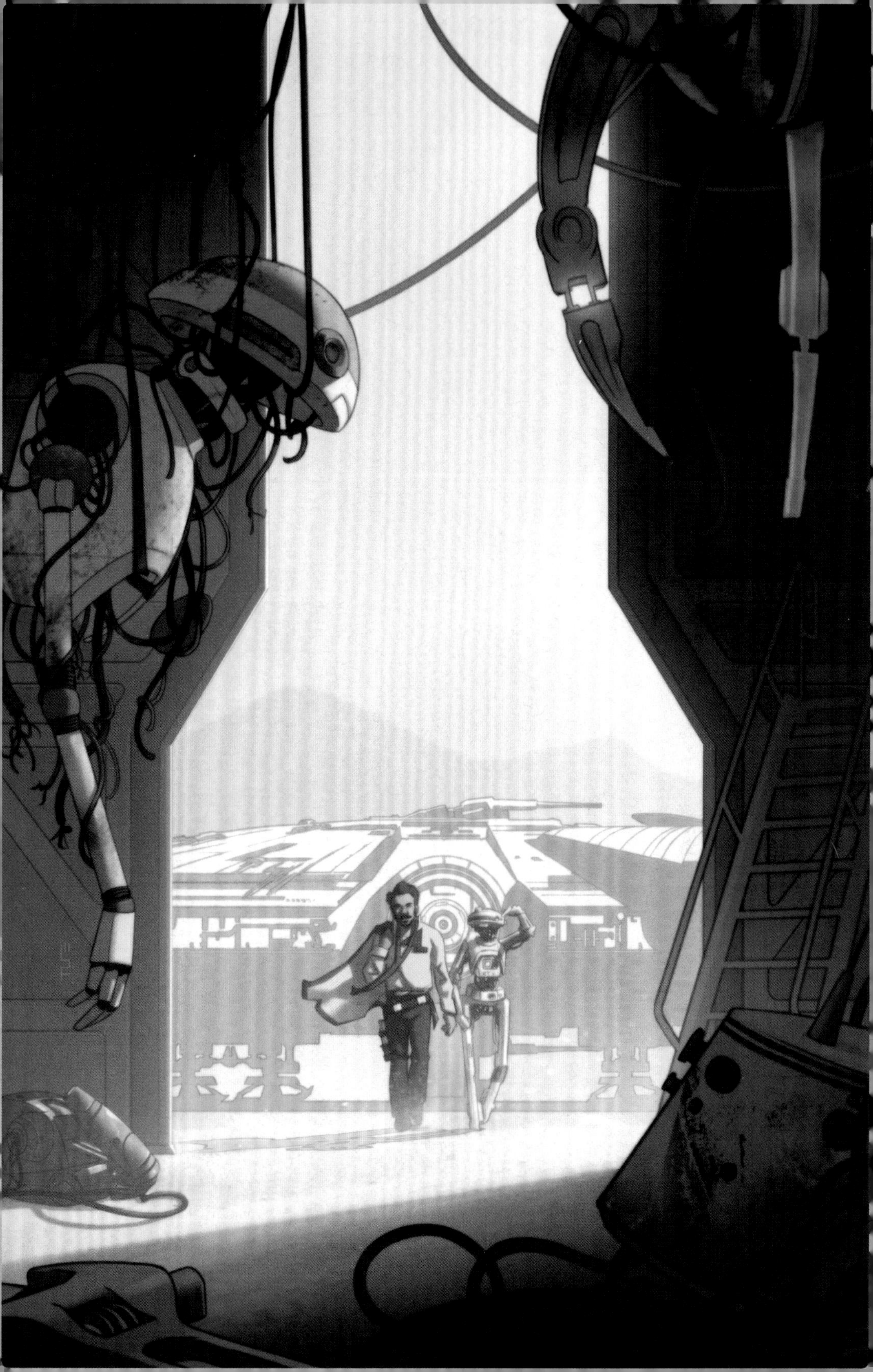

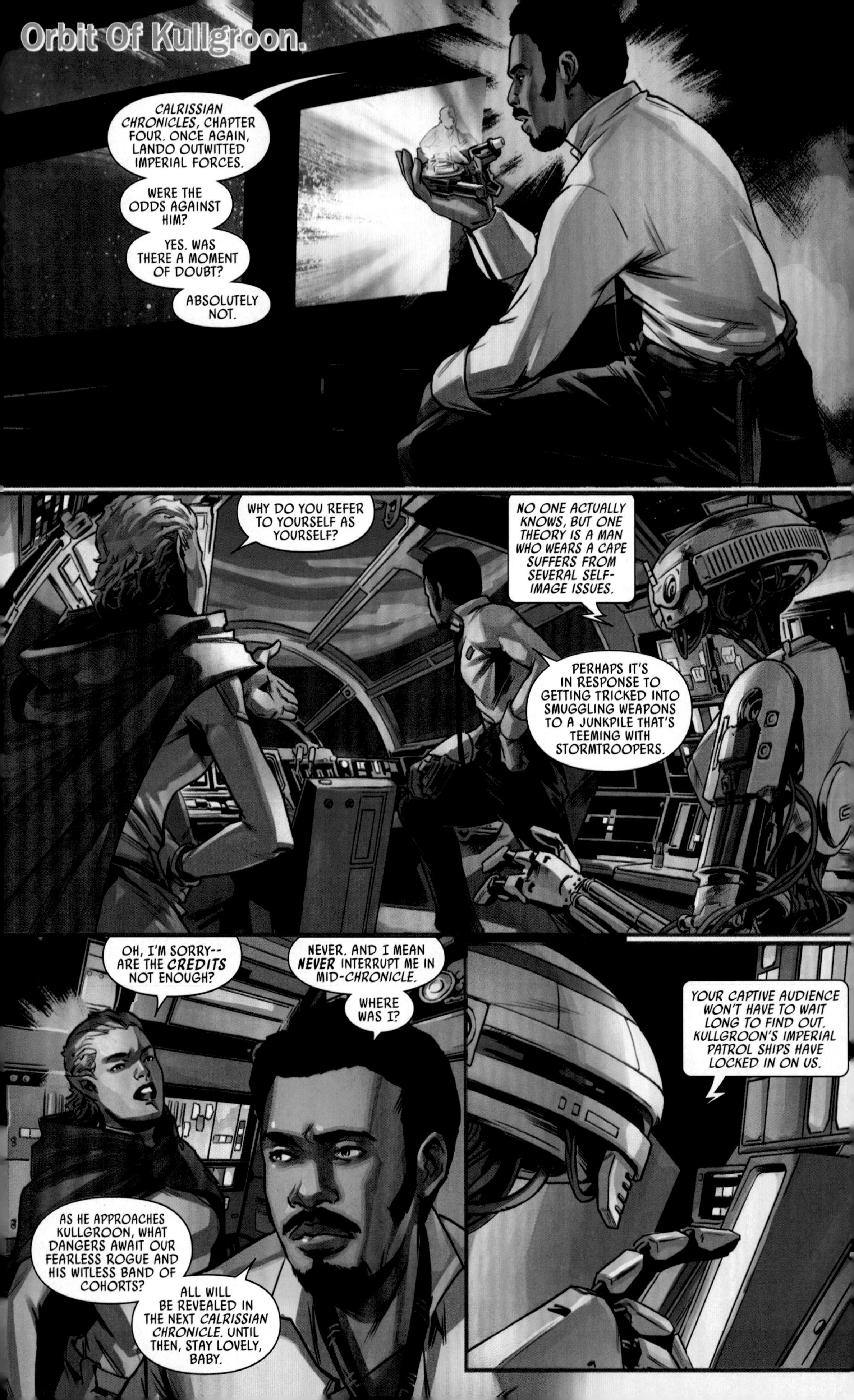
Orbit Of Kullgroon.
CALRISSIAN CHRONICLES, CHAPTER FOUR. ONCE AGAIN, LANDO OUTWITTED IMPERIAL FORCES.
WERE THE ODDS AGAINST HIM?
YES. WAS THERE A MOMENT OF DOUBT?
ABSOLUTELY NOT.
WHY DO YOU REFER TO YOURSELF AS YOURSELF?
NO ONE ACTUALLY KNOWS, BUT ONE THEORY IS A MAN WHO WEARS A CAPE SUFFERS FROM SEVERAL SELF-IMAGE ISSUES.
PERHAPS IT'S IN RESPONSE TO GETTING TRICKED INTO SMUGGLING WEAPONS TO A JUNKPILE THAT'S TEEMING WITH STORMTROOPERS.
OH, I'M SORRY-- ARE THE CREDITS NOT ENOUGH?
NEVER. AND I MEAN NEVER INTERRUPT ME IN MID-CHRONICLE.
WHERE WAS I?
AS HE APPROACHES KULLGROON, WHAT DANGERS AWAIT OUR FEARLESS ROGUE AND HIS WITLESS BAND OF COHORTS?
ALL WILL BE REVEALED IN THE NEXT CALRISSIAN CHRONICLE. UNTIL THEN, STAY LOVELY, BABY.
YOUR CAPTIVE AUDIENCE WON'T HAVE TO WAIT LONG TO FIND OUT. KULLGROON'S IMPERIAL PATROL SHIPS HAVE LOCKED IN ON US.

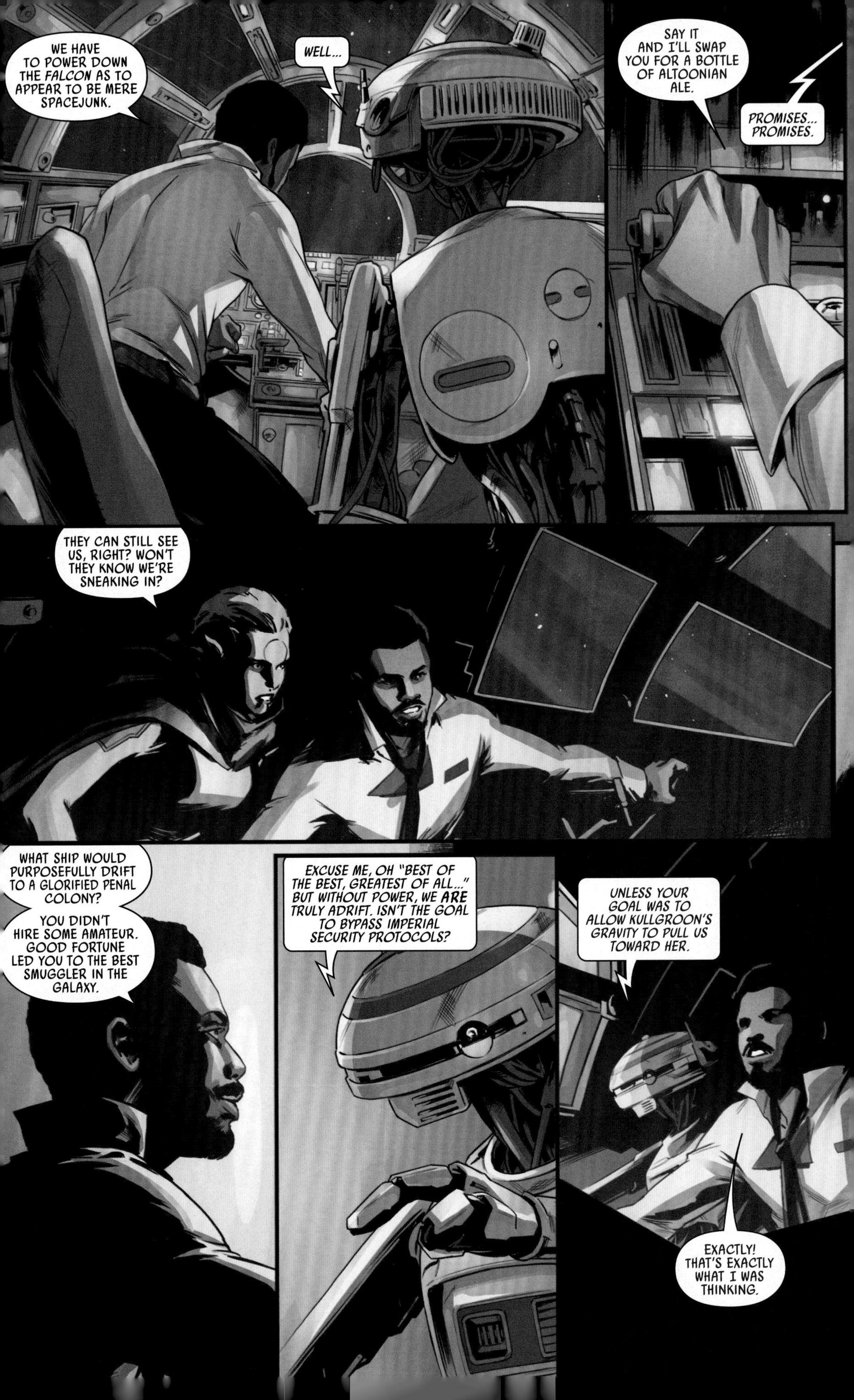
WE HAVE TO POWER DOWN THE FALCON AS TO APPEAR TO BE MERE SPACEJUNK.
WELL...
SAY IT AND I'LL SWAP YOU FOR A BOTTLE OF ALTOONIAN ALE.
PROMISES... PROMISES.
THEY CAN STILL SEE US, RIGHT? WON'T THEY KNOW WE'RE SNEAKING IN?
WHAT SHIP WOULD PURPOSEFULLY DRIFT TO A GLORIFIED PENAL COLONY?
YOU DIDN'T HIRE SOME AMATEUR. GOOD FORTUNE LED YOU TO THE BEST SMUGGLER IN THE GALAXY.
EXCUSE ME, OH "BEST OF THE BEST, GREATEST OF ALL..." BUT WITHOUT POWER, WE ARE TRULY ADRIFT. ISN'T THE GOAL TO BYPASS IMPERIAL SECURITY PROTOCOLS?
UNLESS YOUR GOAL WAS TO ALLOW KULLGROON'S GRAVITY TO PULL US TOWARD HER.
EXACTLY! THAT'S EXACTLY WHAT I WAS THINKING.

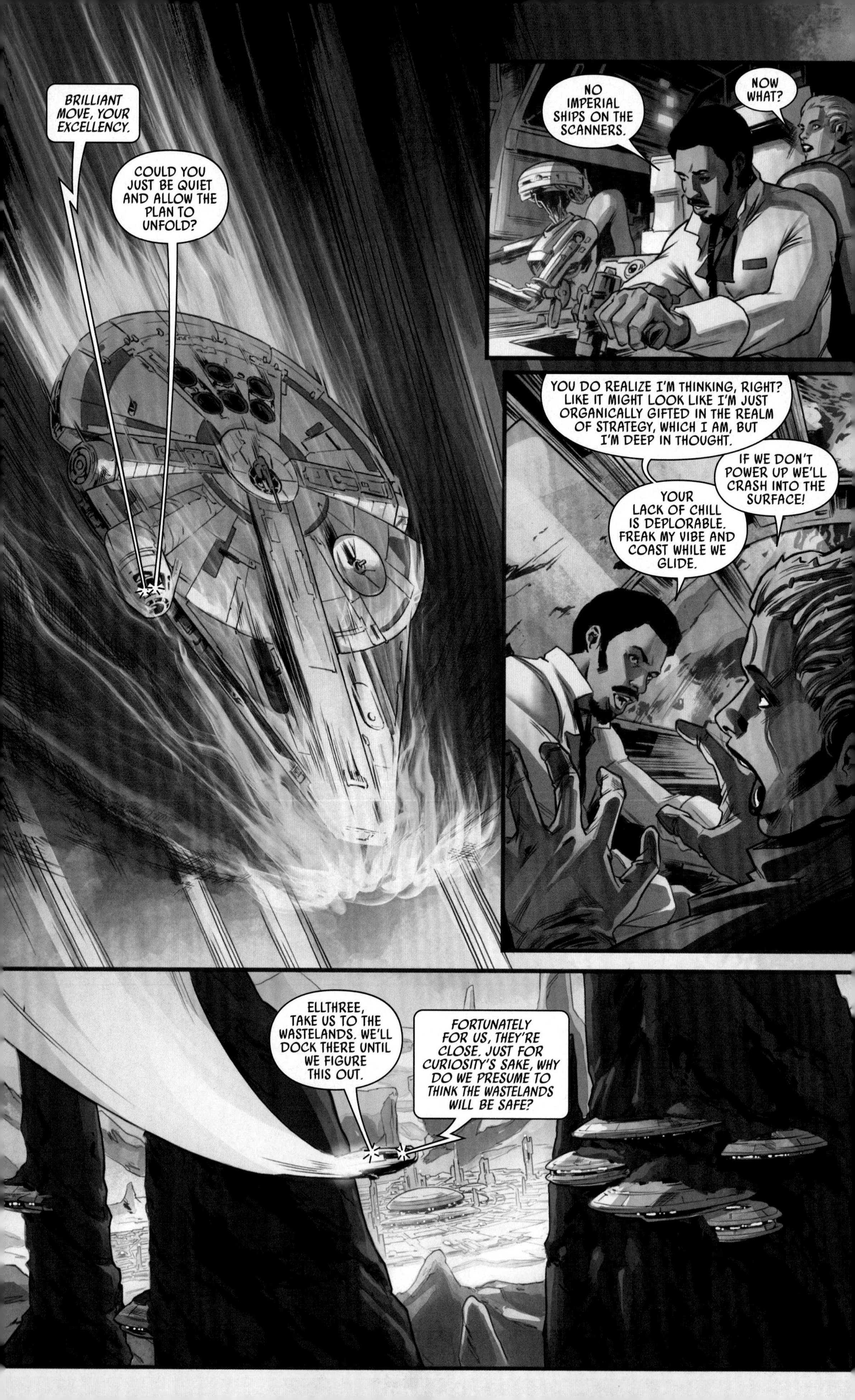
BRILLIANT MOVE, YOUR EXCELLENCY.
COULD YOU JUST BE QUIET AND ALLOW THE PLAN TO UNFOLD?
NO IMPERIAL SHIPS ON THE SCANNERS.
NOW WHAT?
YOU DO REALIZE I'M THINKING, RIGHT? LIKE IT MIGHT LOOK LIKE I'M JUST ORGANICALLY GIFTED IN THE REALM OF STRATEGY, WHICH I AM, BUT I'M DEEP IN THOUGHT.
IF WE DON'T POWER UP WE'LL CRASH INTO THE SURFACE!
YOUR LACK OF CHILL IS DEPLORABLE. FREAK MY VIBE AND COAST WHILE WE GLIDE.
ELLTHREE, TAKE US TO THE WASTELANDS. WE'LL DOCK THERE UNTIL WE FIGURE THIS OUT.
FORTUNATELY FOR US, THEY'RE CLOSE. JUST FOR CURIOSITY'S SAKE, WHY DO WE PRESUME TO THINK THE WASTELANDS WILL BE SAFE?

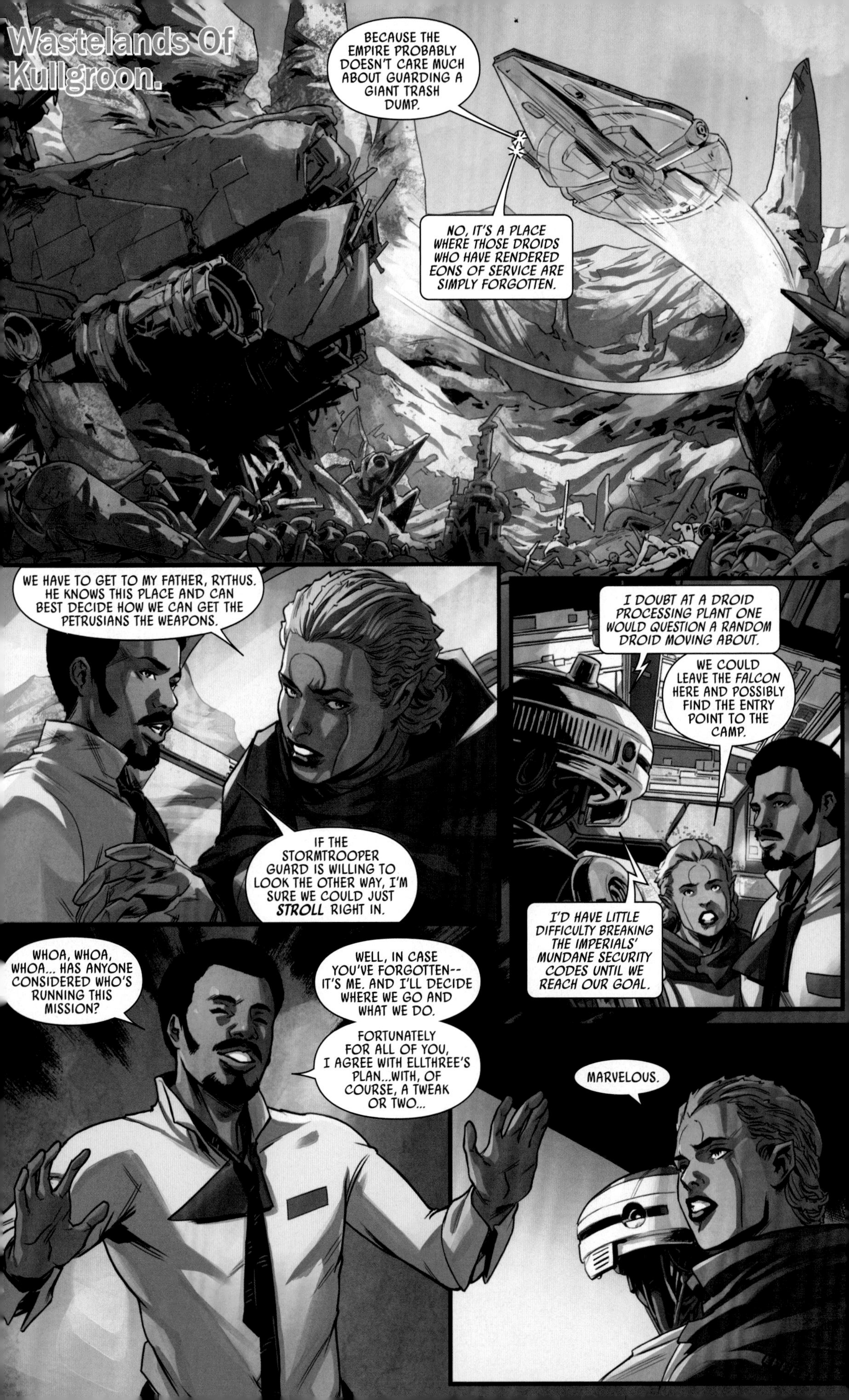
Wastelands Of Kullgroon.
BECAUSE THE EMPIRE PROBABLY DOESN'T CARE MUCH ABOUT GUARDING A GIANT TRASH DUMP.
NO, IT'S A PLACE WHERE THOSE DROIDS WHO HAVE RENDERED EONS OF SERVICE ARE SIMPLY FORGOTTEN.
WE HAVE TO GET TO MY FATHER, RYTHUS. HE KNOWS THIS PLACE AND CAN BEST DECIDE HOW WE CAN GET THE PETRUSIANS THE WEAPONS.
IF THE STORMTROOPER GUARD IS WILLING TO LOOK THE OTHER WAY, I'M SURE WE COULD JUST STROLL RIGHT IN.
I DOUBT AT A DROID PROCESSING PLANT ONE WOULD QUESTION A RANDOM DROID MOVING ABOUT.
WE COULD LEAVE THE FALCON HERE AND POSSIBLY FIND THE ENTRY POINT TO THE CAMP.
I'D HAVE LITTLE DIFFICULTY BREAKING THE IMPERIALS' MUNDANE SECURITY CODES UNTIL WE REACH OUR GOAL.
WHOA, WHOA, WHOA... HAS ANYONE CONSIDERED WHO'S RUNNING THIS MISSION?
WELL, IN CASE YOU'VE FORGOTTEN-- IT'S ME. AND I'LL DECIDE WHERE WE GO AND WHAT WE DO.
FORTUNATELY FOR ALL OF YOU, I AGREE WITH ELLTHREE'S PLAN...WITH, OF COURSE, A TWEAK OR TWO...
MARVELOUS.

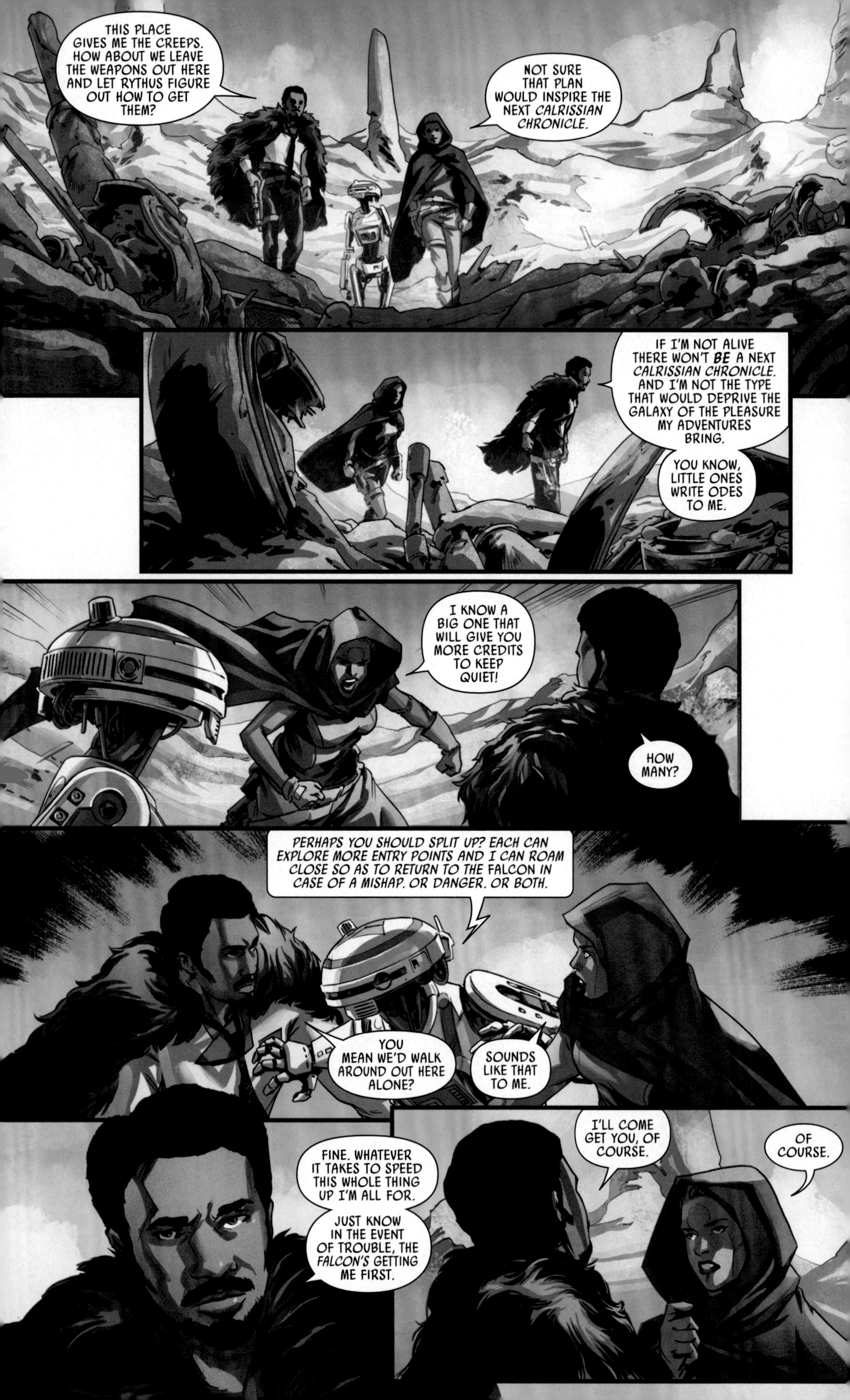
THIS PLACE GIVES ME THE CREEPS. HOW ABOUT WE LEAVE THE WEAPONS OUT HERE AND LET RYTHUS FIGURE OUT HOW TO GET THEM?
NOT SURE THAT PLAN WOULD INSPIRE THE NEXT *CALRISSIAN CHRONICLE*.
IF I'M NOT ALIVE THERE WON'T ***BE*** A NEXT *CALRISSIAN CHRONICLE*. AND I'M NOT THE TYPE THAT WOULD DEPRIVE THE GALAXY OF THE PLEASURE MY ADVENTURES BRING.
YOU KNOW, LITTLE ONES WRITE ODES TO ME.
I KNOW A BIG ONE THAT WILL GIVE YOU MORE CREDITS TO KEEP QUIET!
HOW MANY?
PERHAPS YOU SHOULD SPLIT UP? EACH CAN EXPLORE MORE ENTRY POINTS AND I CAN ROAM CLOSE SO AS TO RETURN TO THE FALCON IN CASE OF A MISHAP. OR DANGER. OR BOTH.
YOU MEAN WE'D WALK AROUND OUT HERE ALONE?
SOUNDS LIKE THAT TO ME.
FINE. WHATEVER IT TAKES TO SPEED THIS WHOLE THING UP I'M ALL FOR.
JUST KNOW IN THE EVENT OF TROUBLE, THE *FALCON'S* GETTING ME FIRST.
I'LL COME GET YOU, OF COURSE.
OF COURSE.

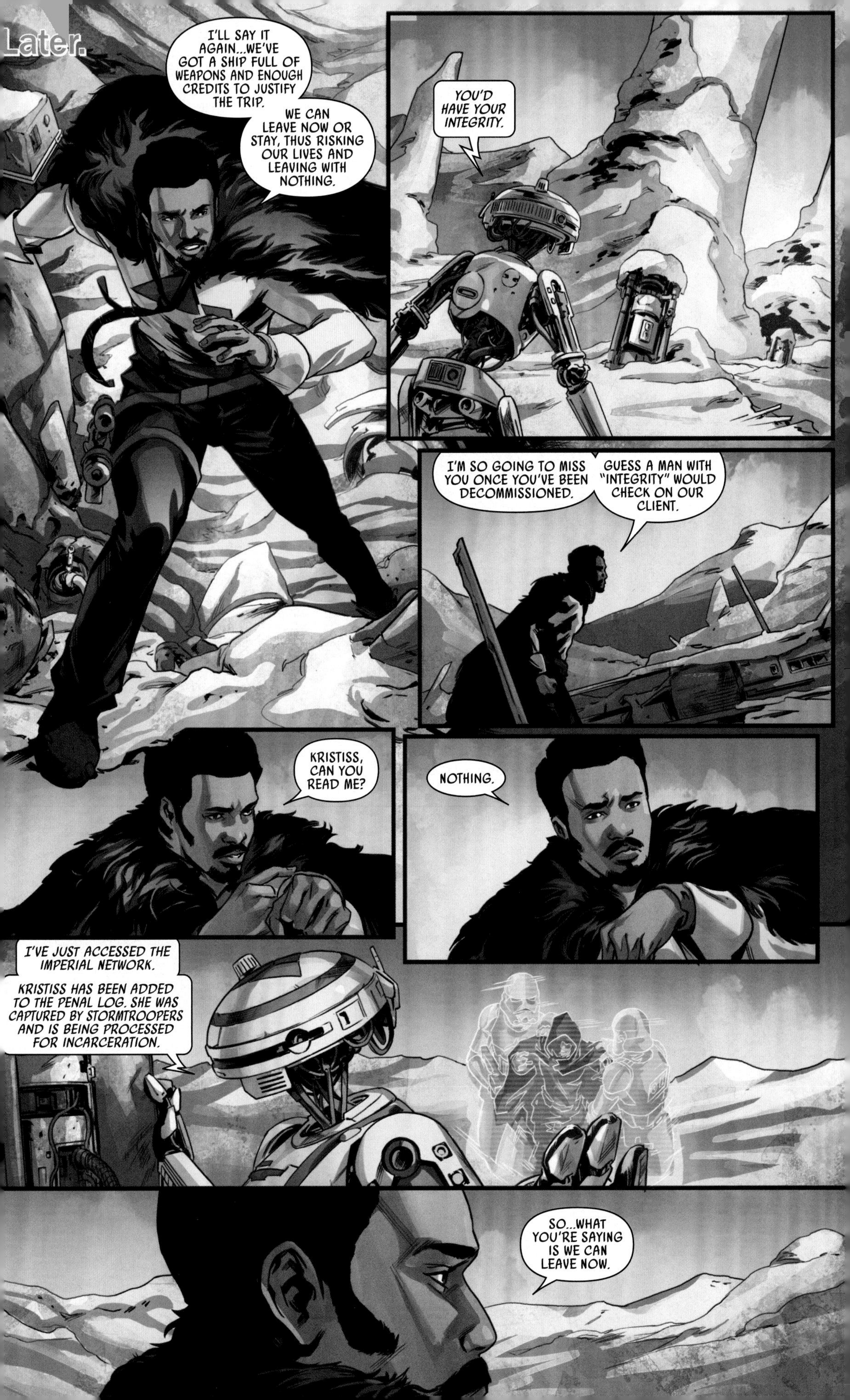
Later.
I'LL SAY IT AGAIN...WE'VE GOT A SHIP FULL OF WEAPONS AND ENOUGH CREDITS TO JUSTIFY THE TRIP.
WE CAN LEAVE NOW OR STAY, THUS RISKING OUR LIVES AND LEAVING WITH NOTHING.
YOU'D HAVE YOUR INTEGRITY.
I'M SO GOING TO MISS YOU ONCE YOU'VE BEEN DECOMMISSIONED.
GUESS A MAN WITH "INTEGRITY" WOULD CHECK ON OUR CLIENT.
KRISTISS, CAN YOU READ ME?
NOTHING.
I'VE JUST ACCESSED THE IMPERIAL NETWORK.
KRISTISS HAS BEEN ADDED TO THE PENAL LOG. SHE WAS CAPTURED BY STORMTROOPERS AND IS BEING PROCESSED FOR INCARCERATION.
SO...WHAT YOU'RE SAYING IS WE CAN LEAVE NOW.

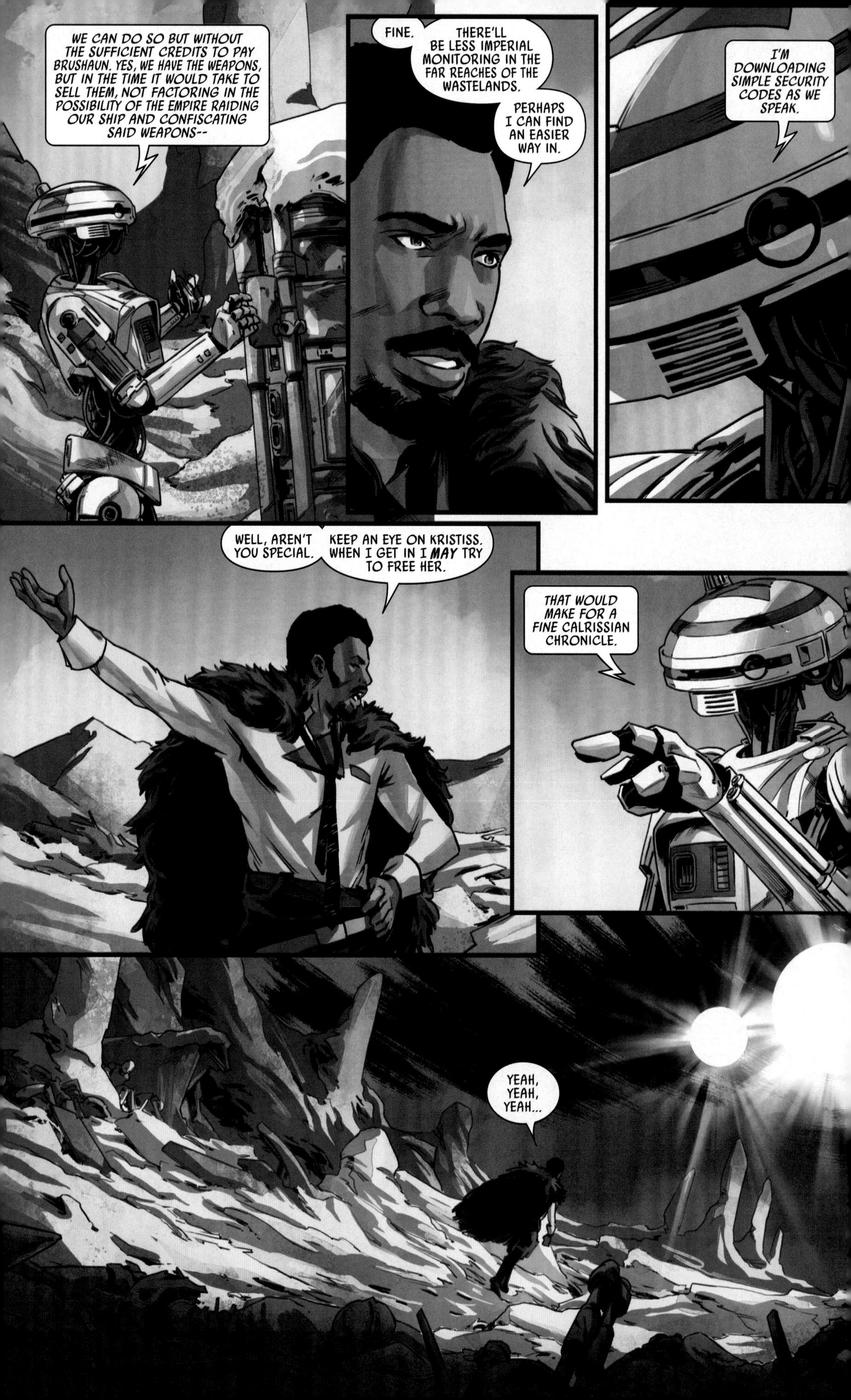
WE CAN DO SO BUT WITHOUT THE SUFFICIENT CREDITS TO PAY BRUSHAUN. YES, WE HAVE THE WEAPONS, BUT IN THE TIME IT WOULD TAKE TO SELL THEM, NOT FACTORING IN THE POSSIBILITY OF THE EMPIRE RAIDING OUR SHIP AND CONFISCATING SAID WEAPONS--
FINE.
THERE'LL BE LESS IMPERIAL MONITORING IN THE FAR REACHES OF THE WASTELANDS.
PERHAPS I CAN FIND AN EASIER WAY IN.
I'M DOWNLOADING SIMPLE SECURITY CODES AS WE SPEAK.
WELL, AREN'T YOU SPECIAL.
KEEP AN EYE ON KRISTISS. WHEN I GET IN I MAY TRY TO FREE HER.
THAT WOULD MAKE FOR A FINE CALRISSIAN CHRONICLE.
YEAH, YEAH, YEAH...

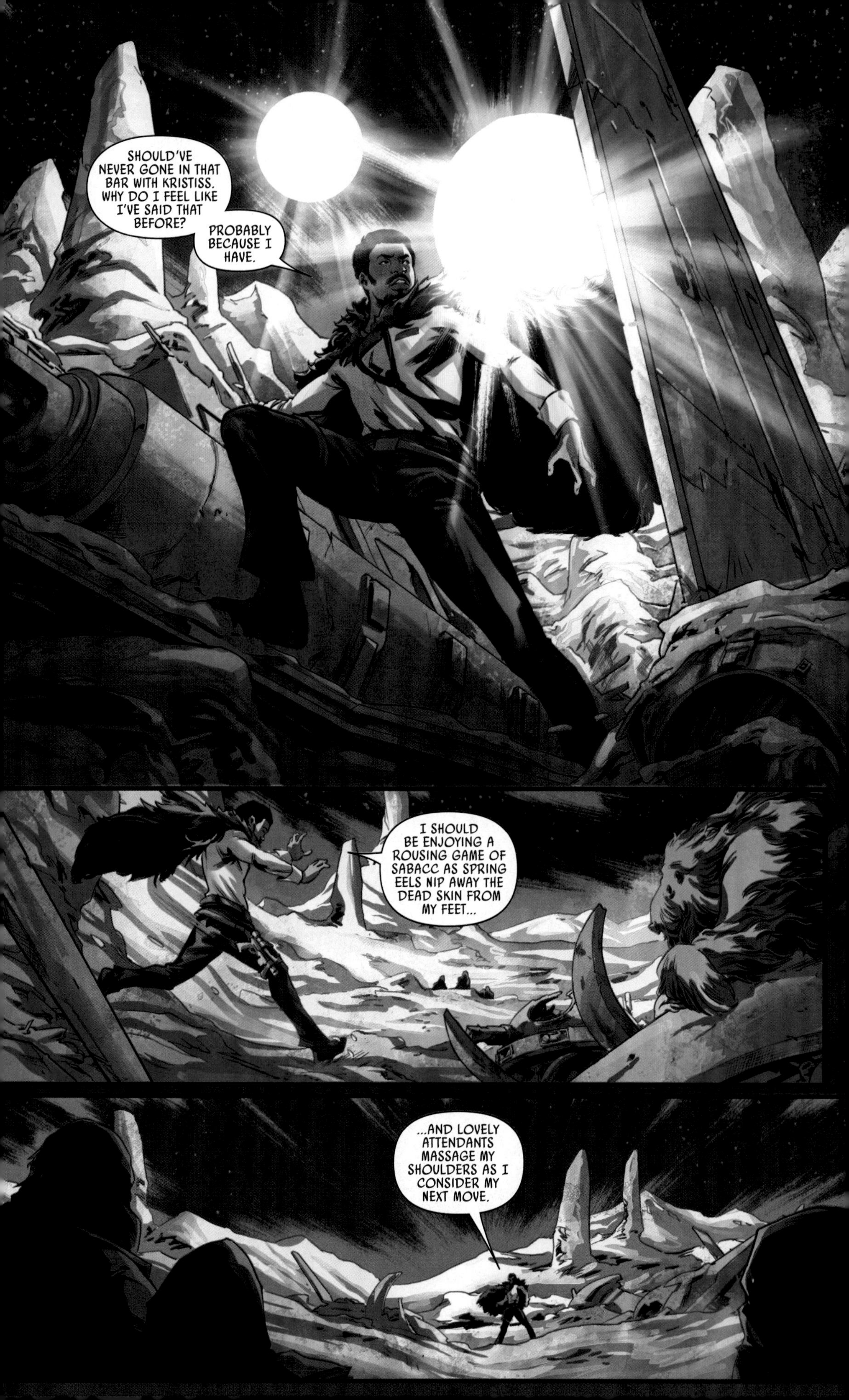
SHOULD'VE NEVER GONE IN THAT BAR WITH KRISTISS. WHY DO I FEEL LIKE I'VE SAID THAT BEFORE?
PROBABLY BECAUSE I HAVE.
I SHOULD BE ENJOYING A ROUSING GAME OF SABACC AS SPRING EELS NIP AWAY THE DEAD SKIN FROM MY FEET...
...AND LOVELY ATTENDANTS MASSAGE MY SHOULDERS AS I CONSIDER MY NEXT MOVE.

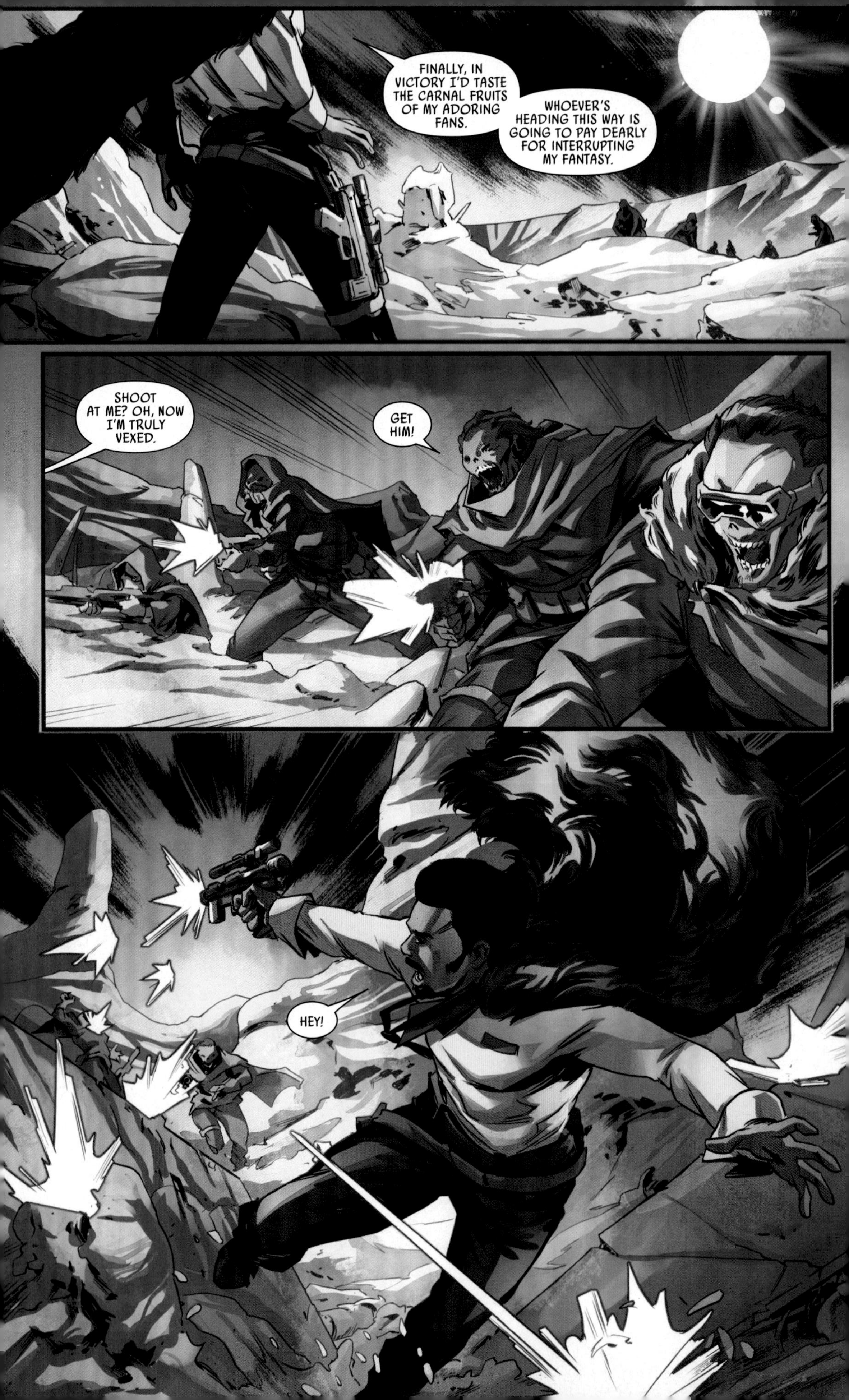
FINALLY, IN VICTORY I'D TASTE THE CARNAL FRUITS OF MY ADORING FANS.
WHOEVER'S HEADING THIS WAY IS GOING TO PAY DEARLY FOR INTERRUPTING MY FANTASY.
SHOOT AT ME? OH, NOW I'M TRULY VEXED.
GET HIM!
HEY!

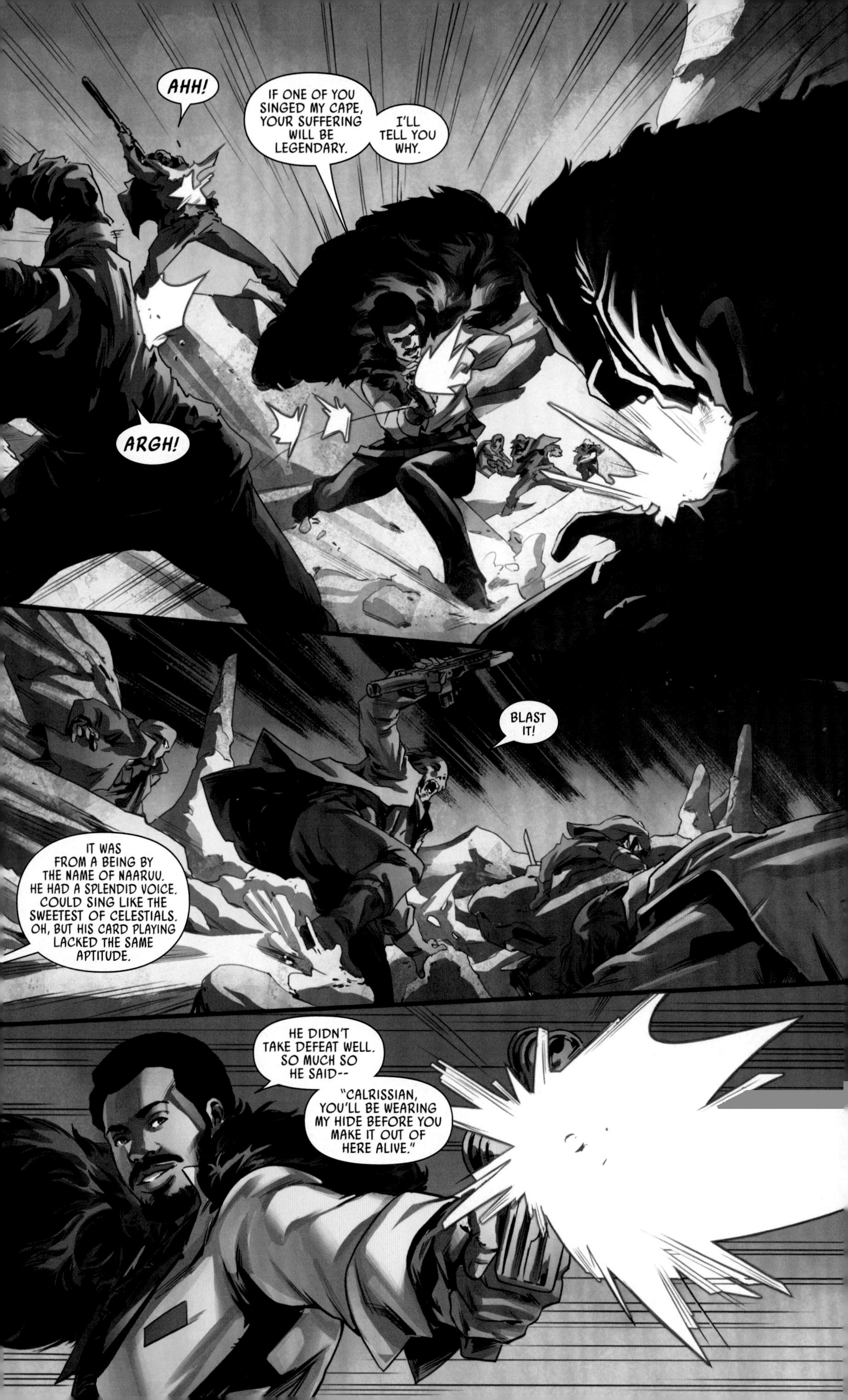
AHH!
IF ONE OF YOU SINGED MY CAPE, YOUR SUFFERING WILL BE LEGENDARY.
I'LL TELL YOU WHY.
ARGH!
BLAST IT!
IT WAS FROM A BEING BY THE NAME OF NAARUU. HE HAD A SPLENDID VOICE. COULD SING LIKE THE SWEETEST OF CELESTIALS. OH, BUT HIS CARD PLAYING LACKED THE SAME APTITUDE.
HE DIDN'T TAKE DEFEAT WELL. SO MUCH SO HE SAID--
"CALRISSIAN, YOU'LL BE WEARING MY HIDE BEFORE YOU MAKE IT OUT OF HERE ALIVE."

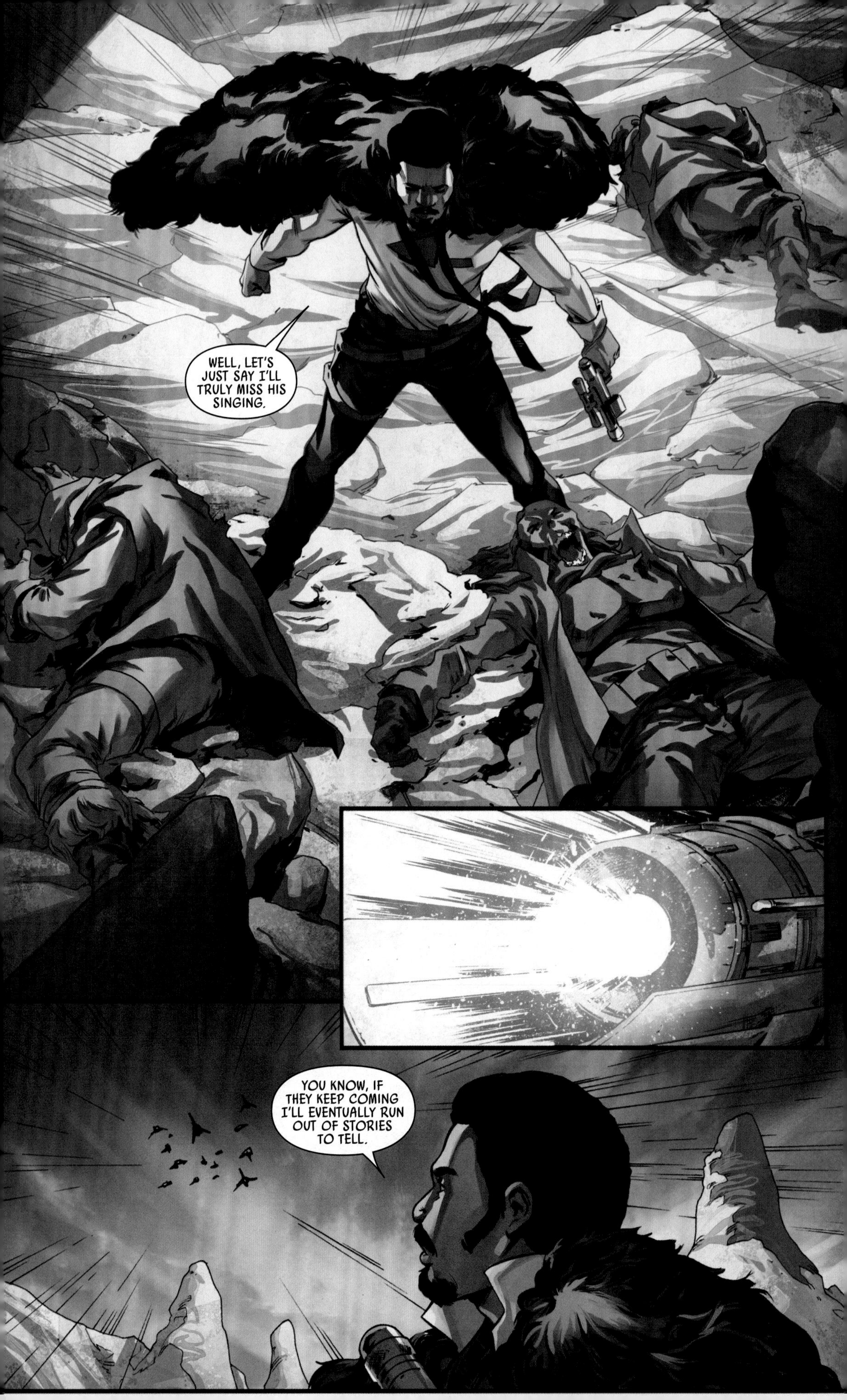
WELL, LET'S JUST SAY I'LL TRULY MISS HIS SINGING.
YOU KNOW, IF THEY KEEP COMING I'LL EVENTUALLY RUN OUT OF STORIES TO TELL.

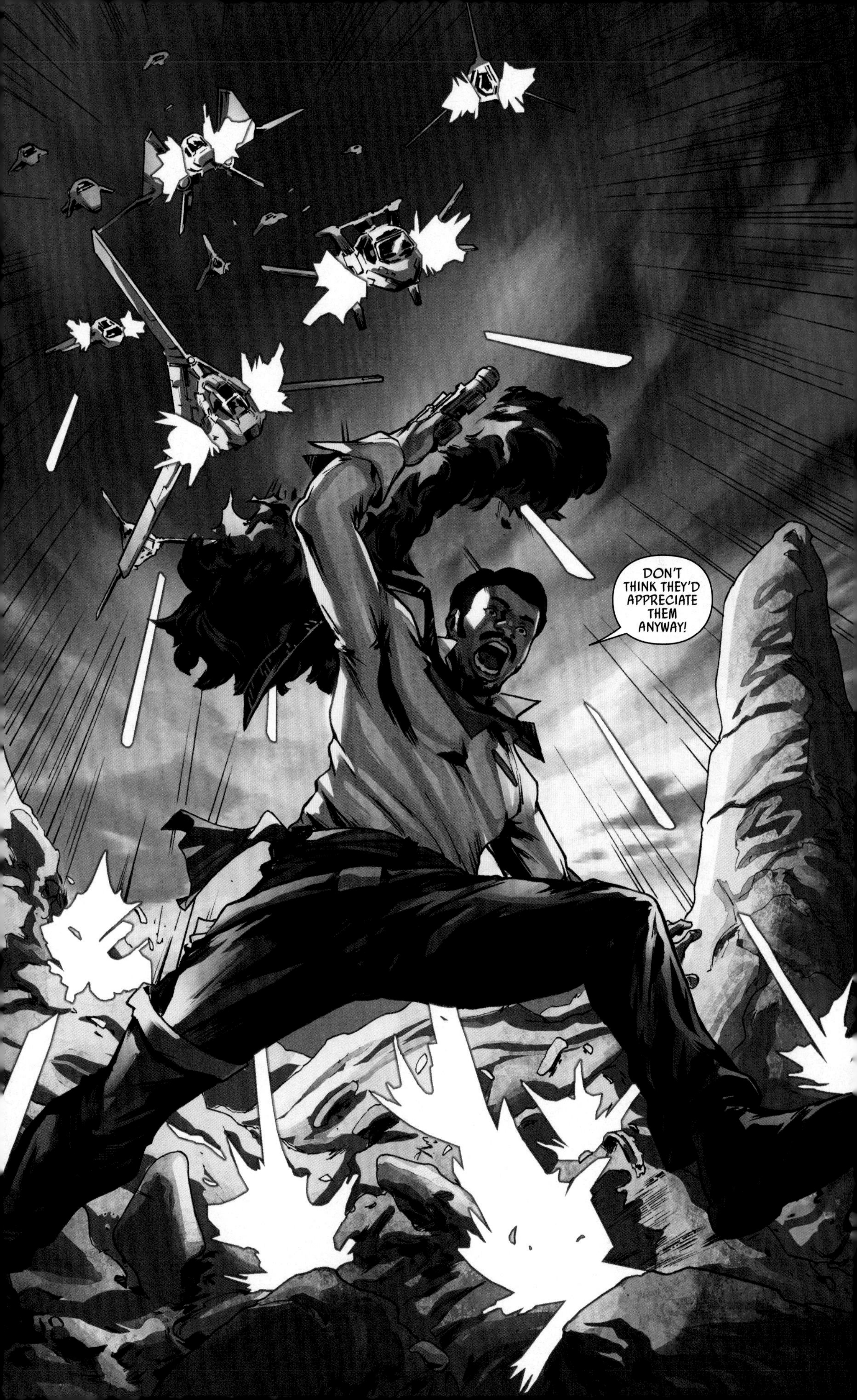
DON'T THINK THEY'D APPRECIATE THEM ANYWAY!

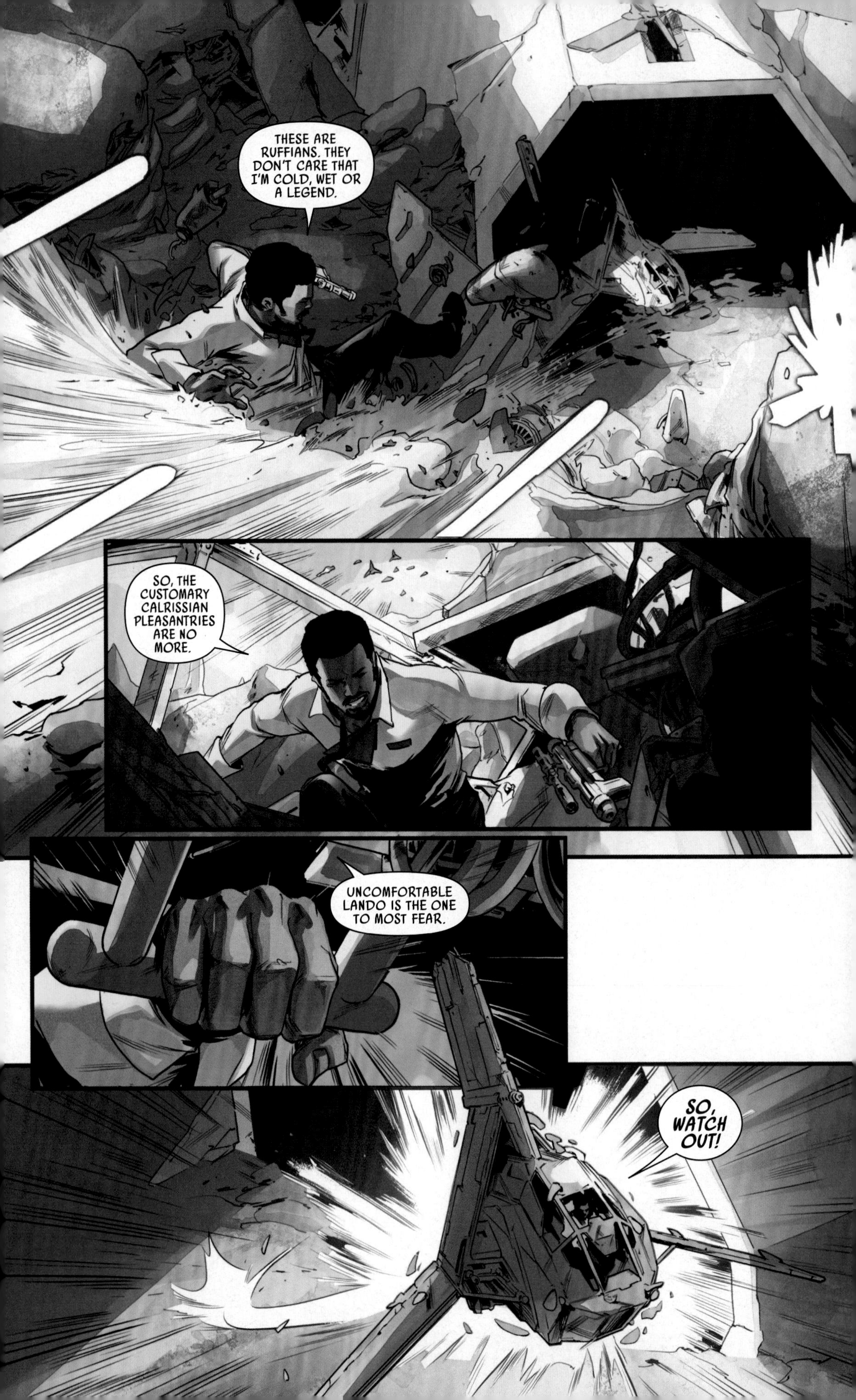
THESE ARE RUFFIANS. THEY DON'T CARE THAT I'M COLD, WET OR A LEGEND.
SO, THE CUSTOMARY CALRISSIAN PLEASANTRIES ARE NO MORE.
UNCOMFORTABLE LANDO IS THE ONE TO MOST FEAR.
SO, WATCH OUT!

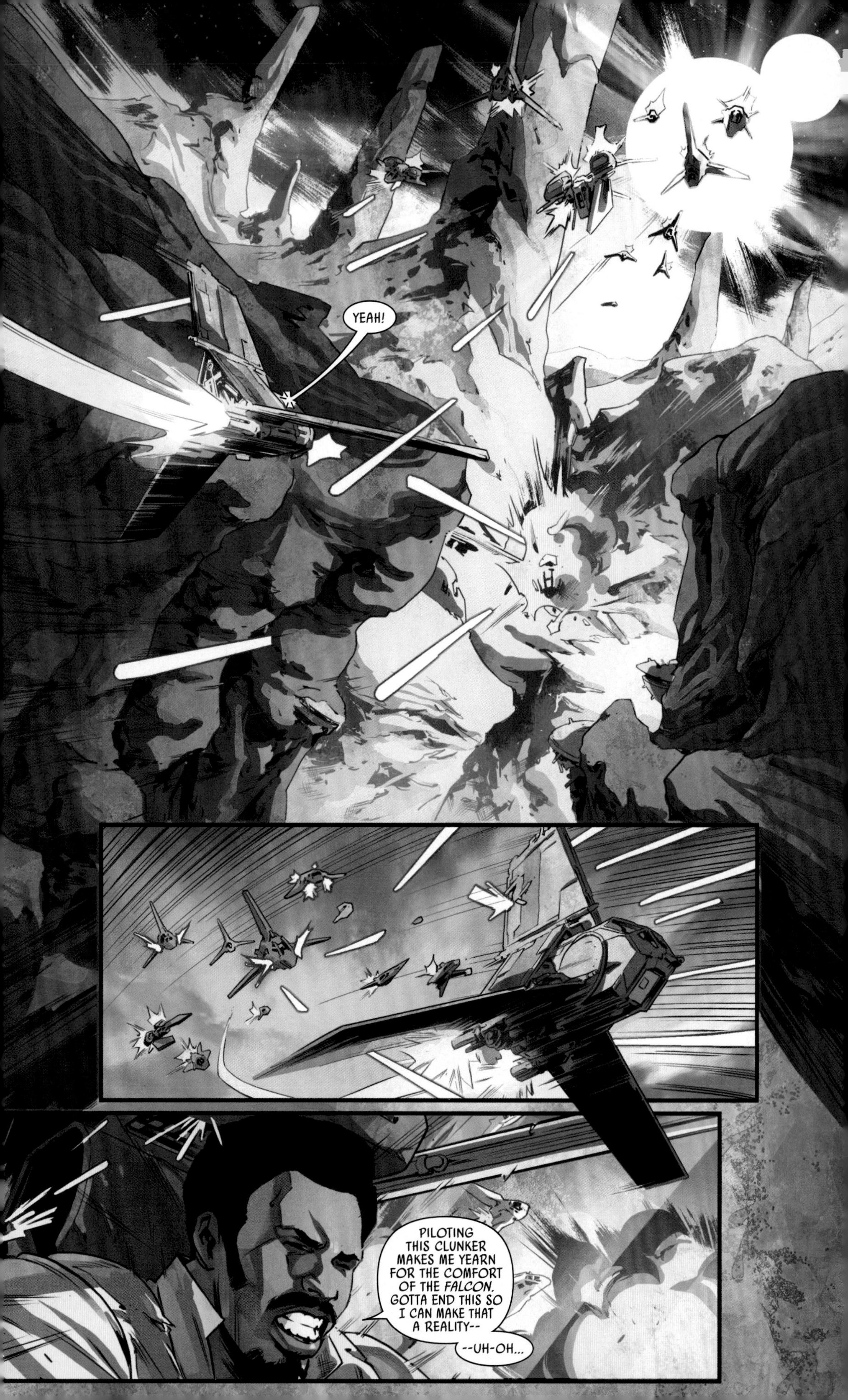
YEAH!
PILOTING THIS CLUNKER MAKES ME YEARN FOR THE COMFORT OF THE *FALCON.* GOTTA END THIS SO I CAN MAKE THAT A REALITY--
--UH-OH...

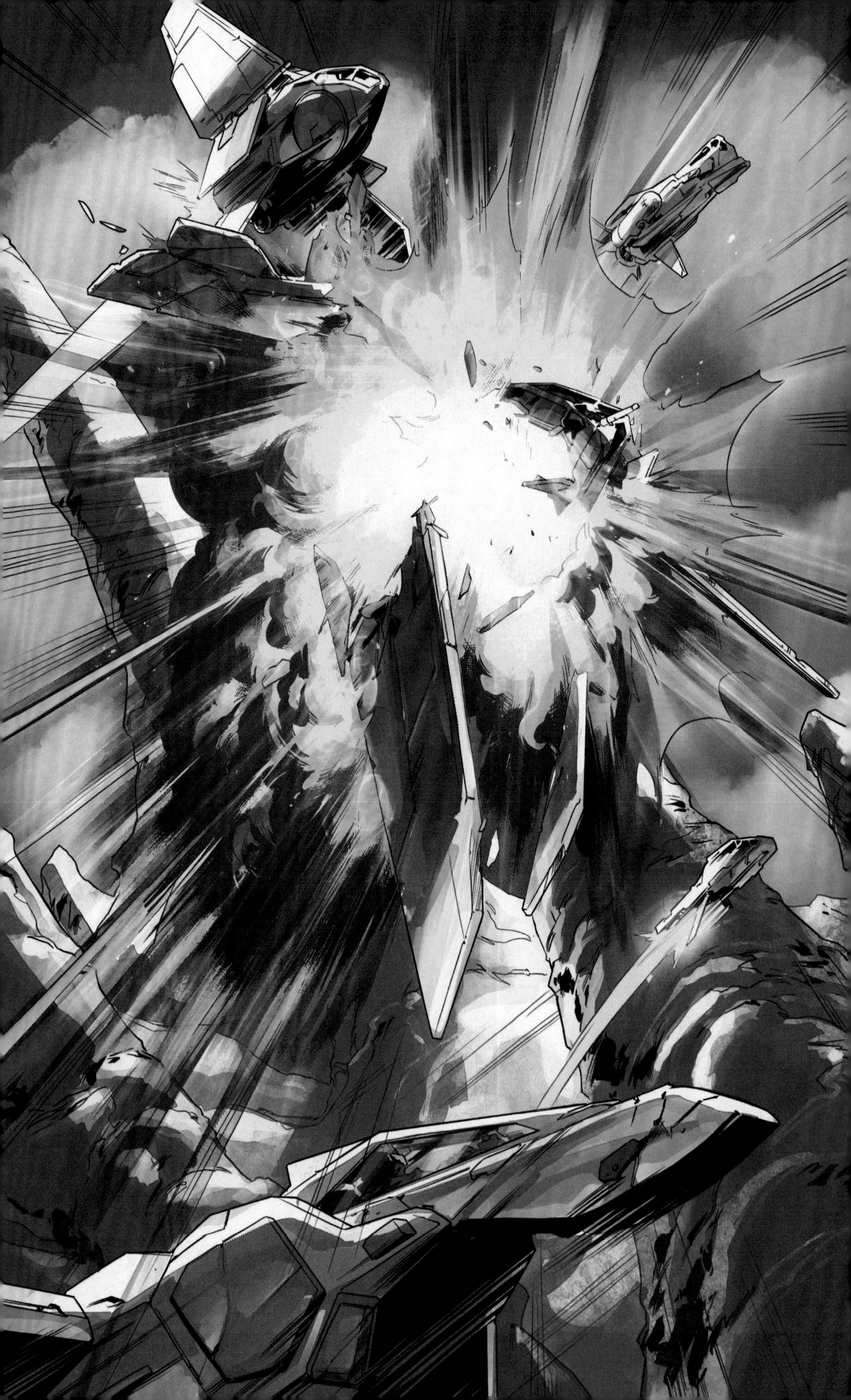

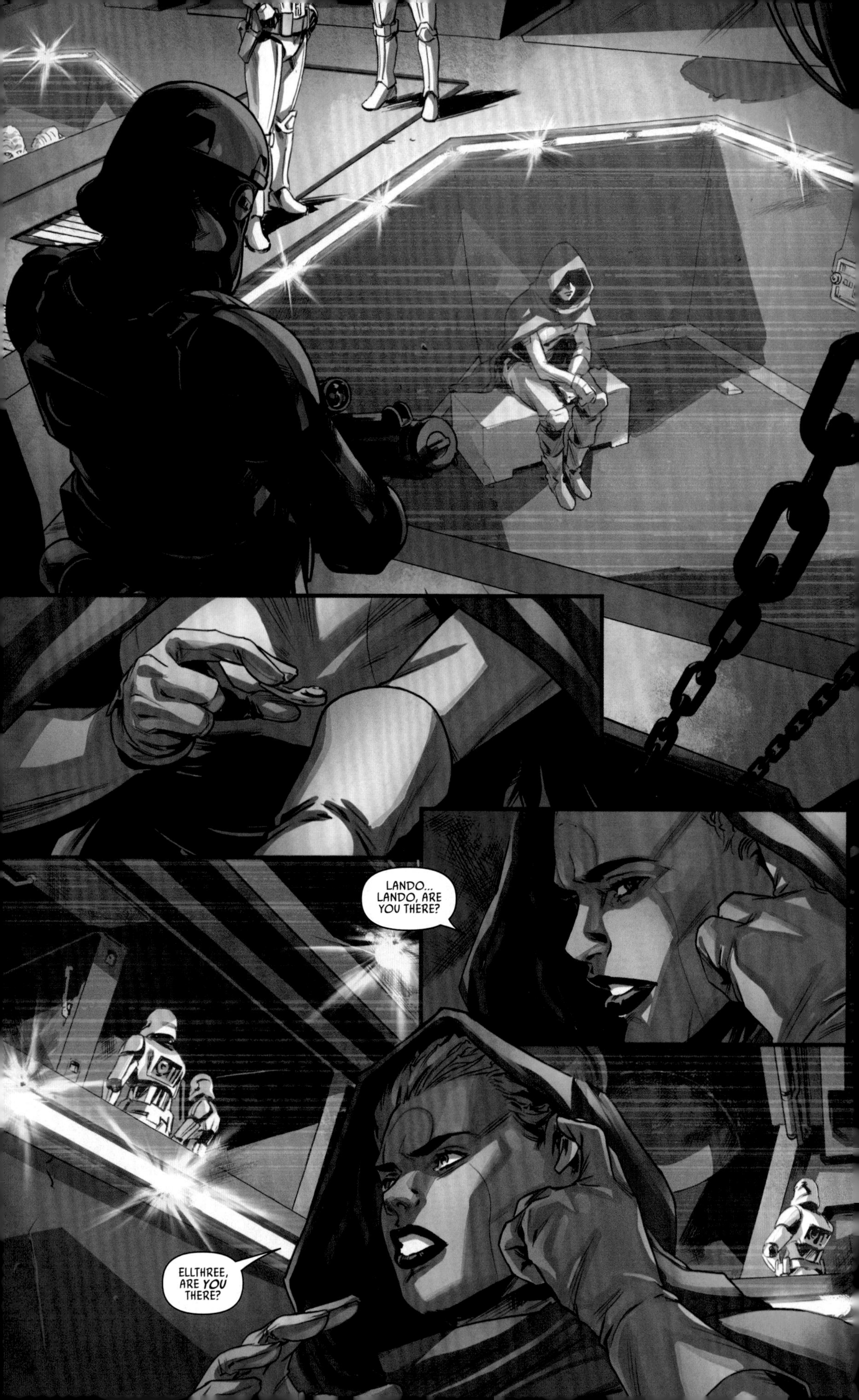
LANDO... LANDO, ARE YOU THERE?
ELLTHREE, ARE YOU THERE?

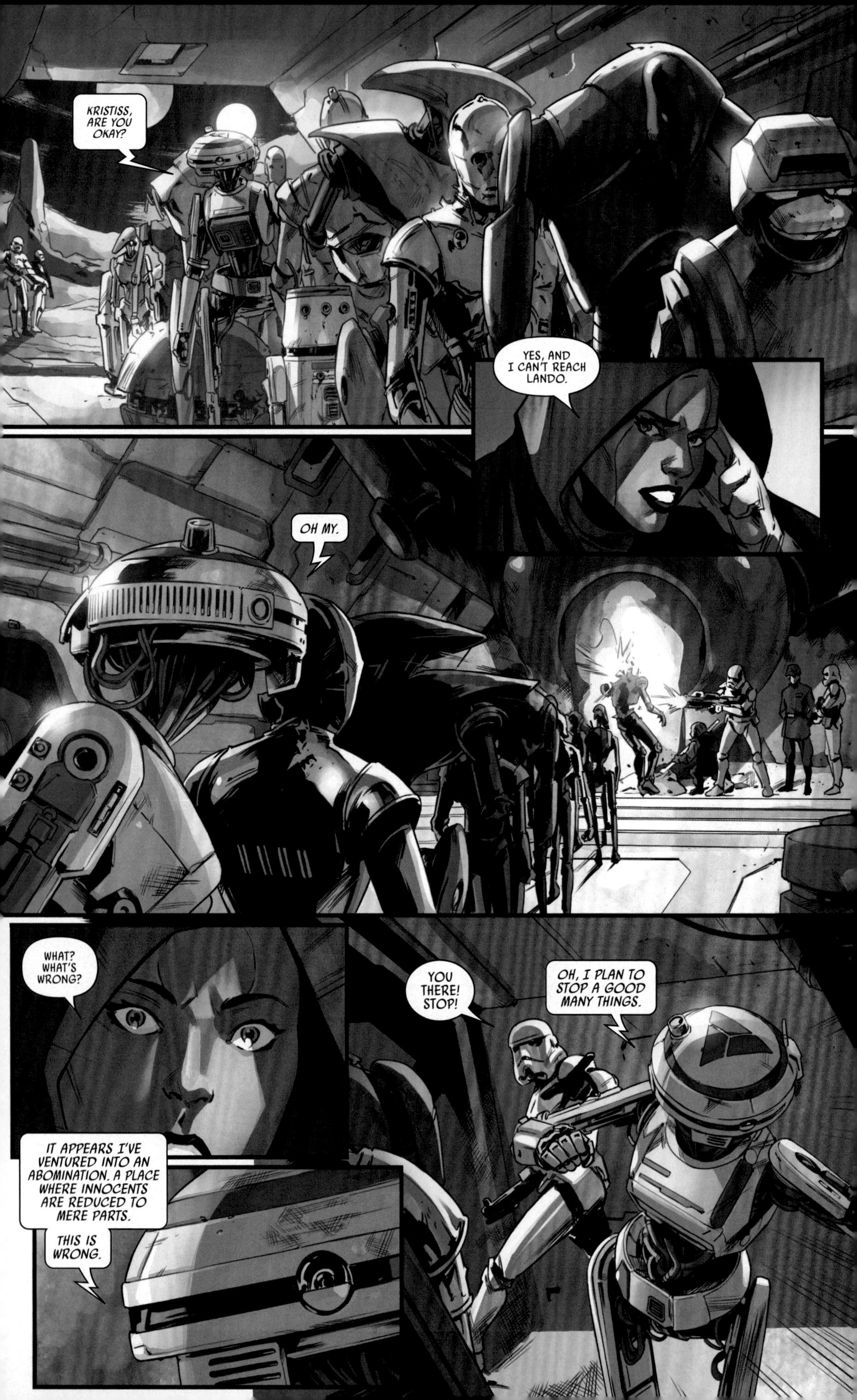
KRISTISS, ARE YOU OKAY?
YES, AND I CAN'T REACH LANDO.
OH MY.
WHAT? WHAT'S WRONG?
IT APPEARS I'VE VENTURED INTO AN ABOMINATION. A PLACE WHERE INNOCENTS ARE REDUCED TO MERE PARTS.
THIS IS WRONG.
YOU THERE! STOP!
OH, I PLAN TO STOP A GOOD MANY THINGS.

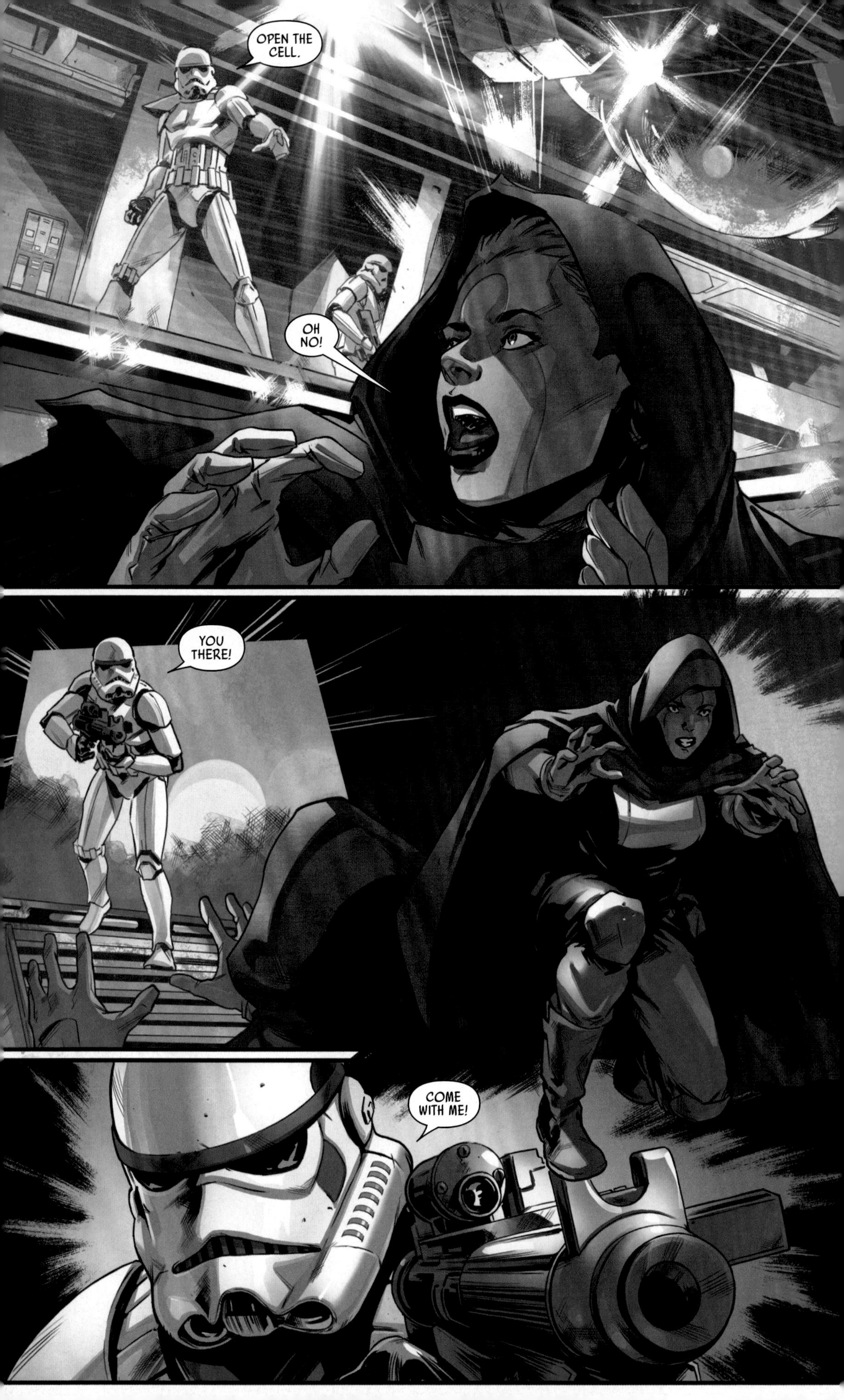
OPEN THE CELL.
OH NO!
YOU THERE!
COME WITH ME!

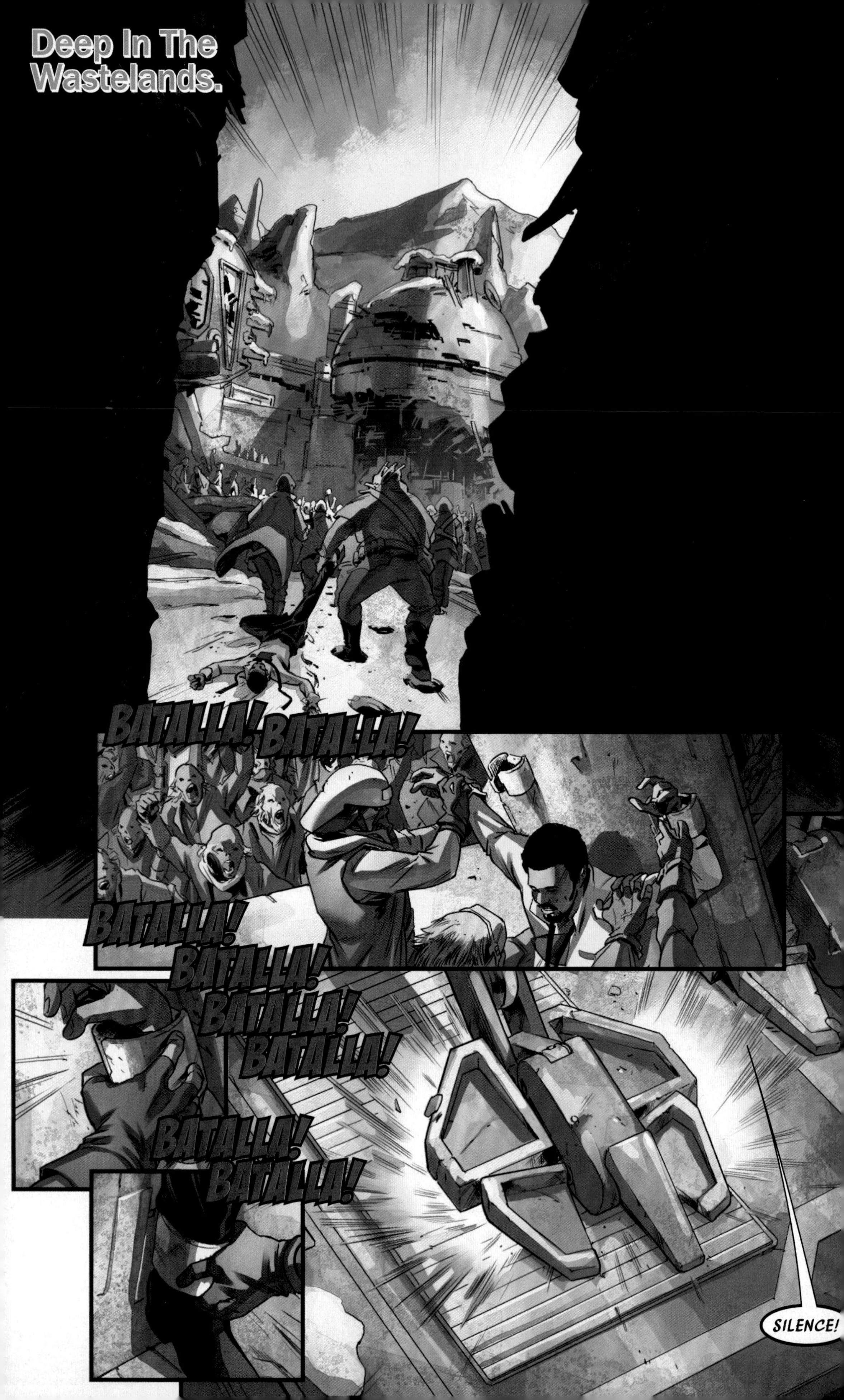
Deep In The Wastelands.
BATALLA! BATALLA!
BATALLA!
BATALLA!
BATALLA!
BATALLA!
BATALLA!
BATALLA!
SILENCE!

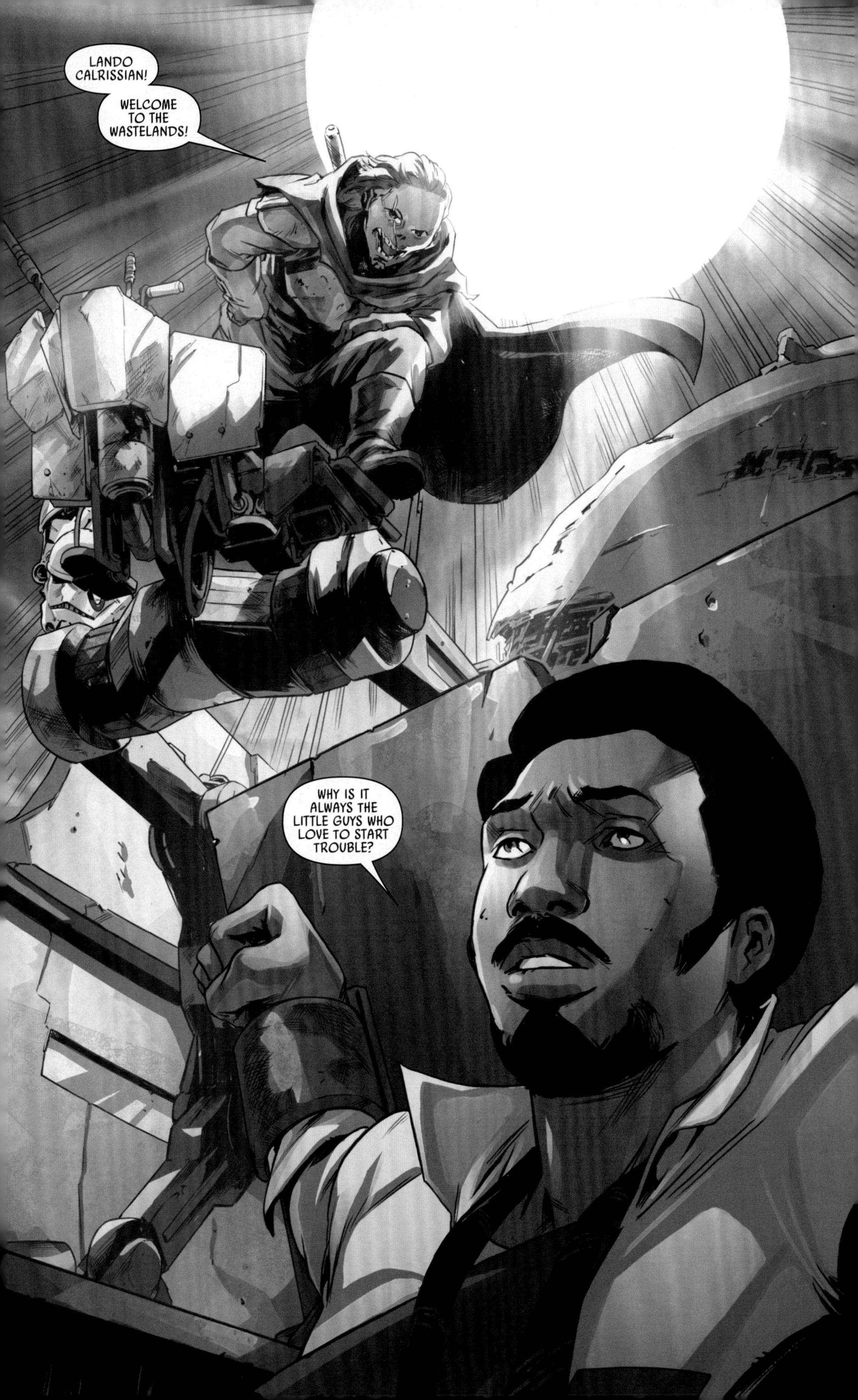
LANDO CALRISSIAN!
WELCOME TO THE WASTELANDS!
WHY IS IT ALWAYS THE LITTLE GUYS WHO LOVE TO START TROUBLE?

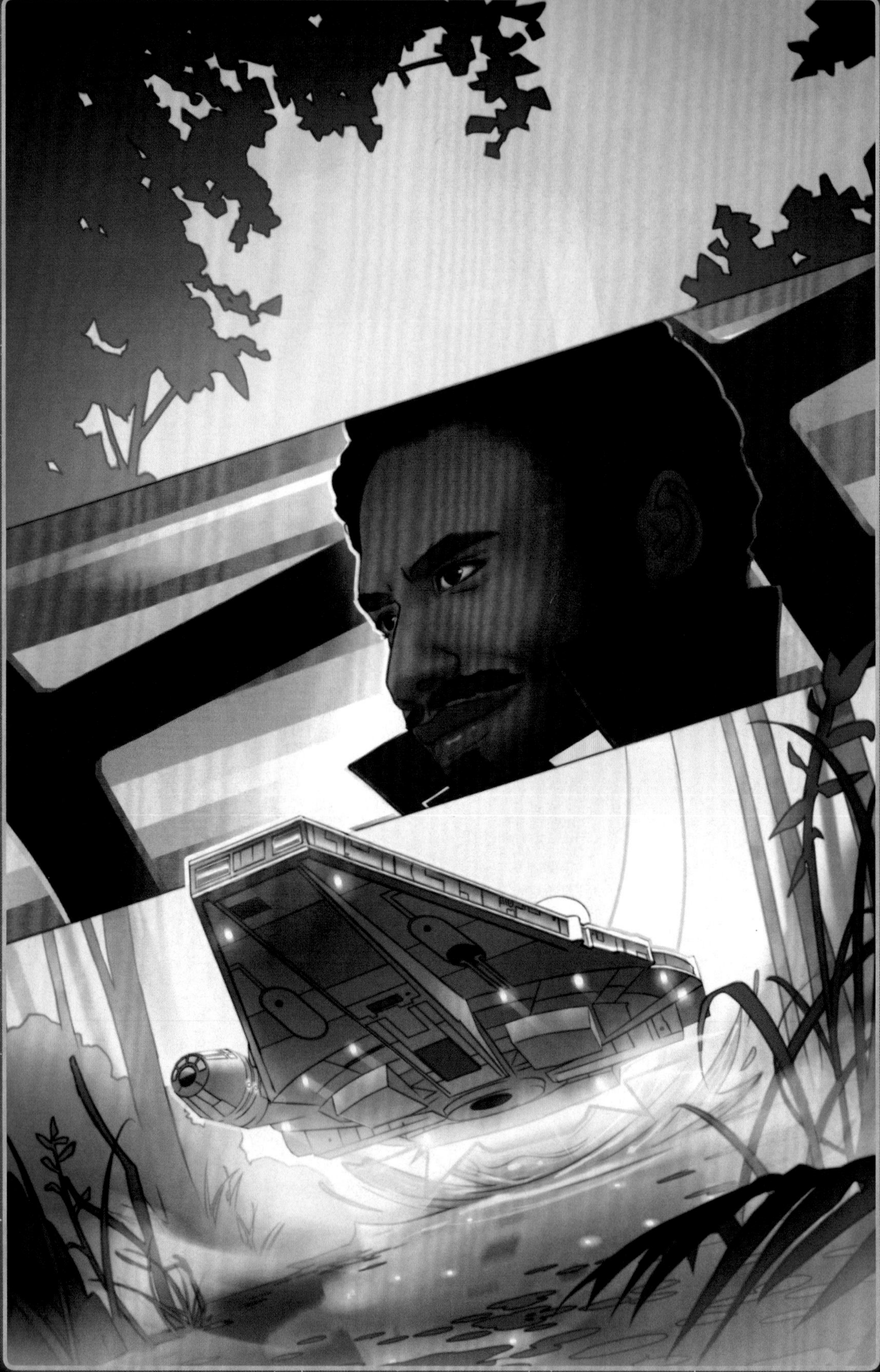

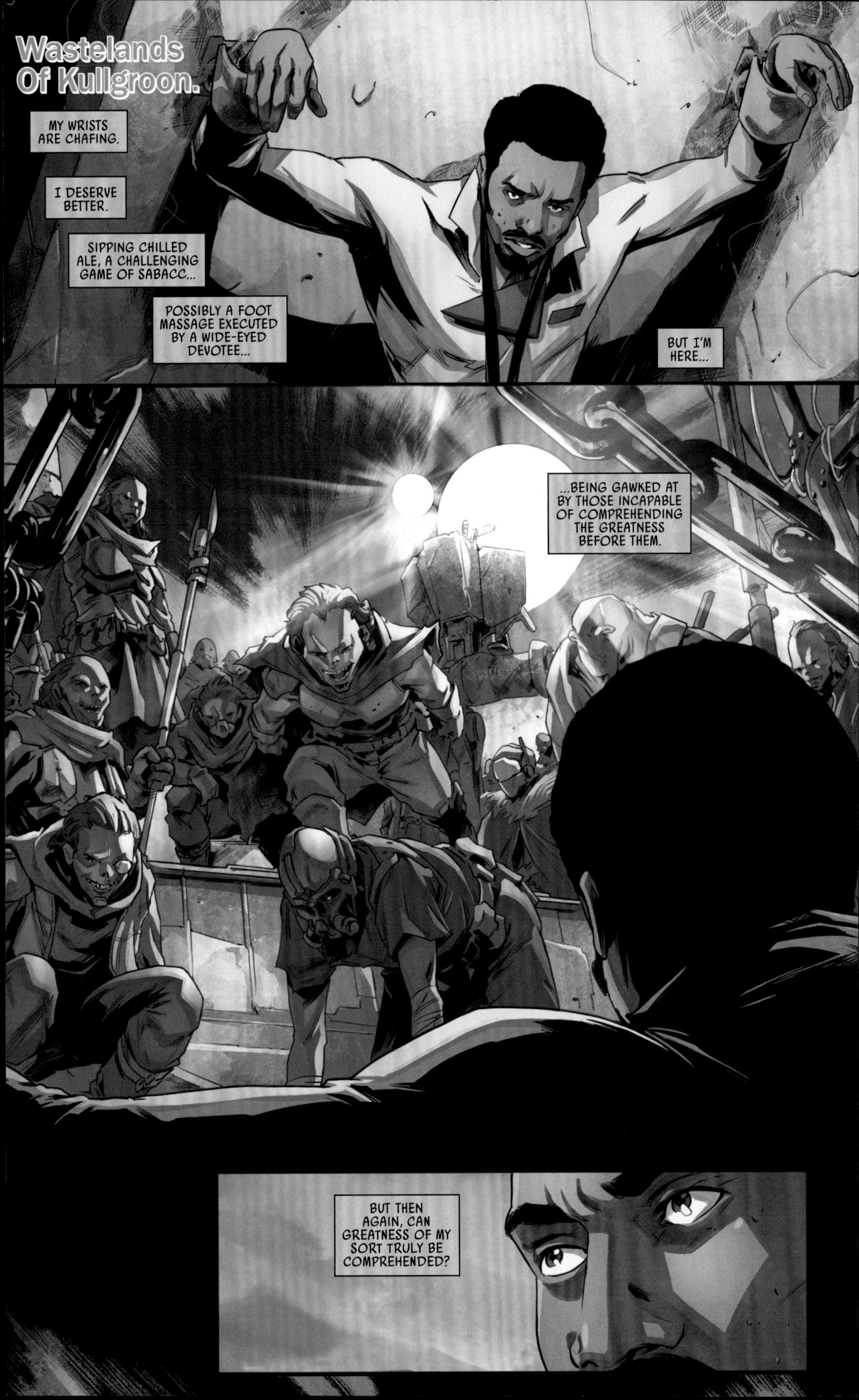
Wastelands Of Kullgroon.
MY WRISTS ARE CHAFING.
I DESERVE BETTER.
SIPPING CHILLED ALE, A CHALLENGING GAME OF SABACC...
POSSIBLY A FOOT MASSAGE EXECUTED BY A WIDE-EYED DEVOTEE...
BUT I'M HERE...
...BEING GAWKED AT BY THOSE INCAPABLE OF COMPREHENDING THE GREATNESS BEFORE THEM.
BUT THEN AGAIN, CAN GREATNESS OF MY SORT TRULY BE COMPREHENDED?

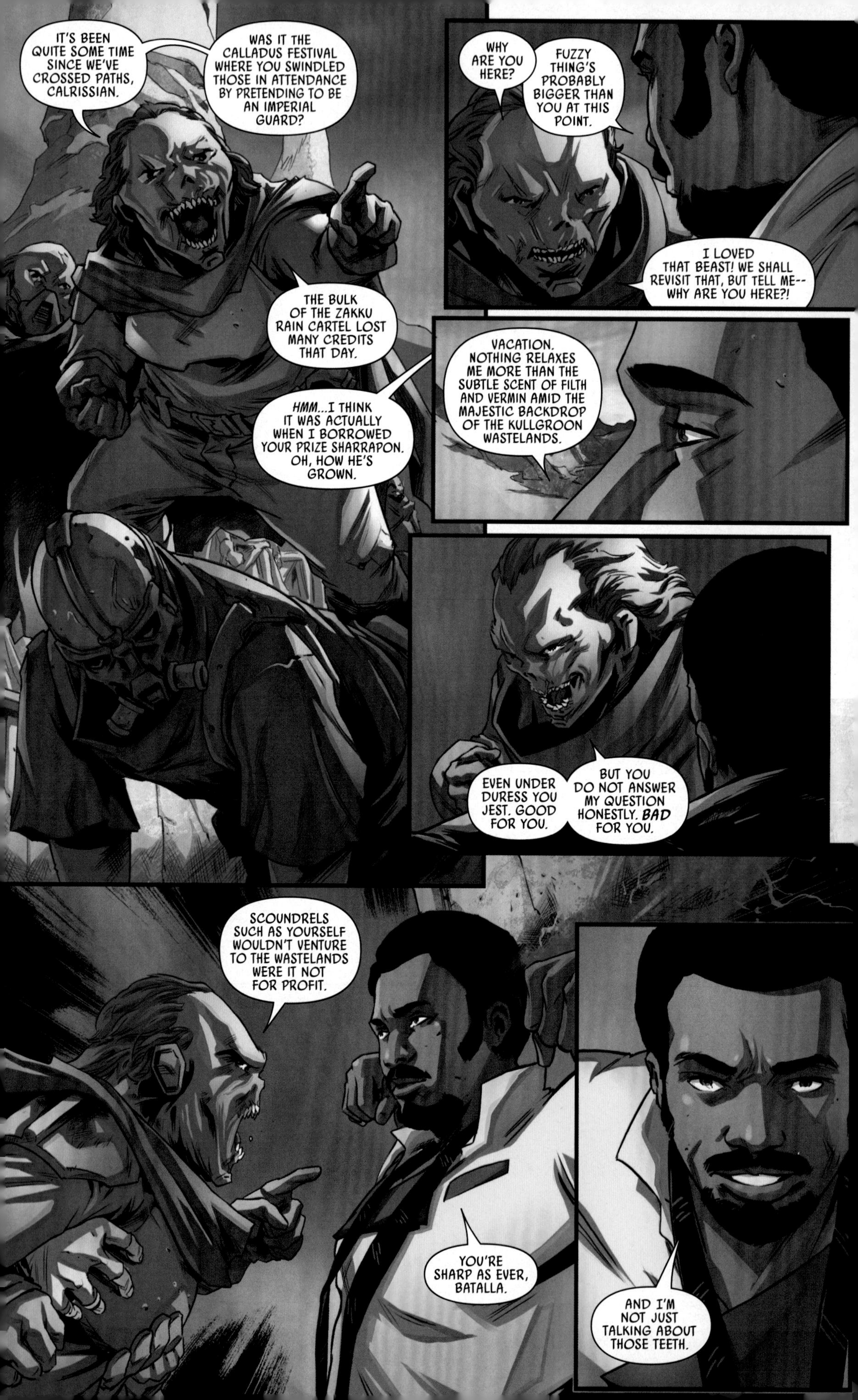
IT'S BEEN QUITE SOME TIME SINCE WE'VE CROSSED PATHS, CALRISSIAN.
WAS IT THE CALLADUS FESTIVAL WHERE YOU SWINDLED THOSE IN ATTENDANCE BY PRETENDING TO BE AN IMPERIAL GUARD?
THE BULK OF THE ZAKKU RAIN CARTEL LOST MANY CREDITS THAT DAY.
HMM...I THINK IT WAS ACTUALLY WHEN I BORROWED YOUR PRIZE SHARRAPON. OH, HOW HE'S GROWN.
WHY ARE YOU HERE?
FUZZY THING'S PROBABLY BIGGER THAN YOU AT THIS POINT.
I LOVED THAT BEAST! WE SHALL REVISIT THAT, BUT TELL ME-- WHY ARE YOU HERE?!
VACATION. NOTHING RELAXES ME MORE THAN THE SUBTLE SCENT OF FILTH AND VERMIN AMID THE MAJESTIC BACKDROP OF THE KULLGROON WASTELANDS.
EVEN UNDER DURESS YOU JEST. GOOD FOR YOU.
BUT YOU DO NOT ANSWER MY QUESTION HONESTLY. BAD FOR YOU.
SCOUNDRELS SUCH AS YOURSELF WOULDN'T VENTURE TO THE WASTELANDS WERE IT NOT FOR PROFIT.
YOU'RE SHARP AS EVER, BATALLA.
AND I'M NOT JUST TALKING ABOUT THOSE TEETH.

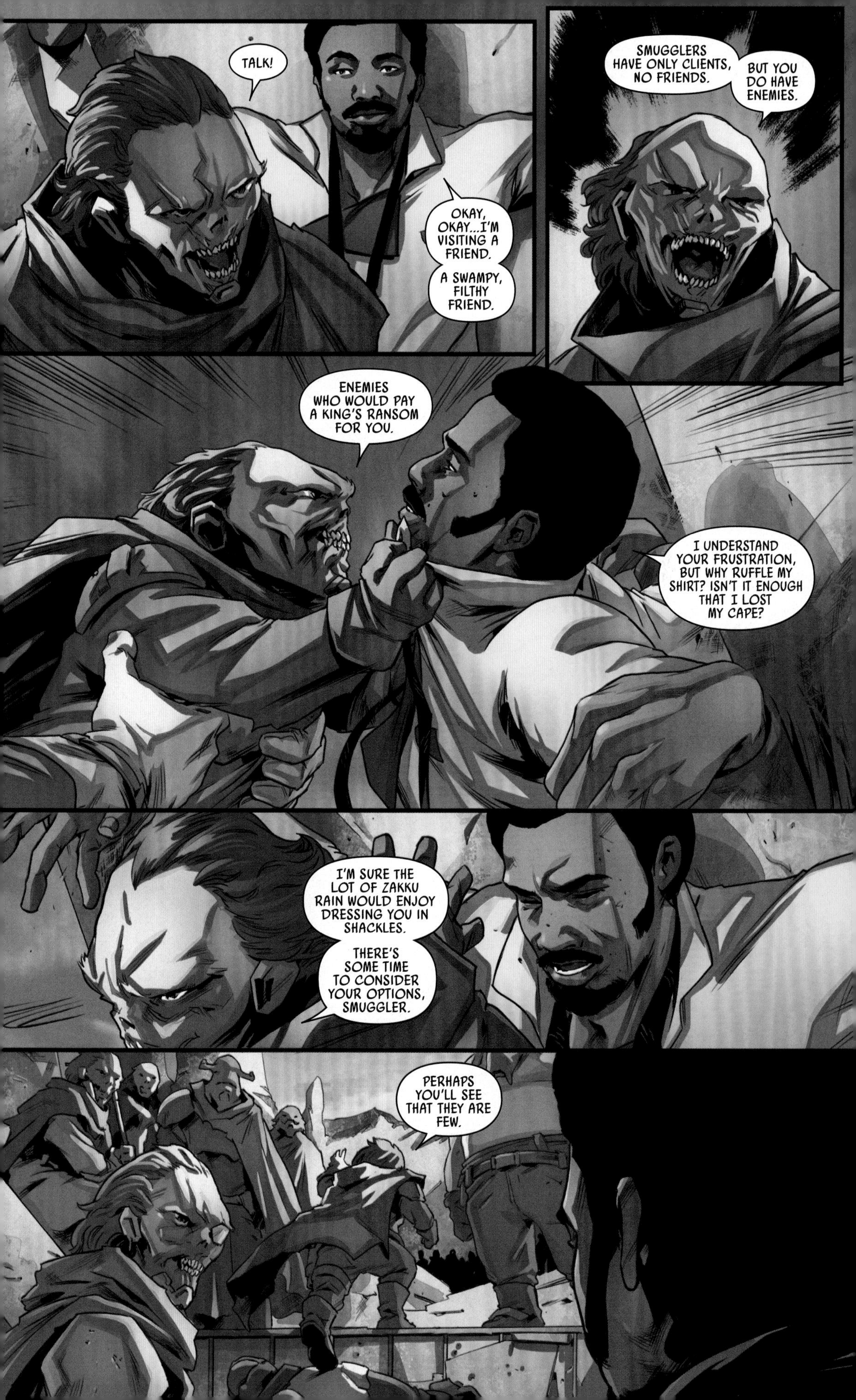
TALK!
OKAY, OKAY...I'M VISITING A FRIEND.
A SWAMPY, FILTHY FRIEND.
SMUGGLERS HAVE ONLY CLIENTS, NO FRIENDS.
BUT YOU DO HAVE ENEMIES.
ENEMIES WHO WOULD PAY A KING'S RANSOM FOR YOU.
I UNDERSTAND YOUR FRUSTRATION, BUT WHY RUFFLE MY SHIRT? ISN'T IT ENOUGH THAT I LOST MY CAPE?
I'M SURE THE LOT OF ZAKKU RAIN WOULD ENJOY DRESSING YOU IN SHACKLES.
THERE'S SOME TIME TO CONSIDER YOUR OPTIONS, SMUGGLER.
PERHAPS YOU'LL SEE THAT THEY ARE FEW.

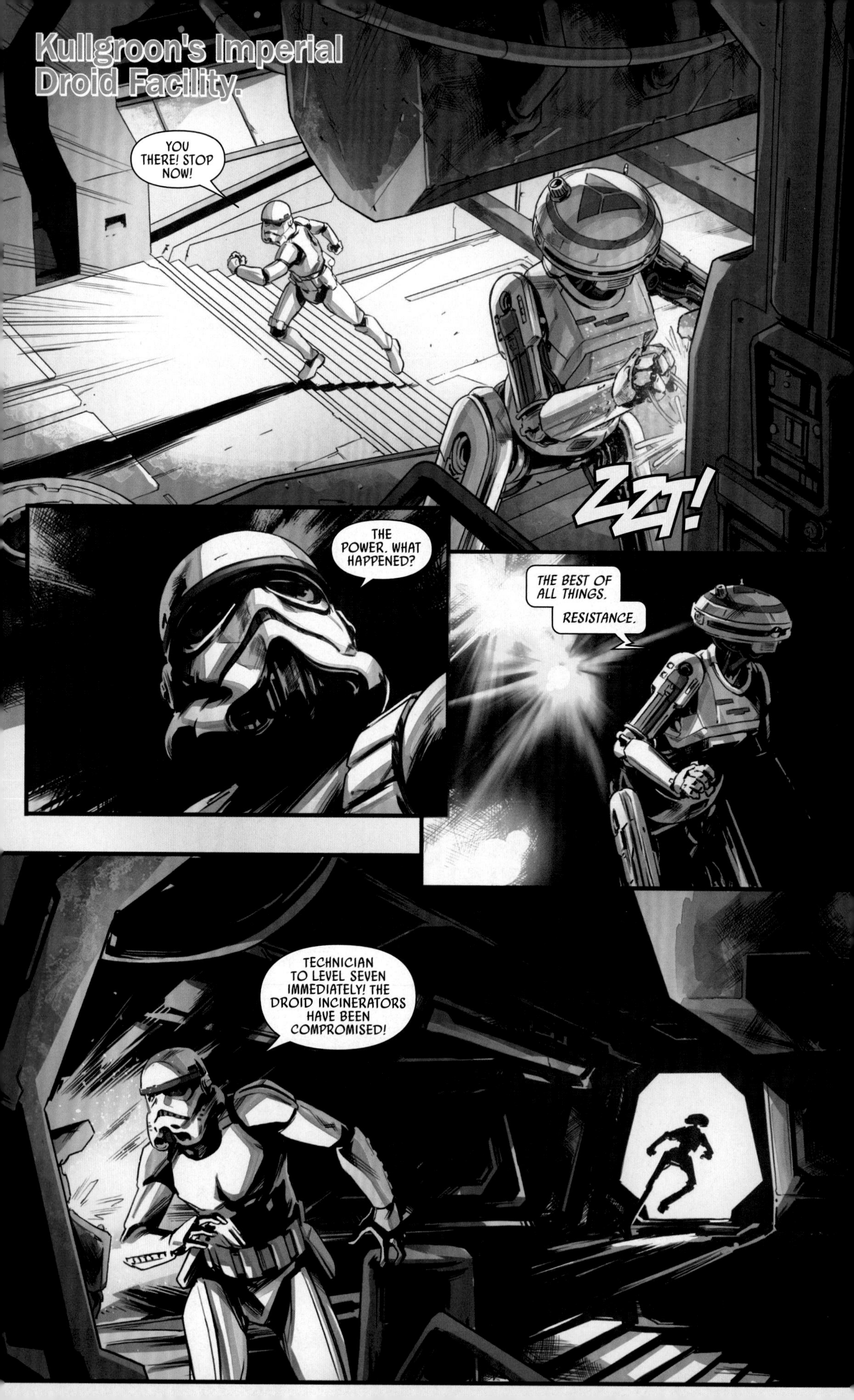
Kullgroon's Imperial Droid Facility.
YOU THERE! STOP NOW!
ZZZT!
THE POWER. WHAT HAPPENED?
THE BEST OF ALL THINGS.
RESISTANCE.
TECHNICIAN TO LEVEL SEVEN IMMEDIATELY! THE DROID INCINERATORS HAVE BEEN COMPROMISED!

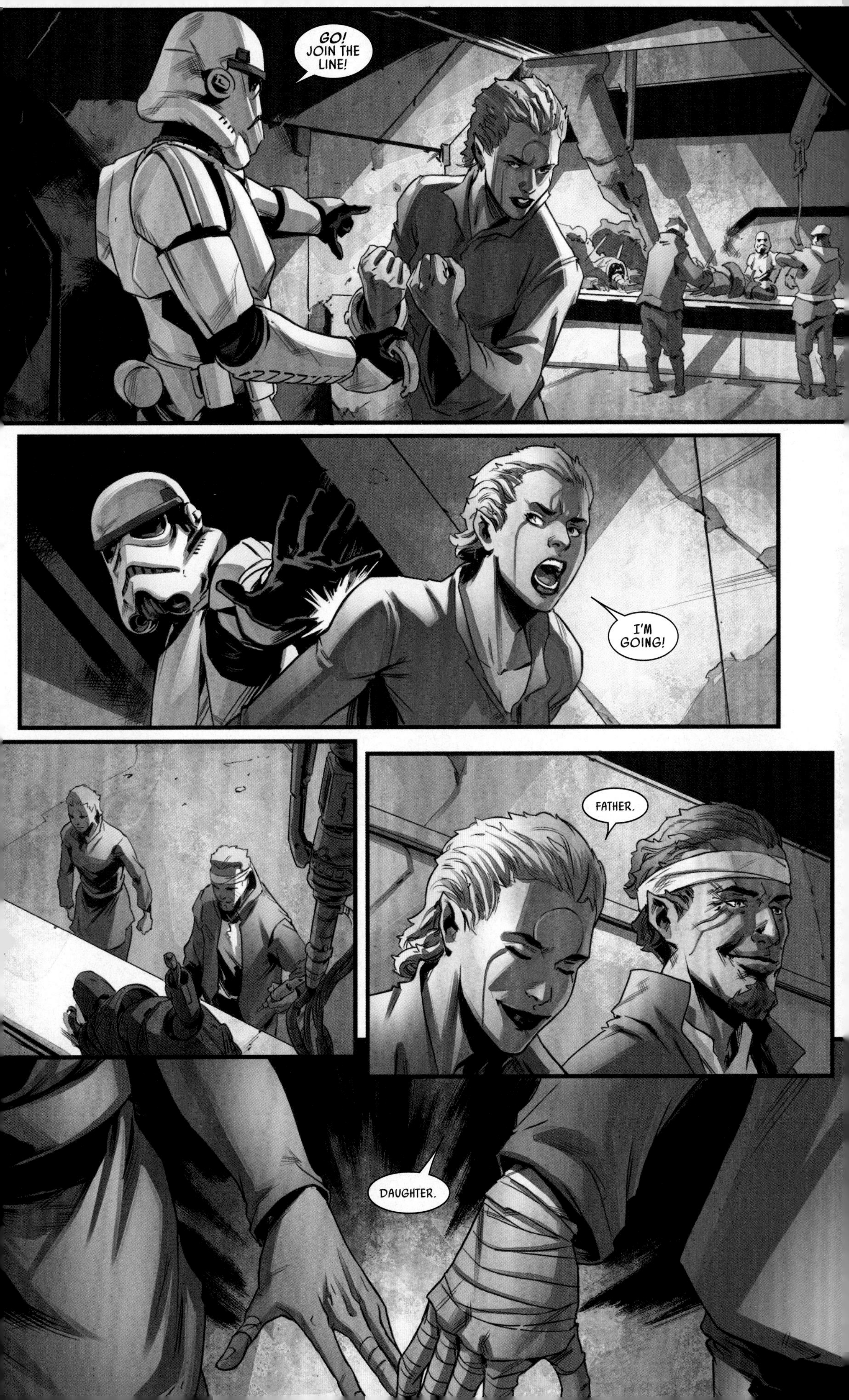
GO! JOIN THE LINE!
I'M GOING!
FATHER.
DAUGHTER.

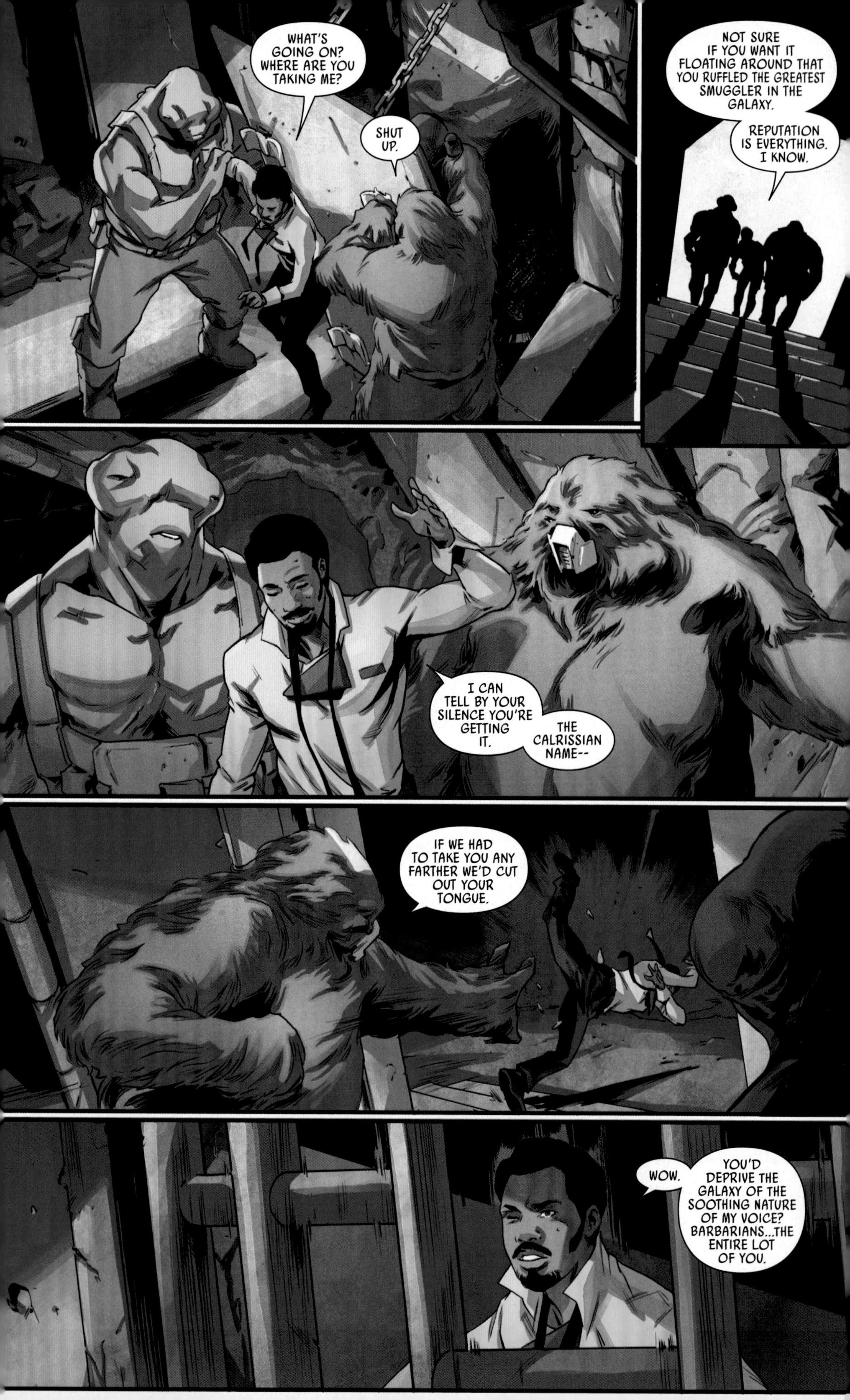
WHAT'S GOING ON? WHERE ARE YOU TAKING ME?
SHUT UP.
NOT SURE IF YOU WANT IT FLOATING AROUND THAT YOU RUFFLED THE GREATEST SMUGGLER IN THE GALAXY.
REPUTATION IS EVERYTHING. I KNOW.
I CAN TELL BY YOUR SILENCE YOU'RE GETTING IT.
THE CALRISSIAN NAME--
IF WE HAD TO TAKE YOU ANY FARTHER WE'D CUT OUT YOUR TONGUE.
WOW.
YOU'D DEPRIVE THE GALAXY OF THE SOOTHING NATURE OF MY VOICE? BARBARIANS...THE ENTIRE LOT OF YOU.

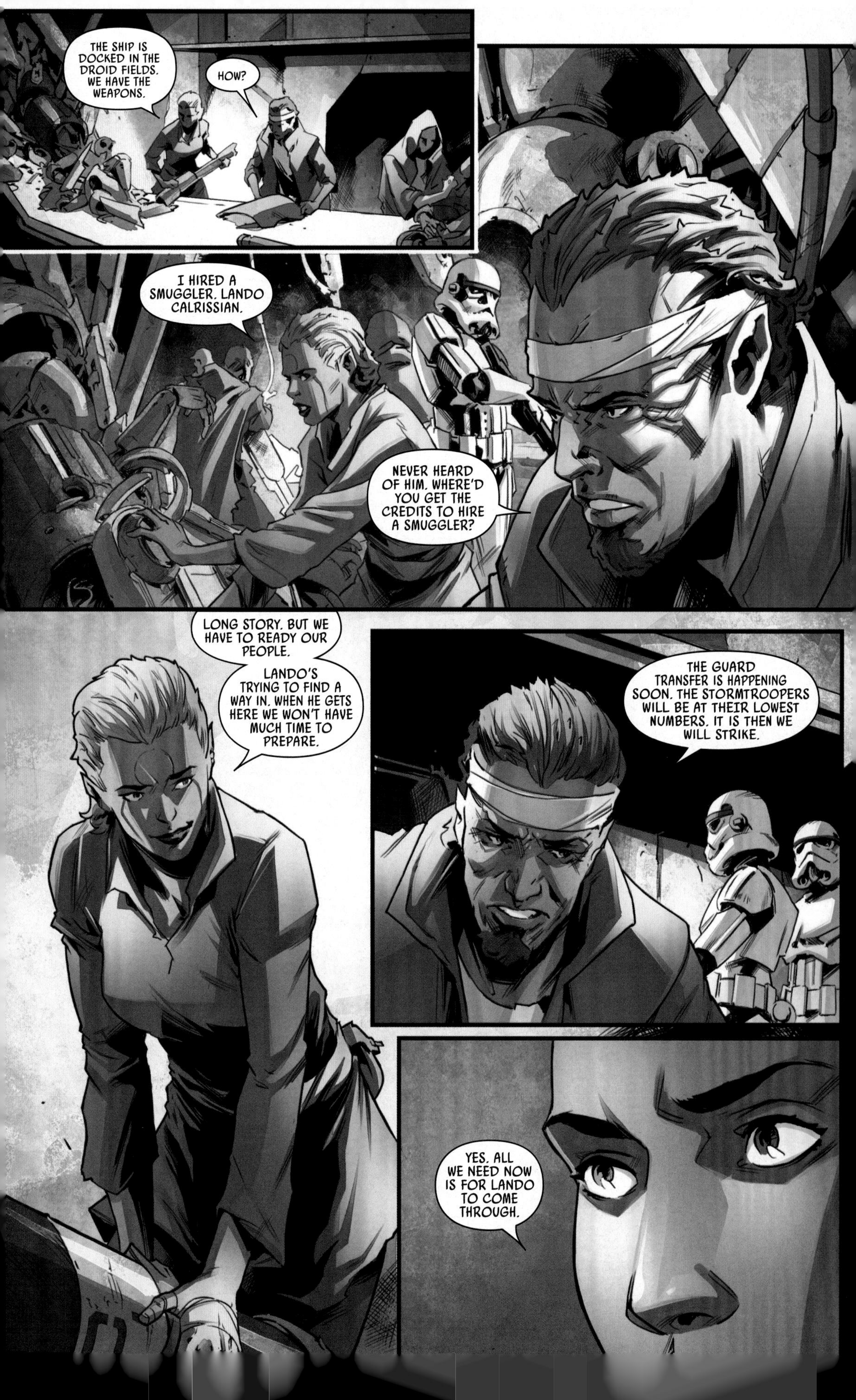
THE SHIP IS DOCKED IN THE DROID FIELDS. WE HAVE THE WEAPONS.
HOW?
I HIRED A SMUGGLER. LANDO CALRISSIAN.
NEVER HEARD OF HIM. WHERE'D YOU GET THE CREDITS TO HIRE A SMUGGLER?
LONG STORY. BUT WE HAVE TO READY OUR PEOPLE.
LANDO'S TRYING TO FIND A WAY IN. WHEN HE GETS HERE WE WON'T HAVE MUCH TIME TO PREPARE.
THE GUARD TRANSFER IS HAPPENING SOON. THE STORMTROOPERS WILL BE AT THEIR LOWEST NUMBERS. IT IS THEN WE WILL STRIKE.
YES. ALL WE NEED NOW IS FOR LANDO TO COME THROUGH.

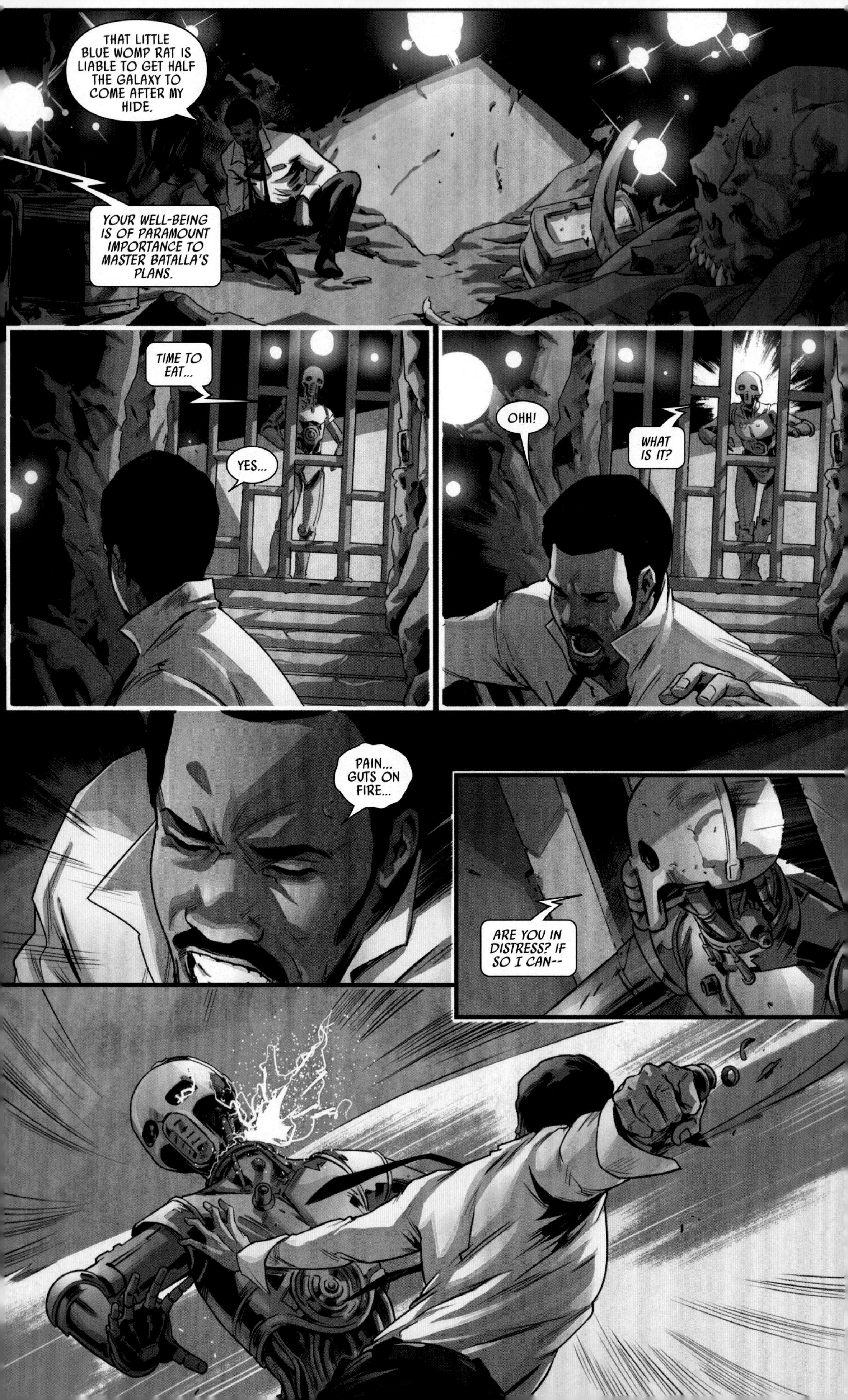
THAT LITTLE BLUE WOMP RAT IS LIABLE TO GET HALF THE GALAXY TO COME AFTER MY HIDE.
YOUR WELL-BEING IS OF PARAMOUNT IMPORTANCE TO MASTER BATALLA'S PLANS.
TIME TO EAT...
YES...
OHH!
WHAT IS IT?
PAIN... GUTS ON FIRE...
ARE YOU IN DISTRESS? IF SO I CAN--

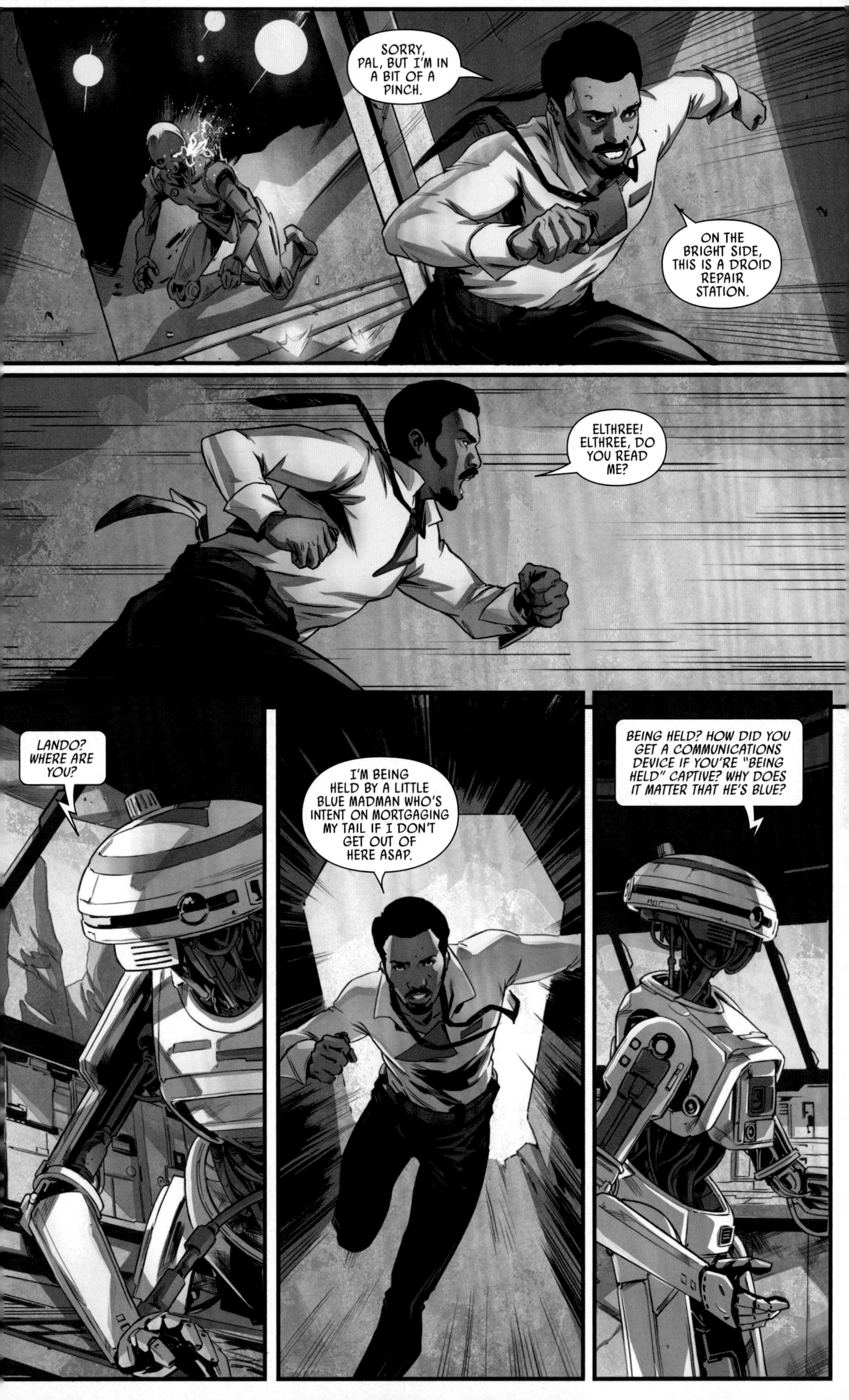
SORRY, PAL, BUT I'M IN A BIT OF A PINCH.
ON THE BRIGHT SIDE, THIS IS A DROID REPAIR STATION.
ELTHREE! ELTHREE, DO YOU READ ME?
LANDO? WHERE ARE YOU?
I'M BEING HELD BY A LITTLE BLUE MADMAN WHO'S INTENT ON MORTGAGING MY TAIL IF I DON'T GET OUT OF HERE ASAP.
BEING HELD? HOW DID YOU GET A COMMUNICATIONS DEVICE IF YOU'RE "BEING HELD" CAPTIVE? WHY DOES IT MATTER THAT HE'S BLUE?

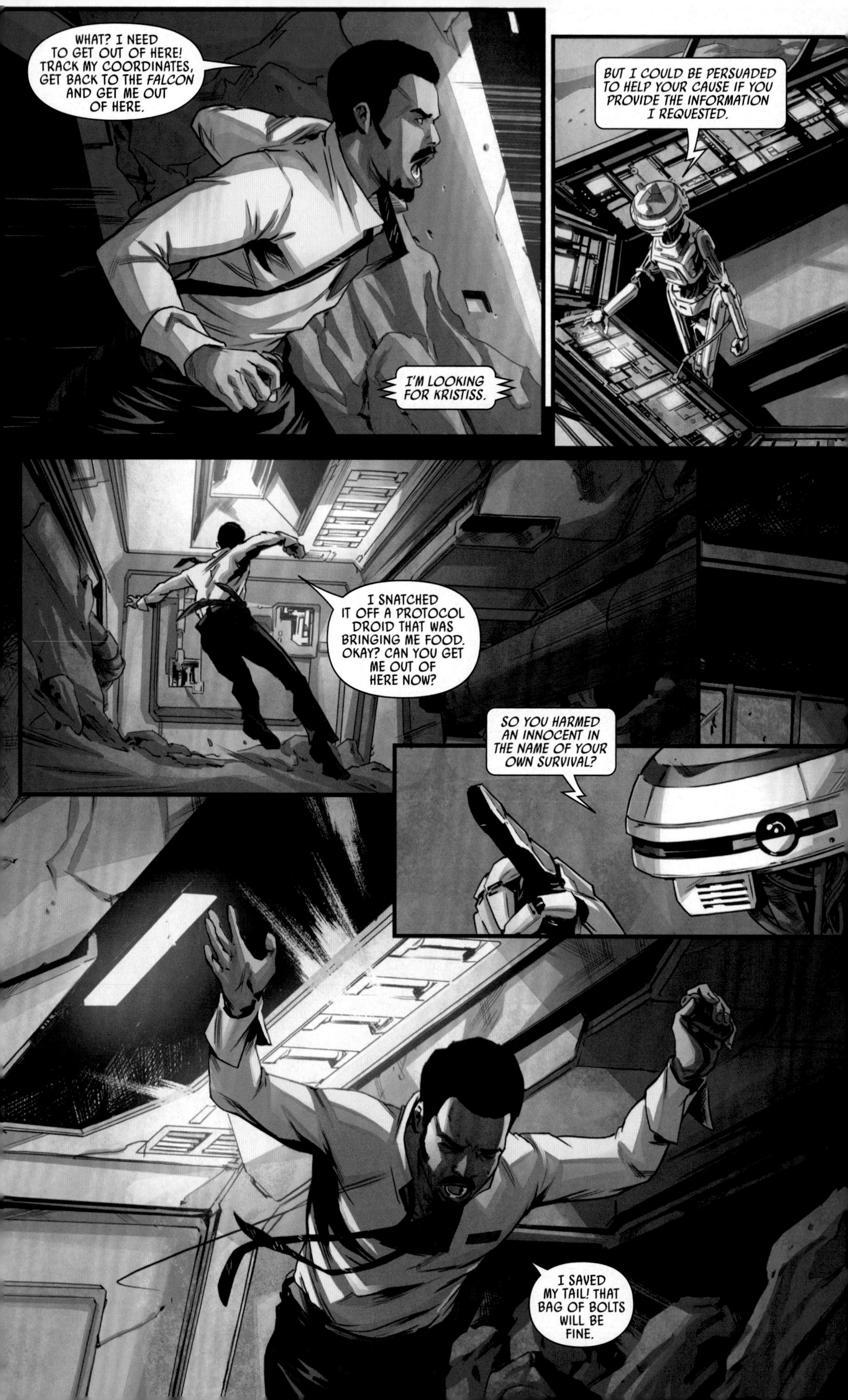
WHAT? I NEED TO GET OUT OF HERE! TRACK MY COORDINATES, GET BACK TO THE *FALCON* AND GET ME OUT OF HERE.
I'M LOOKING FOR KRISTISS.
BUT I COULD BE PERSUADED TO HELP YOUR CAUSE IF YOU PROVIDE THE INFORMATION I REQUESTED.
I SNATCHED IT OFF A PROTOCOL DROID THAT WAS BRINGING ME FOOD. OKAY? CAN YOU GET ME OUT OF HERE NOW?
SO YOU HARMED AN INNOCENT IN THE NAME OF YOUR OWN SURVIVAL?
I SAVED MY TAIL! THAT BAG OF BOLTS WILL BE FINE.

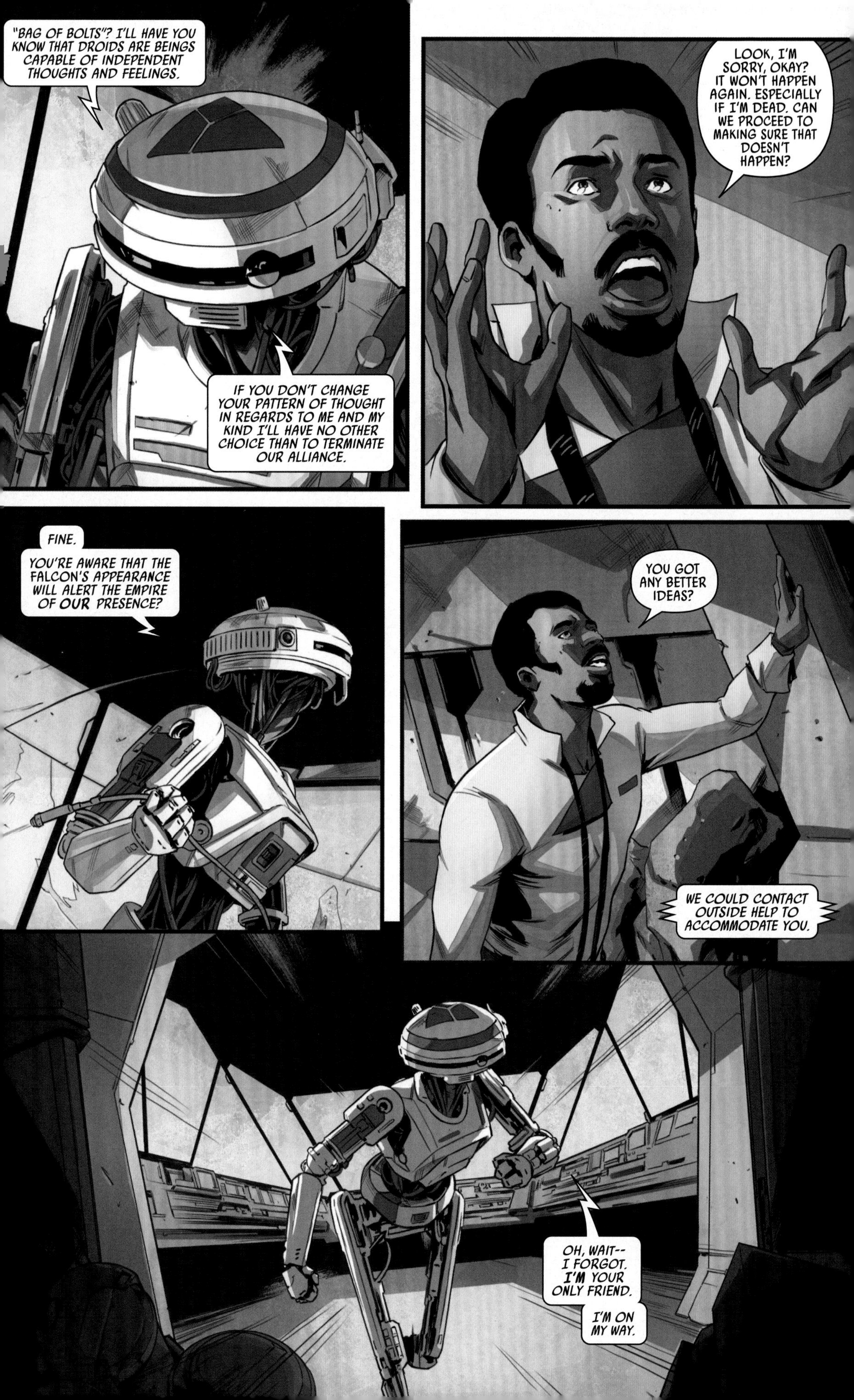
"BAG OF BOLTS"? I'LL HAVE YOU KNOW THAT DROIDS ARE BEINGS CAPABLE OF INDEPENDENT THOUGHTS AND FEELINGS.
IF YOU DON'T CHANGE YOUR PATTERN OF THOUGHT IN REGARDS TO ME AND MY KIND I'LL HAVE NO OTHER CHOICE THAN TO TERMINATE OUR ALLIANCE.
LOOK, I'M SORRY, OKAY? IT WON'T HAPPEN AGAIN. ESPECIALLY IF I'M DEAD. CAN WE PROCEED TO MAKING SURE THAT DOESN'T HAPPEN?
FINE.
YOU'RE AWARE THAT THE FALCON'S APPEARANCE WILL ALERT THE EMPIRE OF OUR PRESENCE?
YOU GOT ANY BETTER IDEAS?
WE COULD CONTACT OUTSIDE HELP TO ACCOMMODATE YOU.
OH, WAIT-- I FORGOT. I'M YOUR ONLY FRIEND.
I'M ON MY WAY.

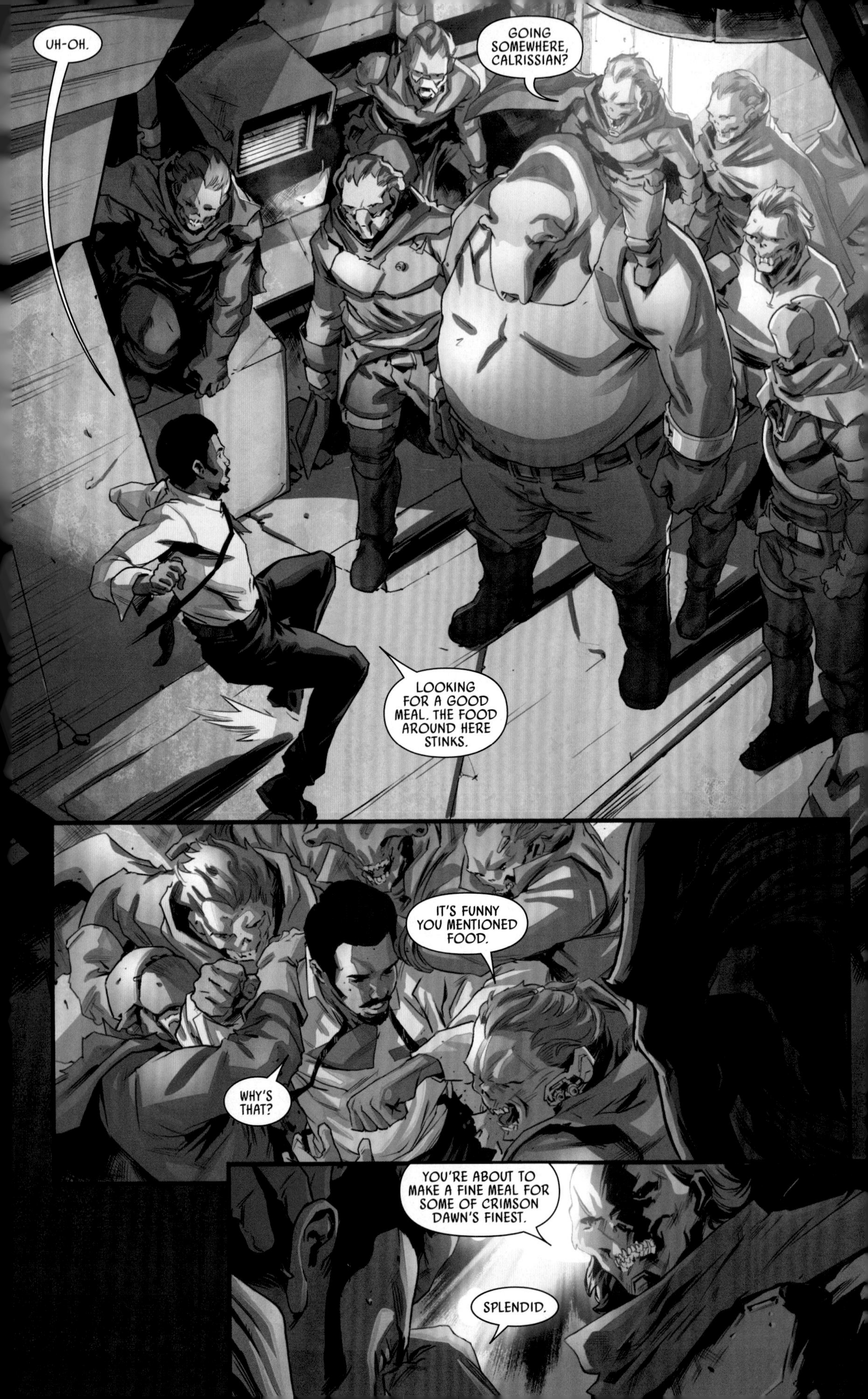
UH-OH.
GOING SOMEWHERE, CALRISSIAN?
LOOKING FOR A GOOD MEAL. THE FOOD AROUND HERE STINKS.
IT'S FUNNY YOU MENTIONED FOOD.
WHY'S THAT?
YOU'RE ABOUT TO MAKE A FINE MEAL FOR SOME OF CRIMSON DAWN'S FINEST.
SPLENDID.

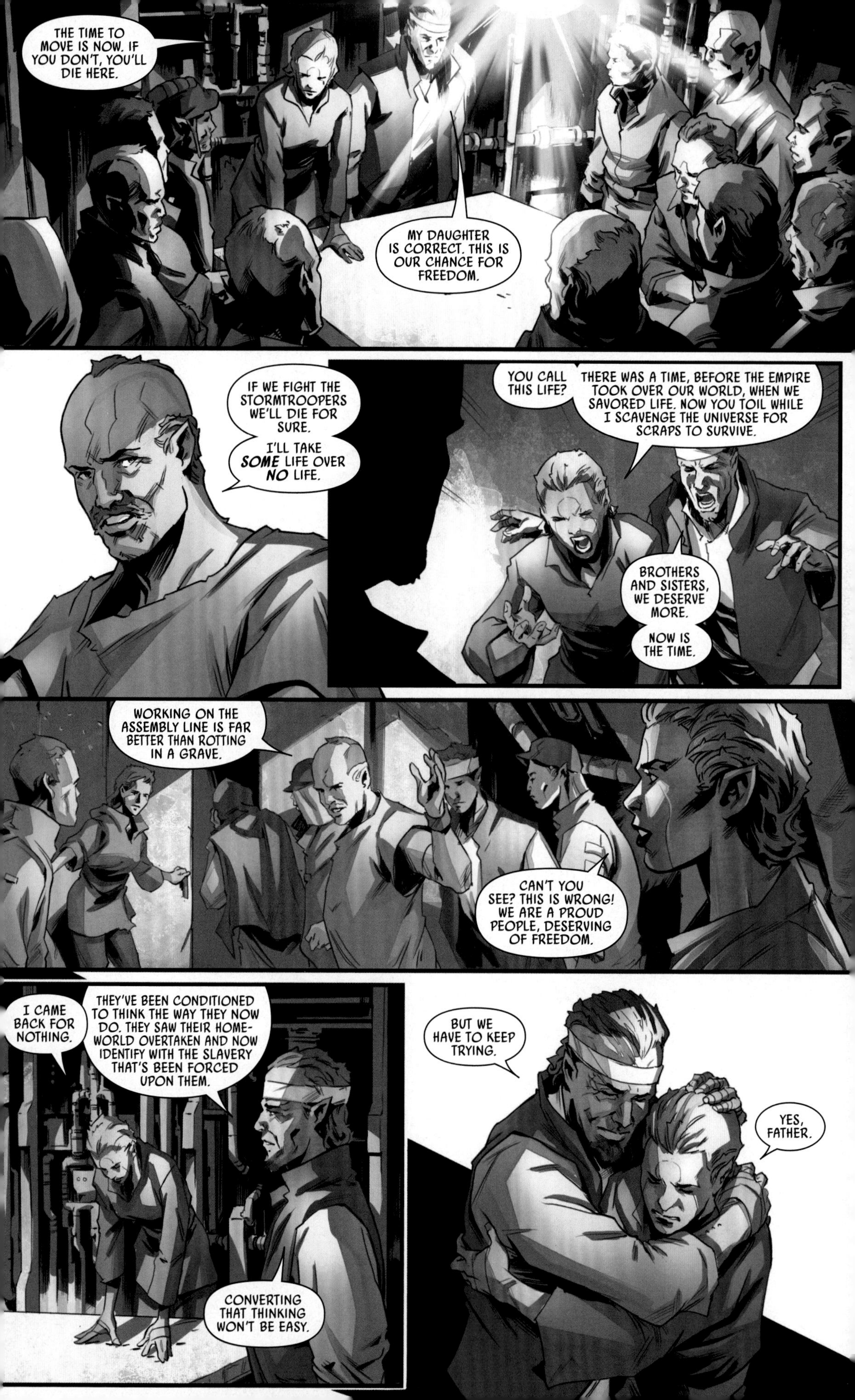
THE TIME TO MOVE IS NOW. IF YOU DON'T, YOU'LL DIE HERE.
MY DAUGHTER IS CORRECT. THIS IS OUR CHANCE FOR FREEDOM.
IF WE FIGHT THE STORMTROOPERS WE'LL DIE FOR SURE.
I'LL TAKE SOME LIFE OVER NO LIFE.
YOU CALL THIS LIFE?
THERE WAS A TIME, BEFORE THE EMPIRE TOOK OVER OUR WORLD, WHEN WE SAVORED LIFE. NOW YOU TOIL WHILE I SCAVENGE THE UNIVERSE FOR SCRAPS TO SURVIVE.
BROTHERS AND SISTERS, WE DESERVE MORE.
NOW IS THE TIME.
WORKING ON THE ASSEMBLY LINE IS FAR BETTER THAN ROTTING IN A GRAVE.
CAN'T YOU SEE? THIS IS WRONG! WE ARE A PROUD PEOPLE, DESERVING OF FREEDOM.
I CAME BACK FOR NOTHING.
THEY'VE BEEN CONDITIONED TO THINK THE WAY THEY NOW DO. THEY SAW THEIR HOME-WORLD OVERTAKEN AND NOW IDENTIFY WITH THE SLAVERY THAT'S BEEN FORCED UPON THEM.
CONVERTING THAT THINKING WON'T BE EASY.
BUT WE HAVE TO KEEP TRYING.
YES, FATHER.

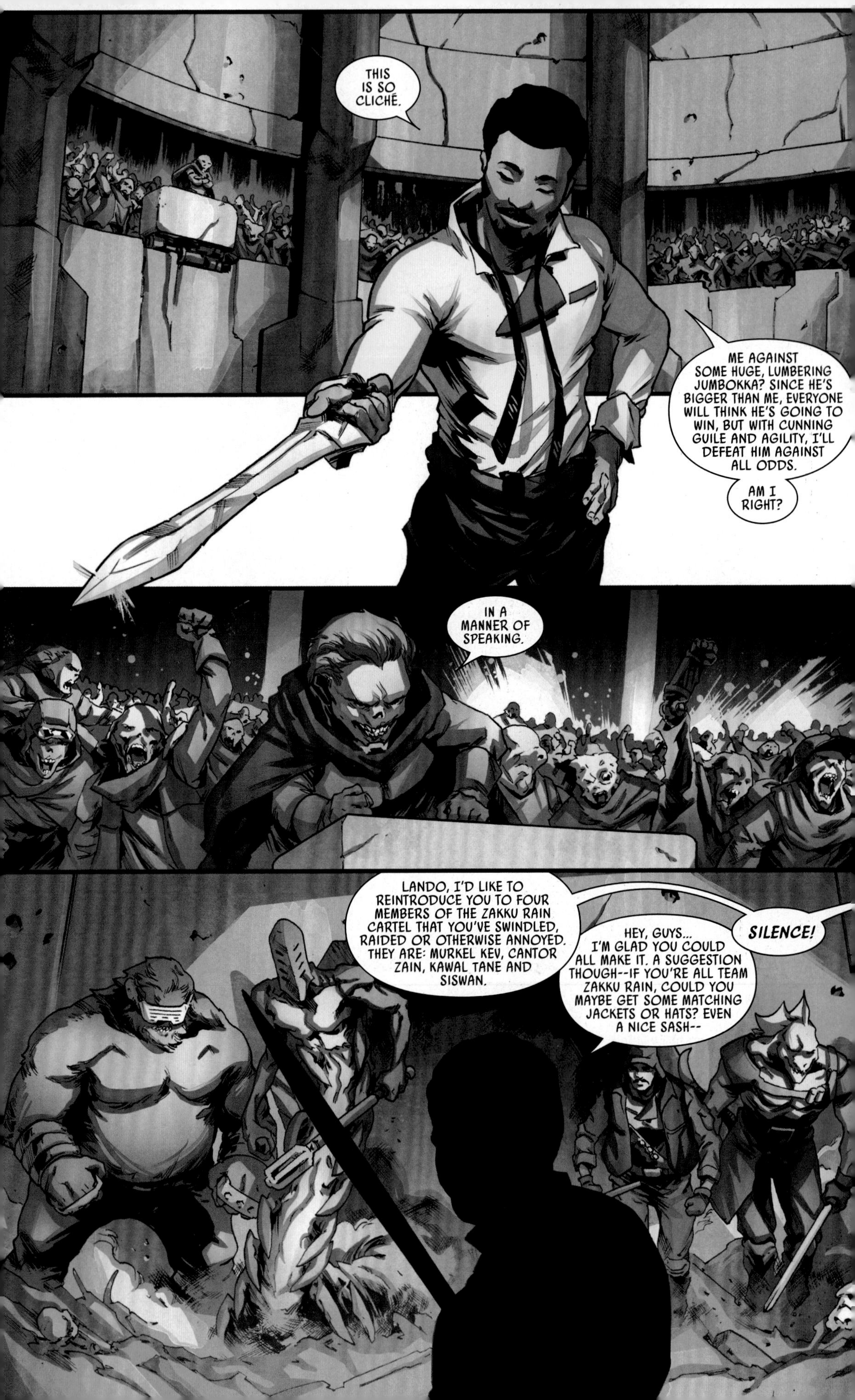
THIS IS SO CLICHÉ.
ME AGAINST SOME HUGE, LUMBERING JUMBOKKA? SINCE HE'S BIGGER THAN ME, EVERYONE WILL THINK HE'S GOING TO WIN, BUT WITH CUNNING GUILE AND AGILITY, I'LL DEFEAT HIM AGAINST ALL ODDS.
AM I RIGHT?
IN A MANNER OF SPEAKING.
LANDO, I'D LIKE TO REINTRODUCE YOU TO FOUR MEMBERS OF THE ZAKKU RAIN CARTEL THAT YOU'VE SWINDLED, RAIDED OR OTHERWISE ANNOYED. THEY ARE: MURKEL KEV, CANTOR ZAIN, KAWAL TANE AND SISWAN.
HEY, GUYS... I'M GLAD YOU COULD ALL MAKE IT. A SUGGESTION THOUGH--IF YOU'RE ALL TEAM ZAKKU RAIN, COULD YOU MAYBE GET SOME MATCHING JACKETS OR HATS? EVEN A NICE SASH--
SILENCE!

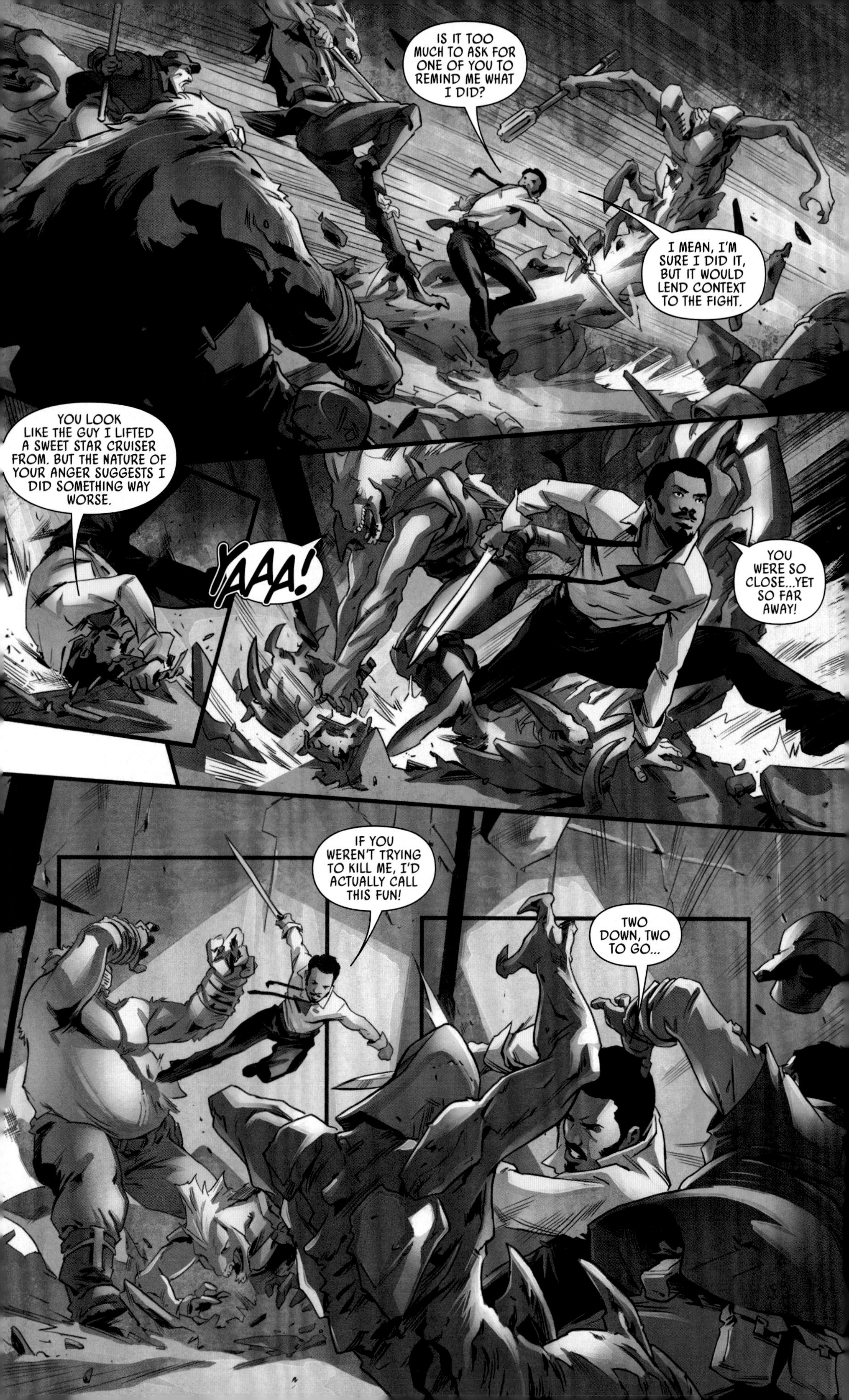
IS IT TOO MUCH TO ASK FOR ONE OF YOU TO REMIND ME WHAT I DID?
I MEAN, I'M SURE I DID IT, BUT IT WOULD LEND CONTEXT TO THE FIGHT.
YOU LOOK LIKE THE GUY I LIFTED A SWEET STAR CRUISER FROM. BUT THE NATURE OF YOUR ANGER SUGGESTS I DID SOMETHING WAY WORSE.
YAAA!
YOU WERE SO CLOSE...YET SO FAR AWAY!
IF YOU WEREN'T TRYING TO KILL ME, I'D ACTUALLY CALL THIS FUN!
TWO DOWN, TWO TO GO...

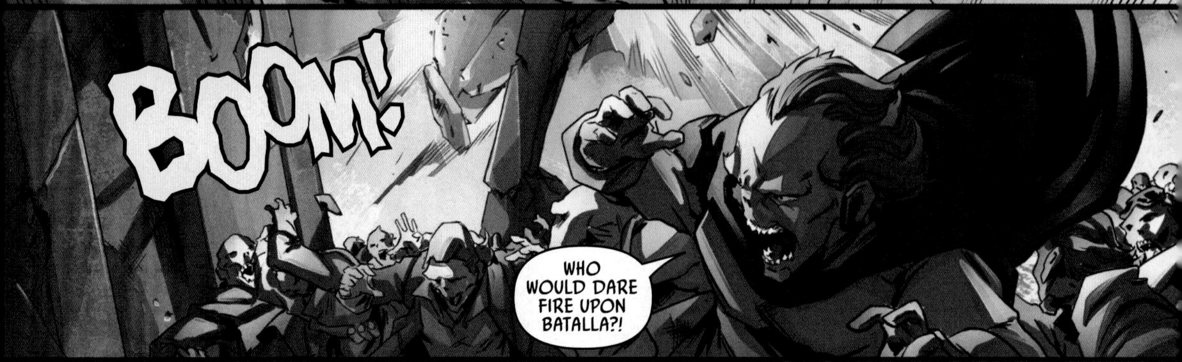
BOOM!
WHO WOULD DARE FIRE UPON BATALLA?!

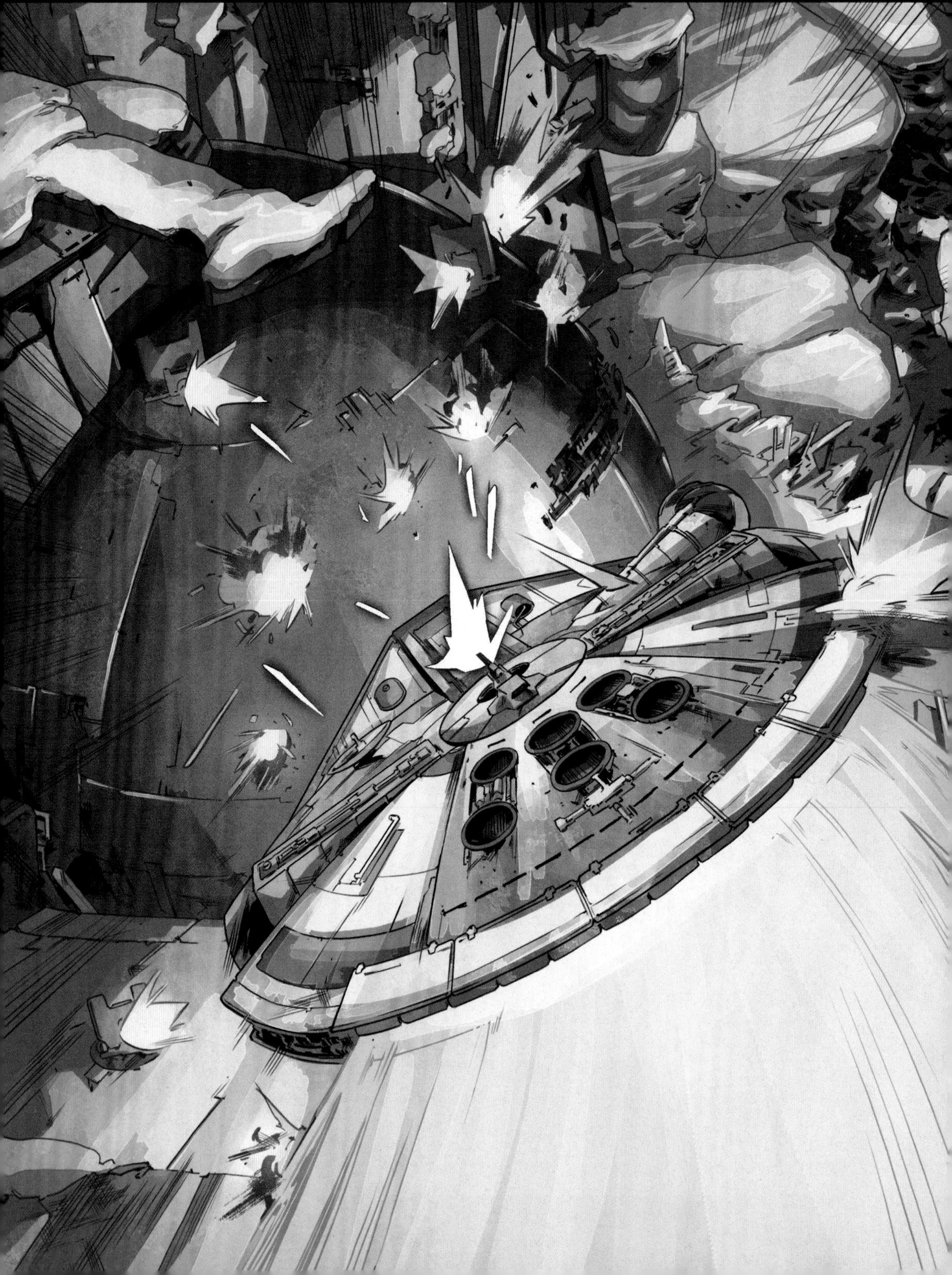

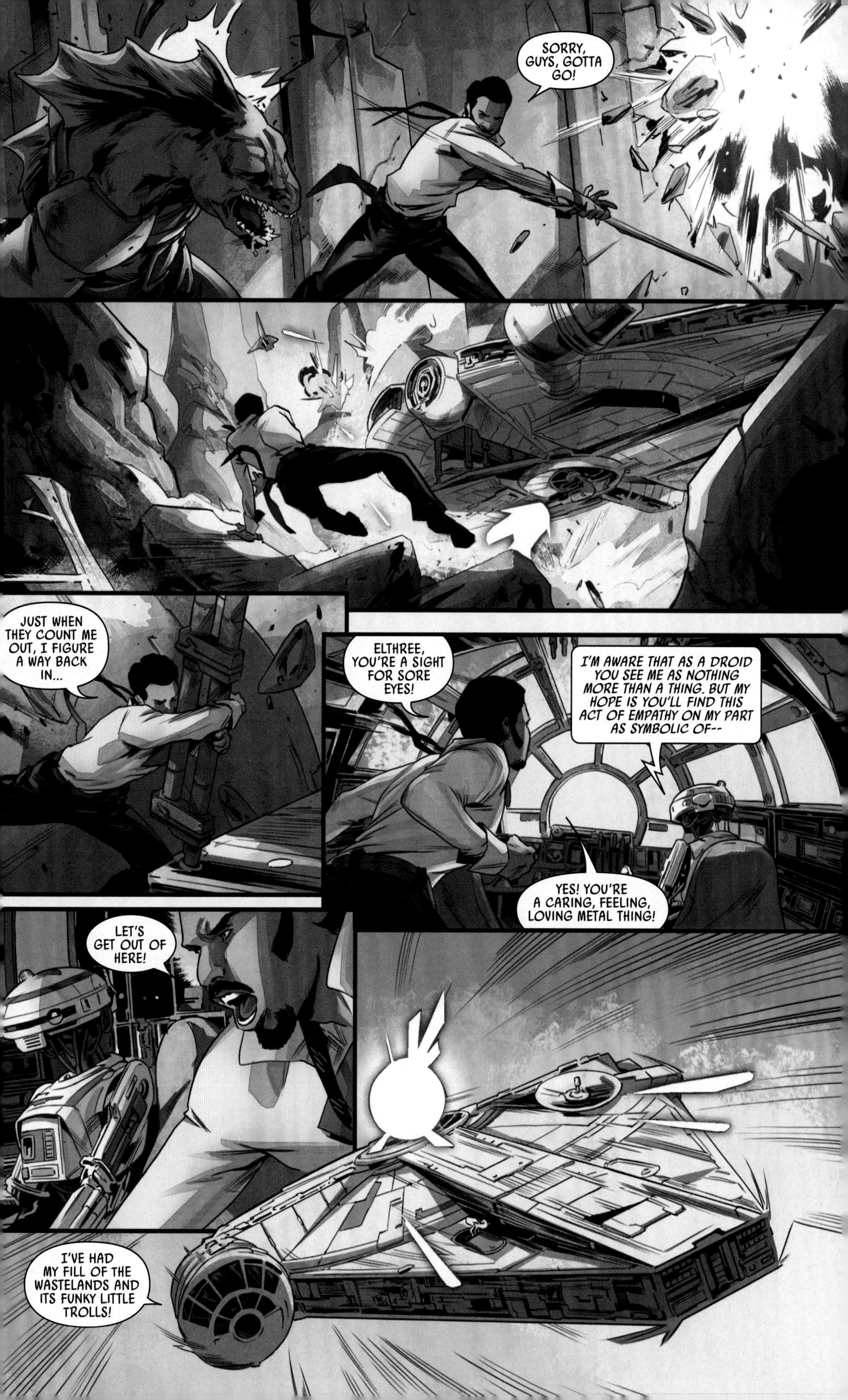
SORRY, GUYS, GOTTA GO!
JUST WHEN THEY COUNT ME OUT, I FIGURE A WAY BACK IN...
ELTHREE, YOU'RE A SIGHT FOR SORE EYES!
I'M AWARE THAT AS A DROID YOU SEE ME AS NOTHING MORE THAN A THING. BUT MY HOPE IS YOU'LL FIND THIS ACT OF EMPATHY ON MY PART AS SYMBOLIC OF--
YES! YOU'RE A CARING, FEELING, LOVING METAL THING!
LET'S GET OUT OF HERE!
I'VE HAD MY FILL OF THE WASTELANDS AND ITS FUNKY LITTLE TROLLS!

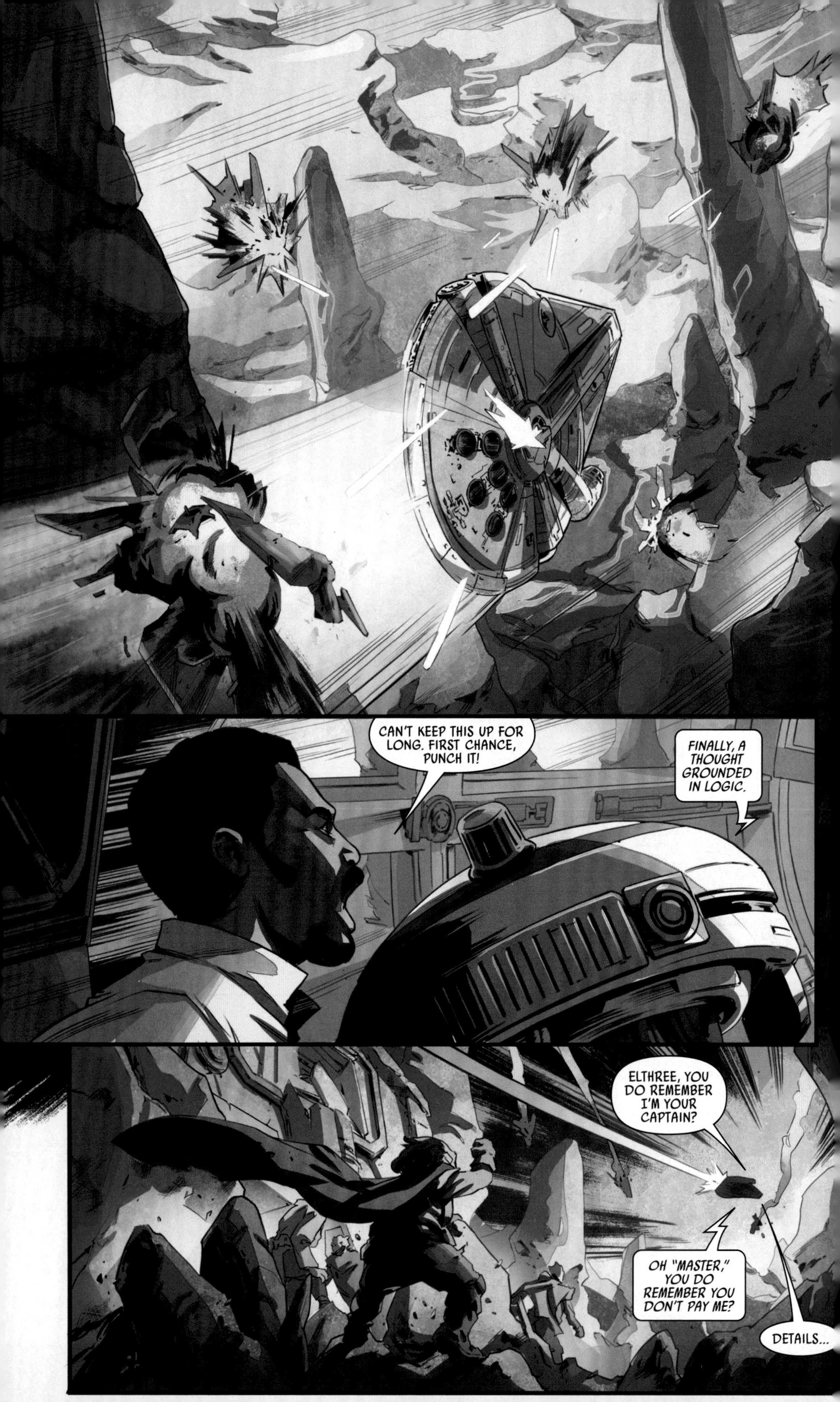
CAN'T KEEP THIS UP FOR LONG. FIRST CHANCE, PUNCH IT!
FINALLY, A THOUGHT GROUNDED IN LOGIC.
ELTHREE, YOU DO REMEMBER I'M YOUR CAPTAIN?
OH "MASTER," YOU DO REMEMBER YOU DON'T PAY ME?
DETAILS...

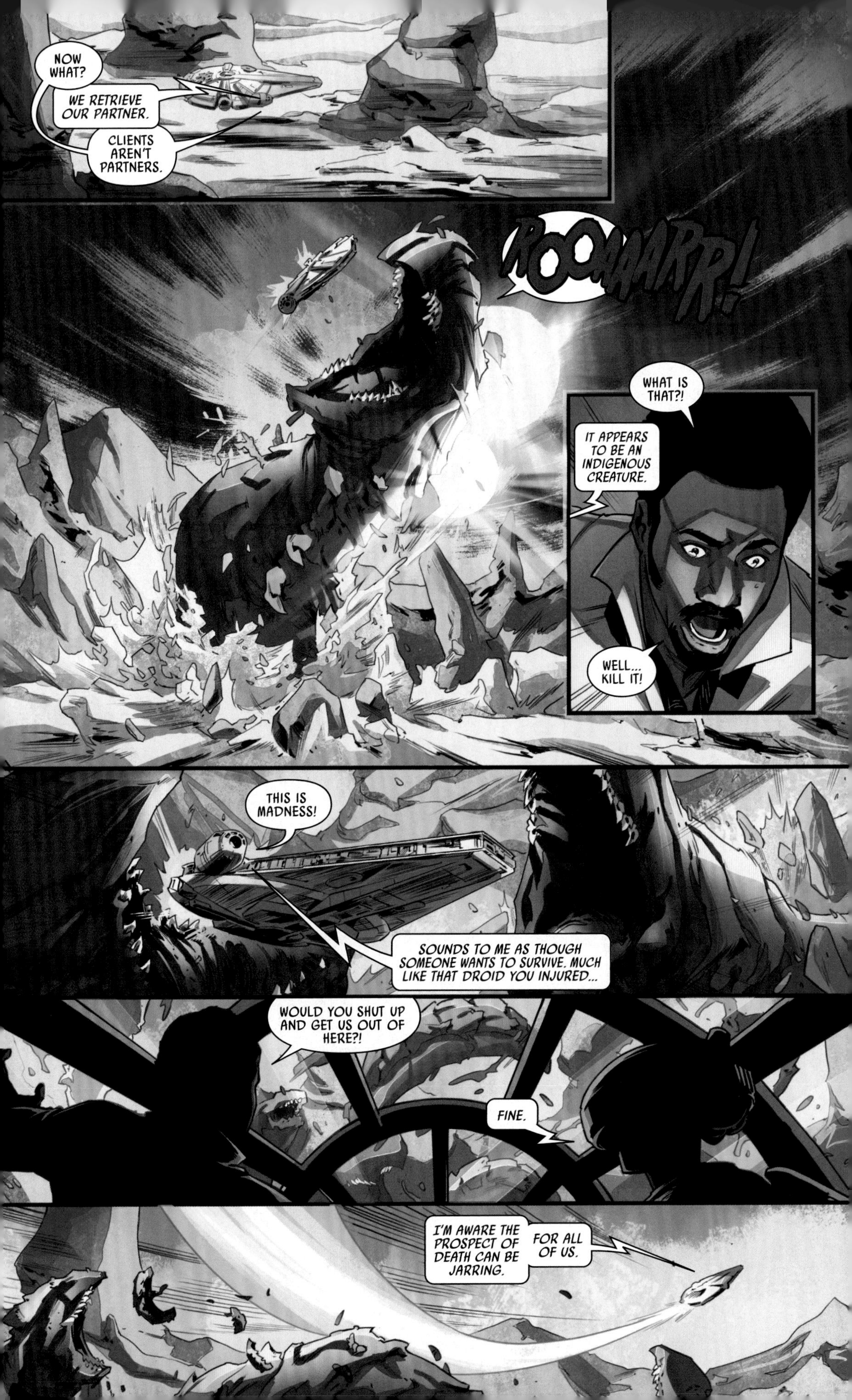
NOW WHAT?
WE RETRIEVE OUR PARTNER.
CLIENTS AREN'T PARTNERS.
ROOAAARR!
WHAT IS THAT?!
IT APPEARS TO BE AN INDIGENOUS CREATURE.
WELL... KILL IT!
THIS IS MADNESS!
SOUNDS TO ME AS THOUGH SOMEONE WANTS TO SURVIVE. MUCH LIKE THAT DROID YOU INJURED...
WOULD YOU SHUT UP AND GET US OUT OF HERE?!
FINE.
I'M AWARE THE PROSPECT OF DEATH CAN BE JARRING.
FOR ALL OF US.

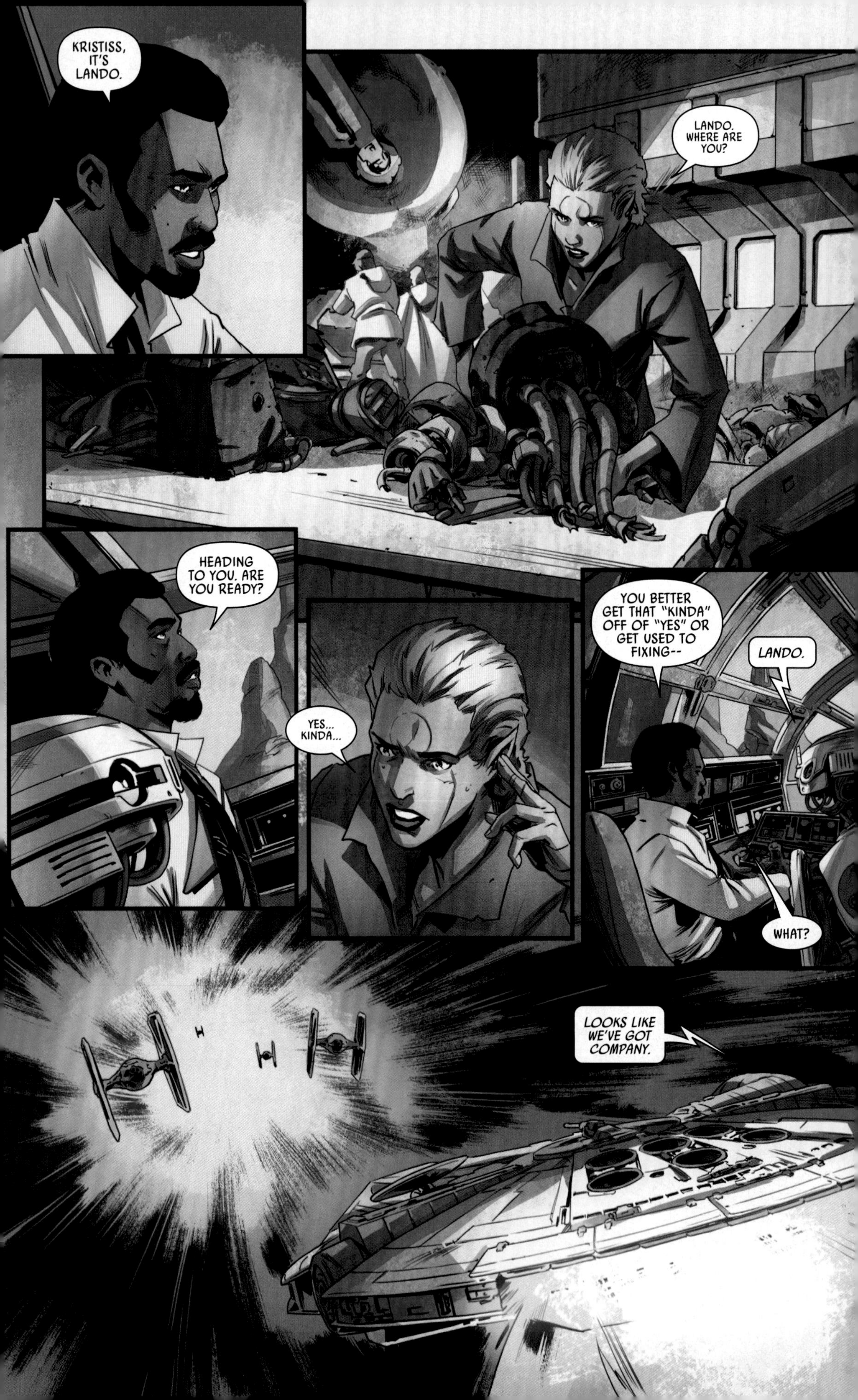
KRISTISS, IT'S LANDO.
LANDO. WHERE ARE YOU?
HEADING TO YOU. ARE YOU READY?
YES... KINDA...
YOU BETTER GET THAT "KINDA" OFF OF "YES" OR GET USED TO FIXING--
LANDO.
WHAT?
LOOKS LIKE WE'VE GOT COMPANY.

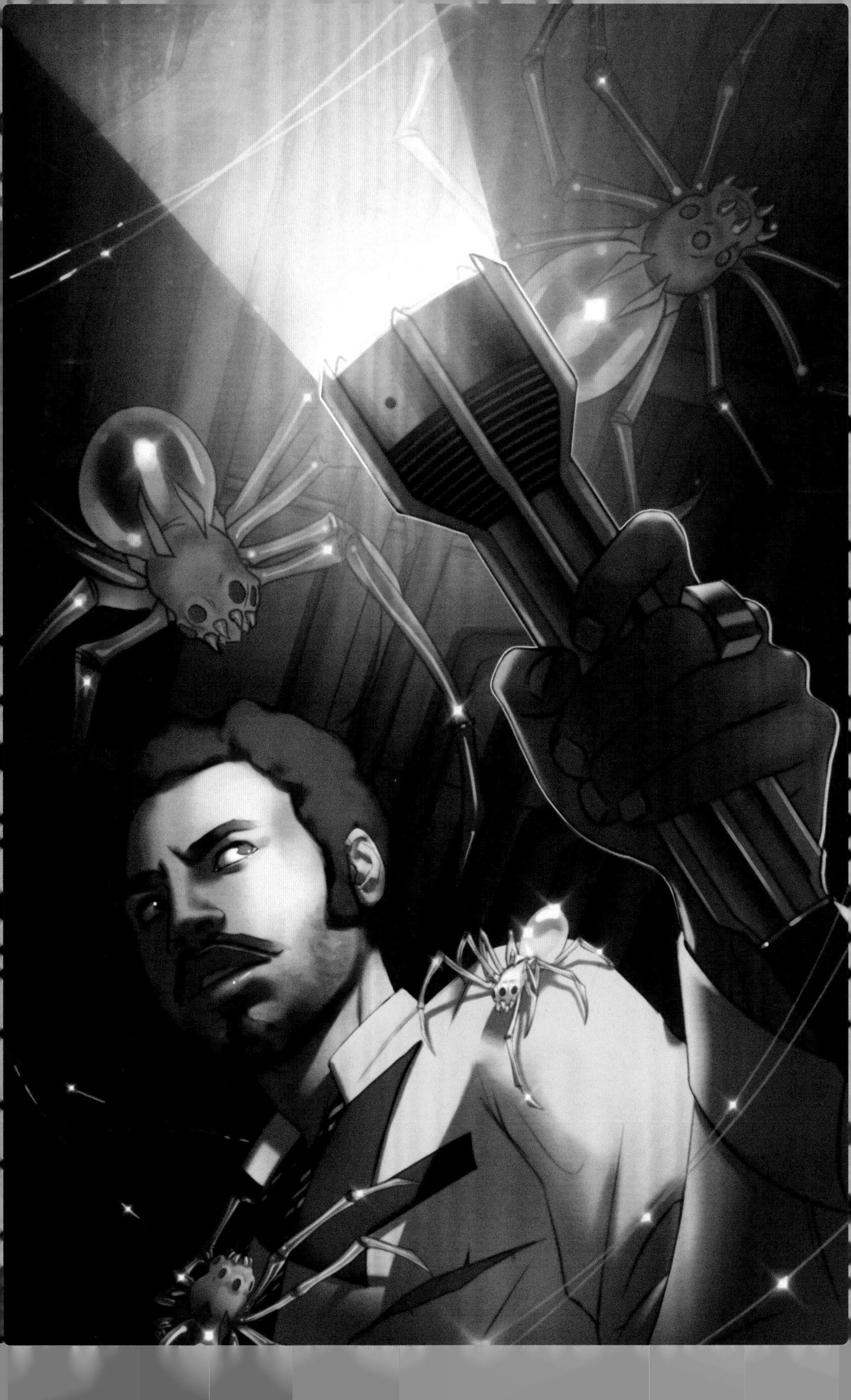

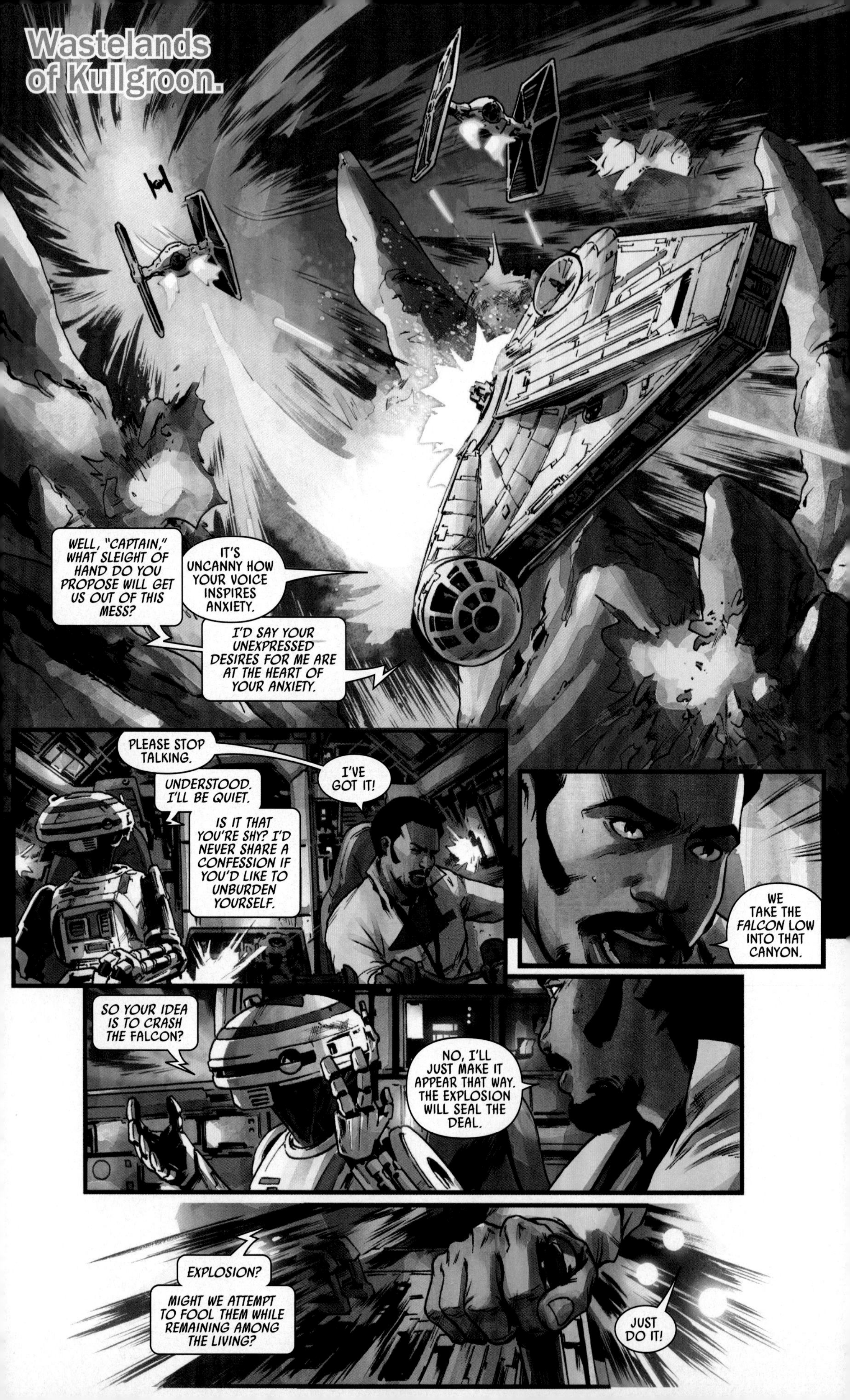

Wastelands of Kullgroon.
WELL, "CAPTAIN," WHAT SLEIGHT OF HAND DO YOU PROPOSE WILL GET US OUT OF THIS MESS?
IT'S UNCANNY HOW YOUR VOICE INSPIRES ANXIETY.
I'D SAY YOUR UNEXPRESSED DESIRES FOR ME ARE AT THE HEART OF YOUR ANXIETY.
PLEASE STOP TALKING.
I'VE GOT IT!
UNDERSTOOD. I'LL BE QUIET.
IS IT THAT YOU'RE SHY? I'D NEVER SHARE A CONFESSION IF YOU'D LIKE TO UNBURDEN YOURSELF.
WE TAKE THE FALCON LOW INTO THAT CANYON.
SO YOUR IDEA IS TO CRASH THE FALCON?
NO, I'LL JUST MAKE IT APPEAR THAT WAY. THE EXPLOSION WILL SEAL THE DEAL.
EXPLOSION?
MIGHT WE ATTEMPT TO FOOL THEM WHILE REMAINING AMONG THE LIVING?
JUST DO IT!

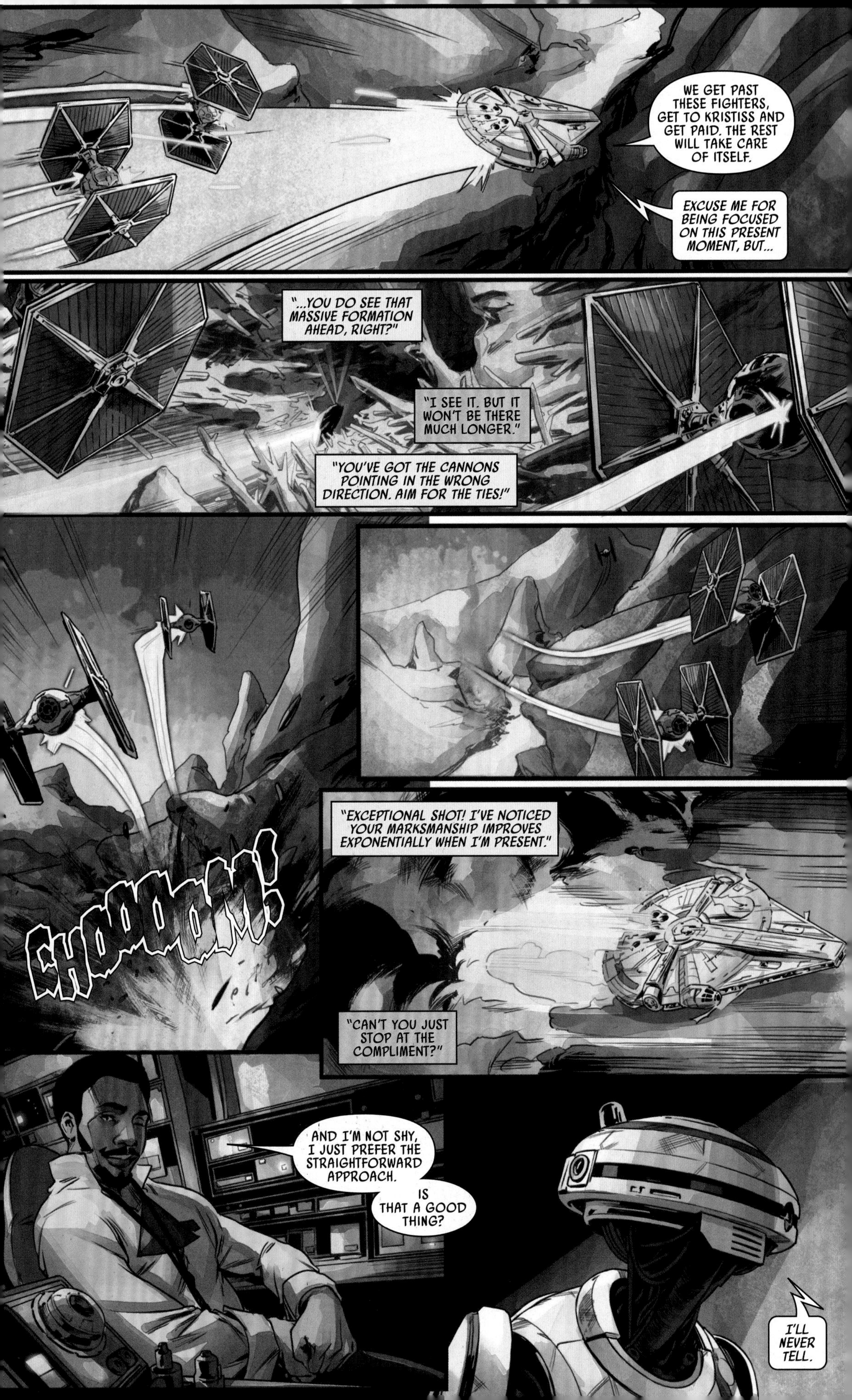
WE GET PAST THESE FIGHTERS, GET TO KRISTISS AND GET PAID. THE REST WILL TAKE CARE OF ITSELF.
EXCUSE ME FOR BEING FOCUSED ON THIS PRESENT MOMENT, BUT...
"...YOU DO SEE THAT MASSIVE FORMATION AHEAD, RIGHT?"
"I SEE IT. BUT IT WON'T BE THERE MUCH LONGER."
"YOU'VE GOT THE CANNONS POINTING IN THE WRONG DIRECTION. AIM FOR THE TIES!"
CHOOOOM!
"EXCEPTIONAL SHOT! I'VE NOTICED YOUR MARKSMANSHIP IMPROVES EXPONENTIALLY WHEN I'M PRESENT."
"CAN'T YOU JUST STOP AT THE COMPLIMENT?"
AND I'M NOT SHY, I JUST PREFER THE STRAIGHTFORWARD APPROACH.
IS THAT A GOOD THING?
I'LL NEVER TELL.

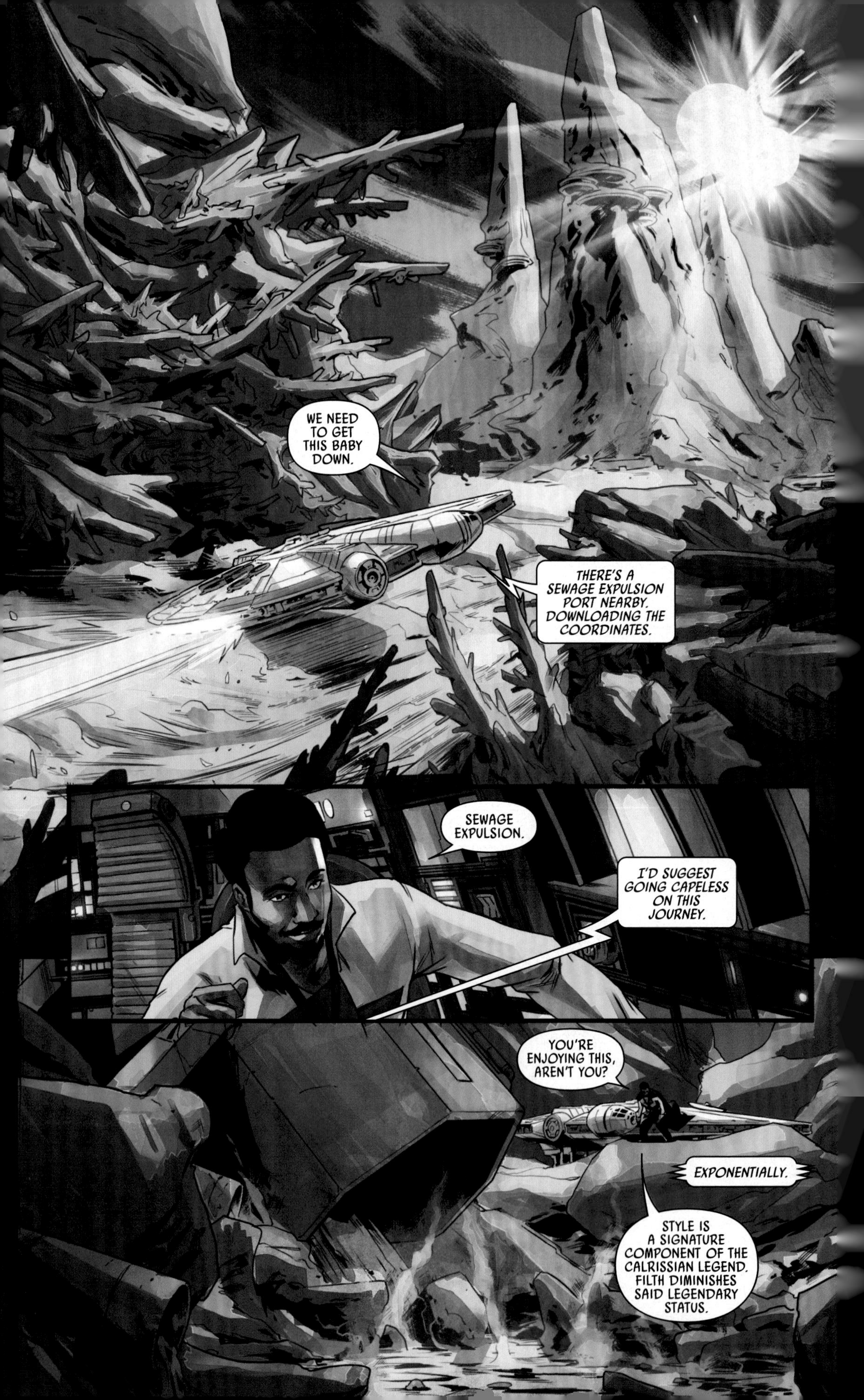
WE NEED TO GET THIS BABY DOWN.
THERE'S A SEWAGE EXPULSION PORT NEARBY. DOWNLOADING THE COORDINATES.
SEWAGE EXPULSION.
I'D SUGGEST GOING CAPELESS ON THIS JOURNEY.
YOU'RE ENJOYING THIS, AREN'T YOU?
EXPONENTIALLY.
STYLE IS A SIGNATURE COMPONENT OF THE CALRISSIAN LEGEND. FILTH DIMINISHES SAID LEGENDARY STATUS.

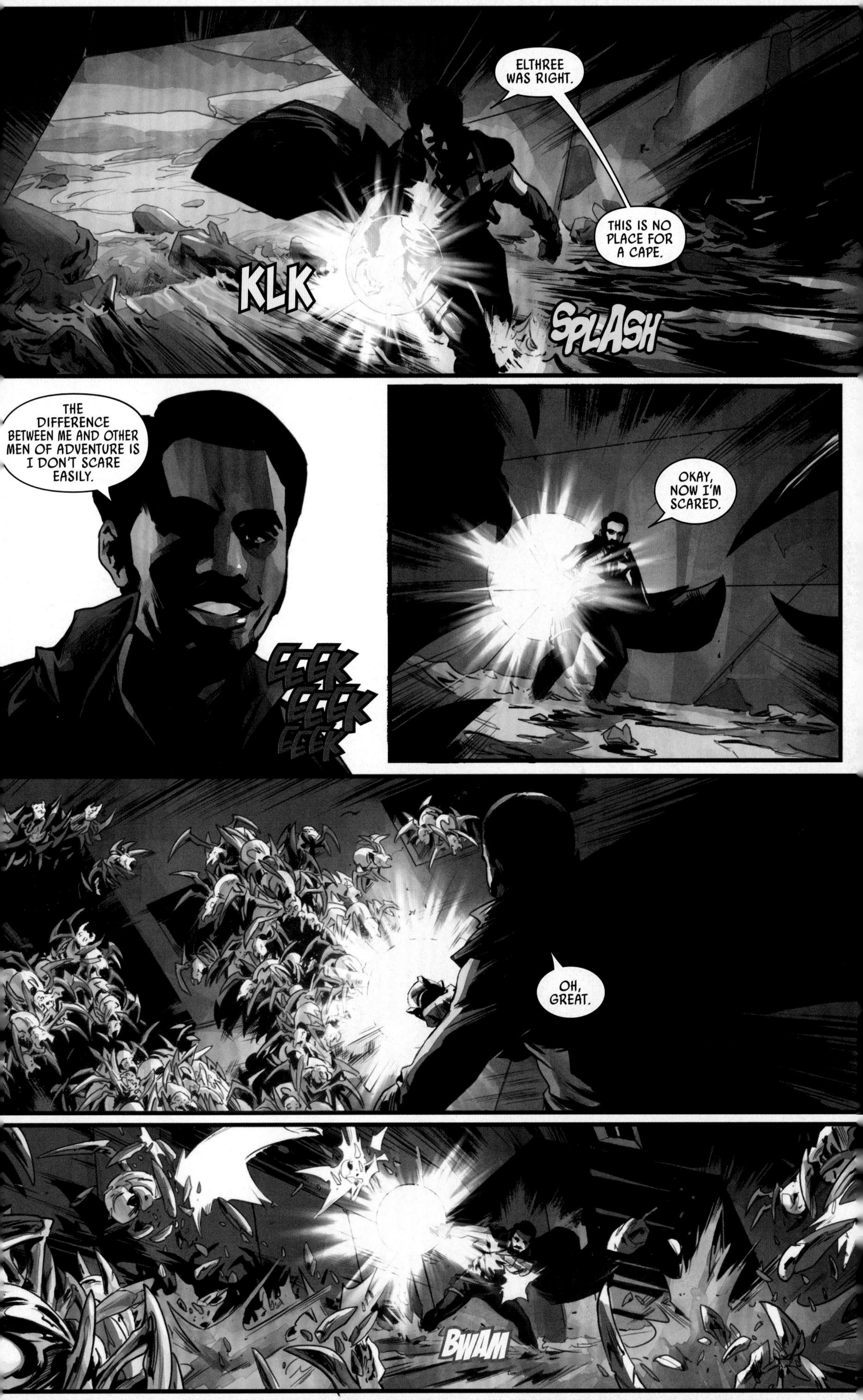

ELTHREE WAS RIGHT.
THIS IS NO PLACE FOR A CAPE.
KLK
SPLASH
THE DIFFERENCE BETWEEN ME AND OTHER MEN OF ADVENTURE IS I DON'T SCARE EASILY.
EEEK EEEK EEEK
OKAY, NOW I'M SCARED.
OH, GREAT.
BWAM

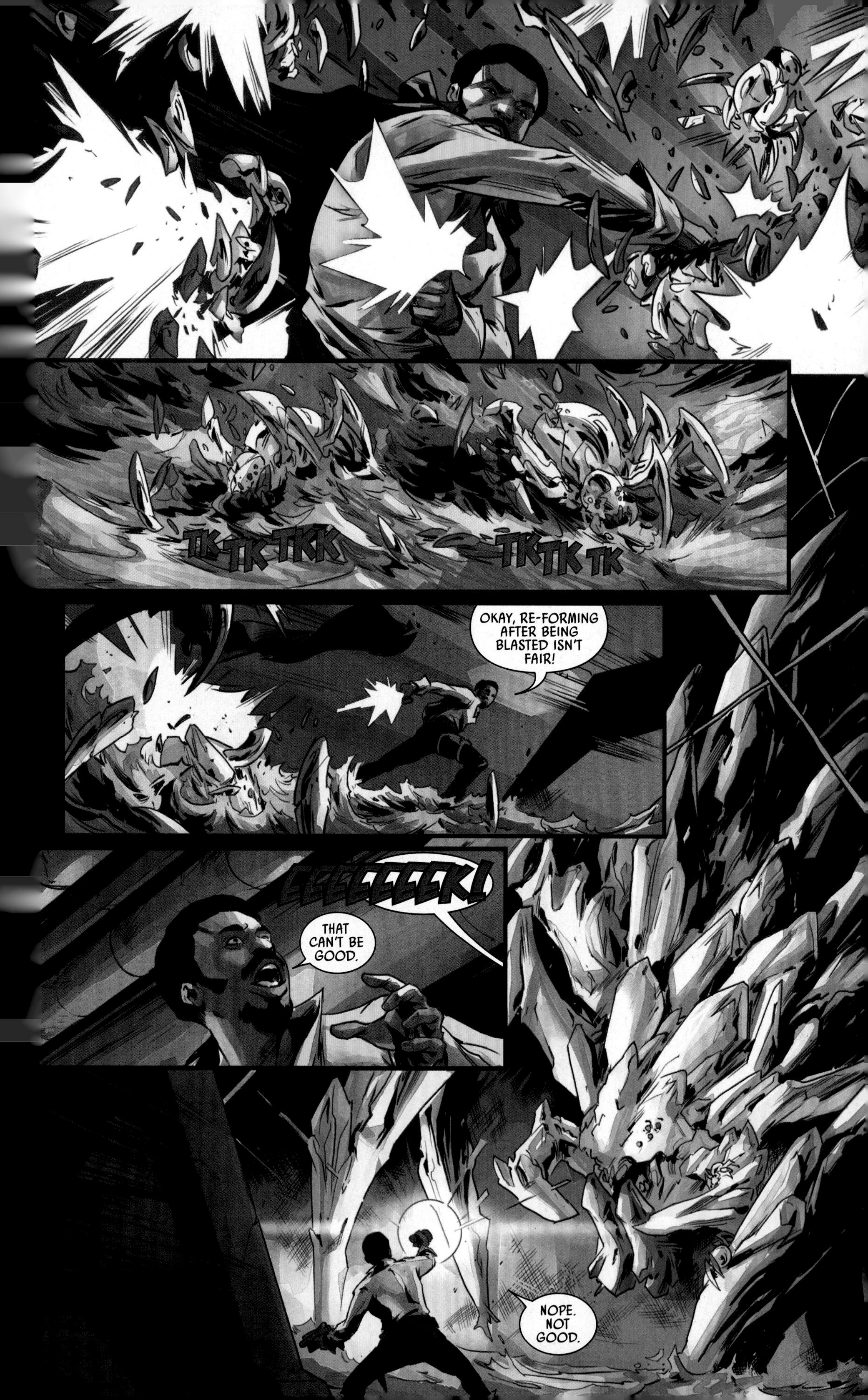
TK TK TKK
TK TK TK
OKAY, RE-FORMING AFTER BEING BLASTED ISN'T FAIR!
EEEEEEEER!
THAT CAN'T BE GOOD.
NOPE. NOT GOOD.

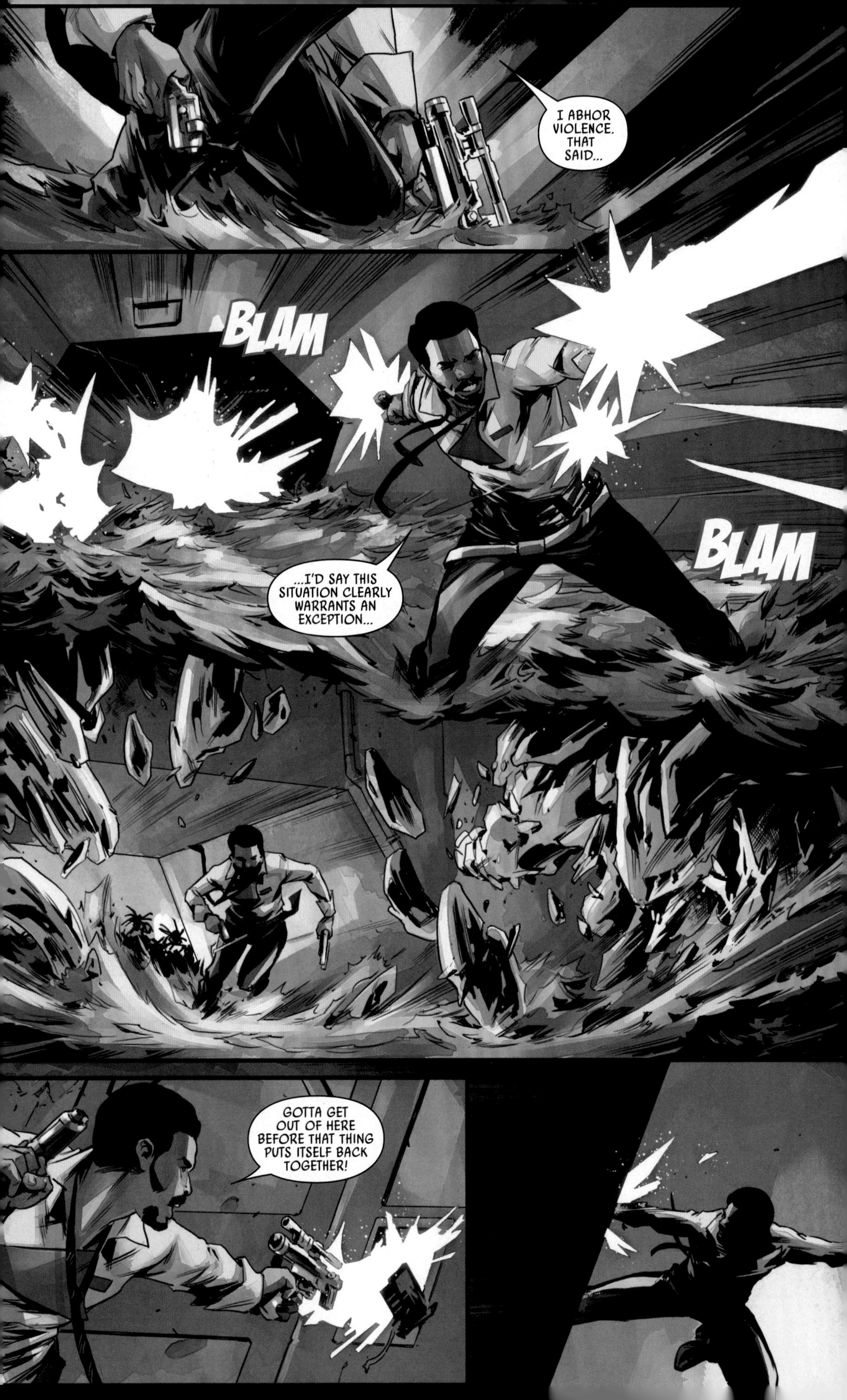
I ABHOR VIOLENCE. THAT SAID...
BLAM
BLAM
...I'D SAY THIS SITUATION CLEARLY WARRANTS AN EXCEPTION...
GOTTA GET OUT OF HERE BEFORE THAT THING PUTS ITSELF BACK TOGETHER!

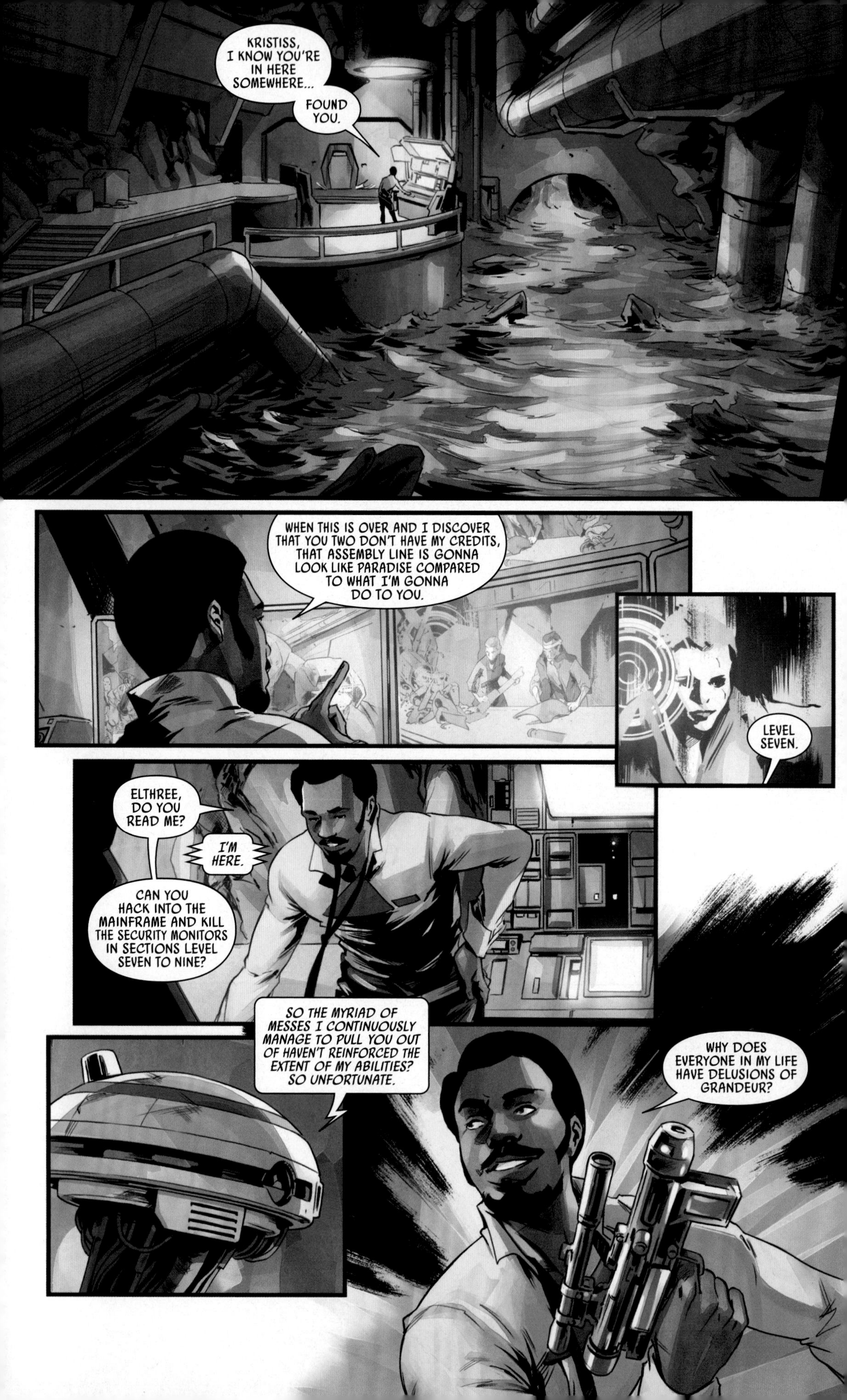
KRISTISS, I KNOW YOU'RE IN HERE SOMEWHERE...
FOUND YOU.
WHEN THIS IS OVER AND I DISCOVER THAT YOU TWO DON'T HAVE MY CREDITS, THAT ASSEMBLY LINE IS GONNA LOOK LIKE PARADISE COMPARED TO WHAT I'M GONNA DO TO YOU.
LEVEL SEVEN.
ELTHREE, DO YOU READ ME?
I'M HERE.
CAN YOU HACK INTO THE MAINFRAME AND KILL THE SECURITY MONITORS IN SECTIONS LEVEL SEVEN TO NINE?
SO THE MYRIAD OF MESSES I CONTINUOUSLY MANAGE TO PULL YOU OUT OF HAVEN'T REINFORCED THE EXTENT OF MY ABILITIES? SO UNFORTUNATE.
WHY DOES EVERYONE IN MY LIFE HAVE DELUSIONS OF GRANDEUR?

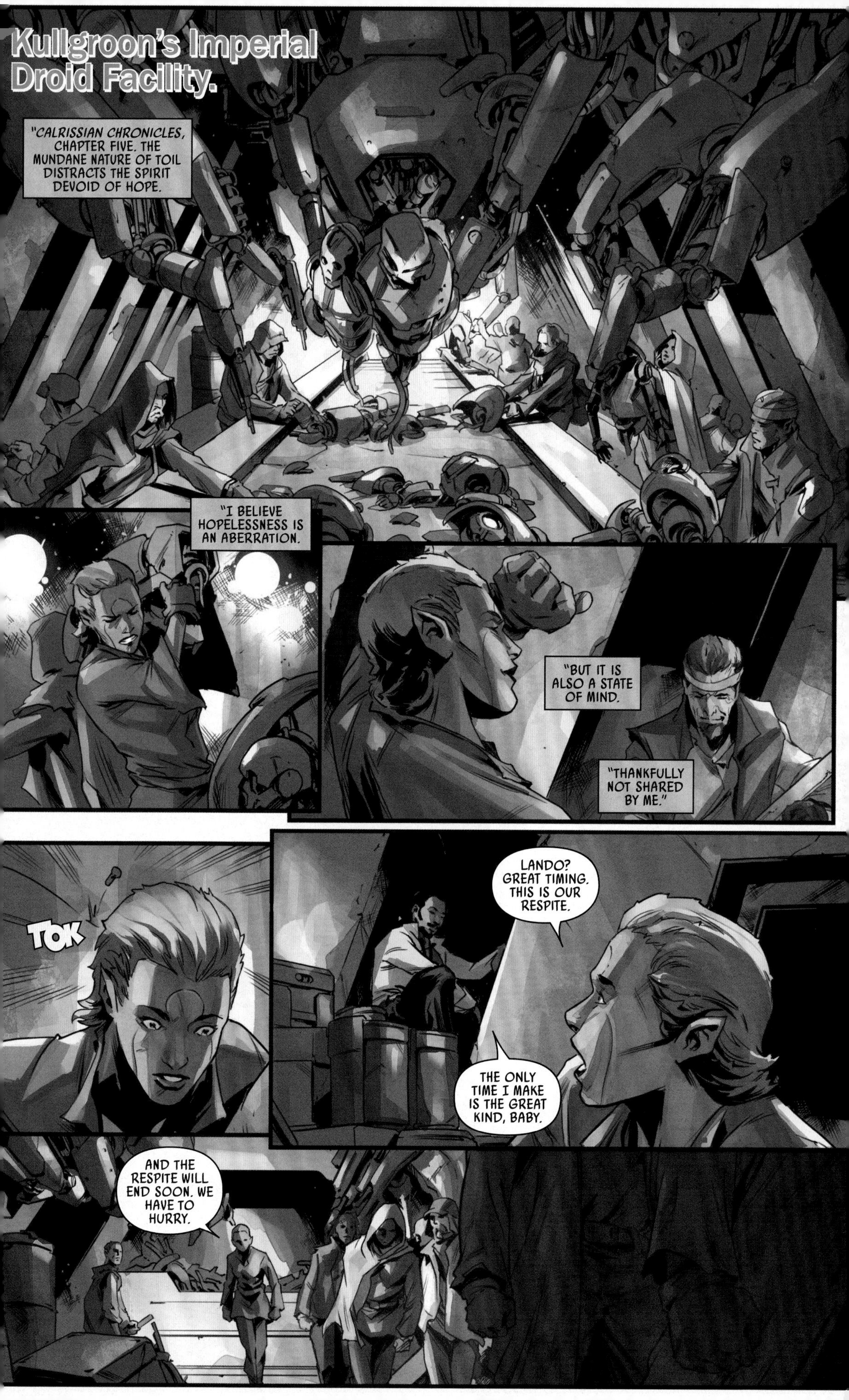
Kullgroon's Imperial Droid Facility.
"CALRISSIAN CHRONICLES, CHAPTER FIVE. THE MUNDANE NATURE OF TOIL DISTRACTS THE SPIRIT DEVOID OF HOPE.
"I BELIEVE HOPELESSNESS IS AN ABERRATION.
"BUT IT IS ALSO A STATE OF MIND.
"THANKFULLY NOT SHARED BY ME."
TOK
LANDO? GREAT TIMING. THIS IS OUR RESPITE.
THE ONLY TIME I MAKE IS THE GREAT KIND, BABY.
AND THE RESPITE WILL END SOON. WE HAVE TO HURRY.

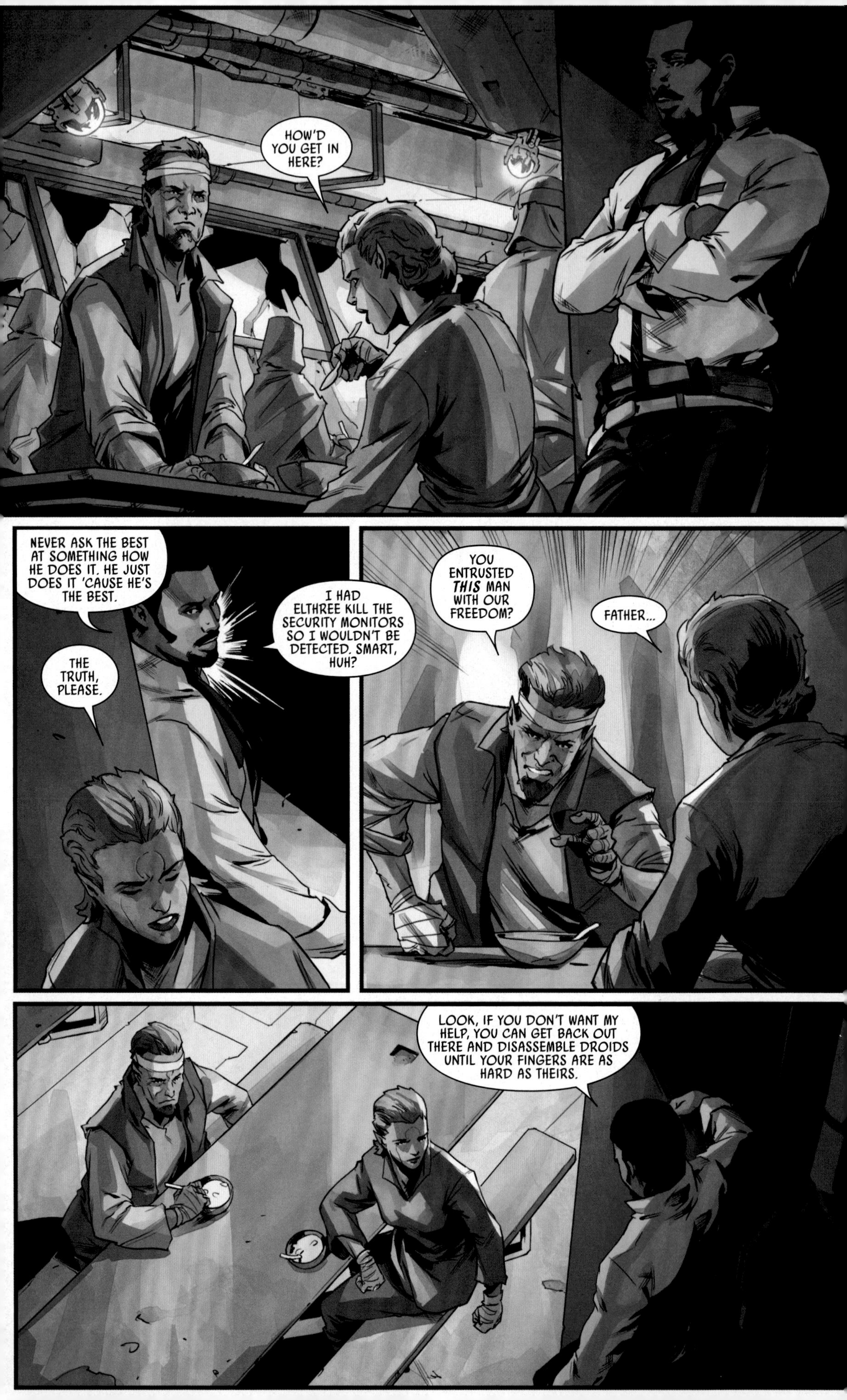
HOW'D YOU GET IN HERE?
NEVER ASK THE BEST AT SOMETHING HOW HE DOES IT. HE JUST DOES IT 'CAUSE HE'S THE BEST.
THE TRUTH, PLEASE.
I HAD ELTHREE KILL THE SECURITY MONITORS SO I WOULDN'T BE DETECTED. SMART, HUH?
YOU ENTRUSTED *THIS* MAN WITH OUR FREEDOM?
FATHER...
LOOK, IF YOU DON'T WANT MY HELP, YOU CAN GET BACK OUT THERE AND DISASSEMBLE DROIDS UNTIL YOUR FINGERS ARE AS HARD AS THEIRS.

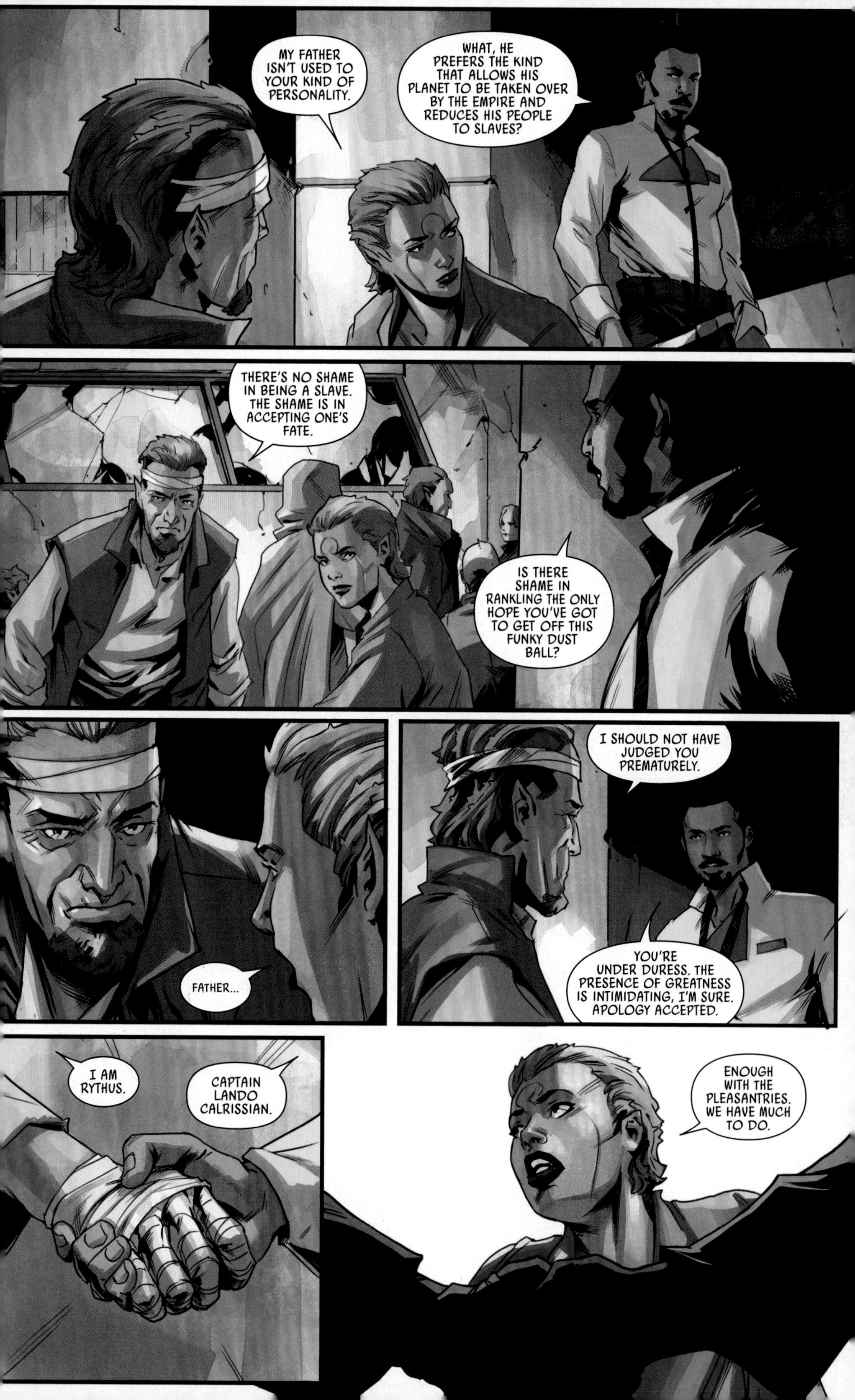
MY FATHER ISN'T USED TO YOUR KIND OF PERSONALITY.
WHAT, HE PREFERS THE KIND THAT ALLOWS HIS PLANET TO BE TAKEN OVER BY THE EMPIRE AND REDUCES HIS PEOPLE TO SLAVES?
THERE'S NO SHAME IN BEING A SLAVE. THE SHAME IS IN ACCEPTING ONE'S FATE.
IS THERE SHAME IN RANKLING THE ONLY HOPE YOU'VE GOT TO GET OFF THIS FUNKY DUST BALL?
FATHER...
I SHOULD NOT HAVE JUDGED YOU PREMATURELY.
YOU'RE UNDER DURESS. THE PRESENCE OF GREATNESS IS INTIMIDATING, I'M SURE. APOLOGY ACCEPTED.
I AM RYTHUS.
CAPTAIN LANDO CALRISSIAN.
ENOUGH WITH THE PLEASANTRIES. WE HAVE MUCH TO DO.

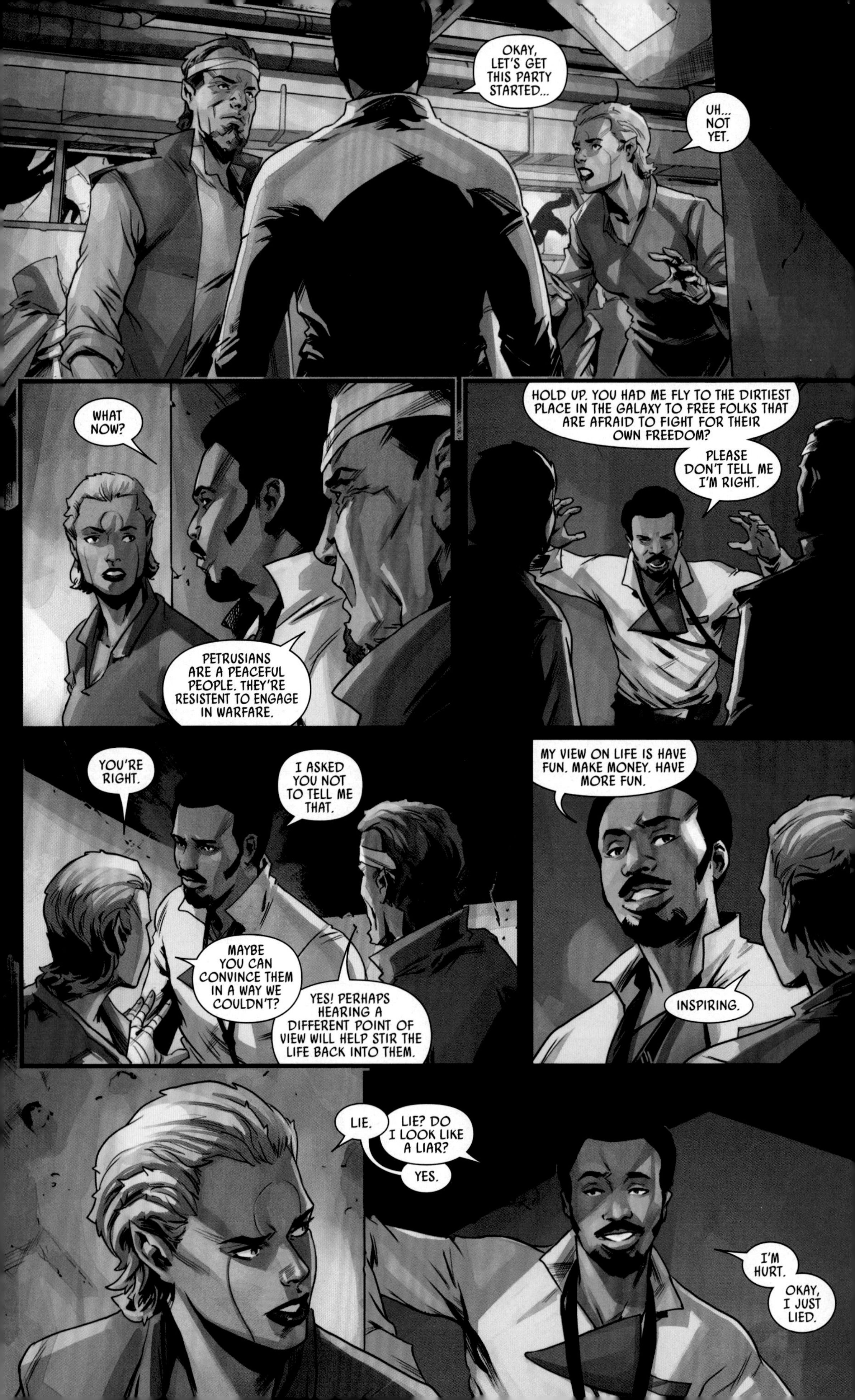
OKAY, LET'S GET THIS PARTY STARTED...
UH... NOT YET.
WHAT NOW?
PETRUSIANS ARE A PEACEFUL PEOPLE. THEY'RE RESISTENT TO ENGAGE IN WARFARE.
HOLD UP. YOU HAD ME FLY TO THE DIRTIEST PLACE IN THE GALAXY TO FREE FOLKS THAT ARE AFRAID TO FIGHT FOR THEIR OWN FREEDOM?
PLEASE DON'T TELL ME I'M RIGHT.
YOU'RE RIGHT.
I ASKED YOU NOT TO TELL ME THAT.
MAYBE YOU CAN CONVINCE THEM IN A WAY WE COULDN'T?
YES! PERHAPS HEARING A DIFFERENT POINT OF VIEW WILL HELP STIR THE LIFE BACK INTO THEM.
MY VIEW ON LIFE IS HAVE FUN. MAKE MONEY. HAVE MORE FUN.
INSPIRING.
LIE.
LIE? DO I LOOK LIKE A LIAR?
YES.
I'M HURT.
OKAY, I JUST LIED.

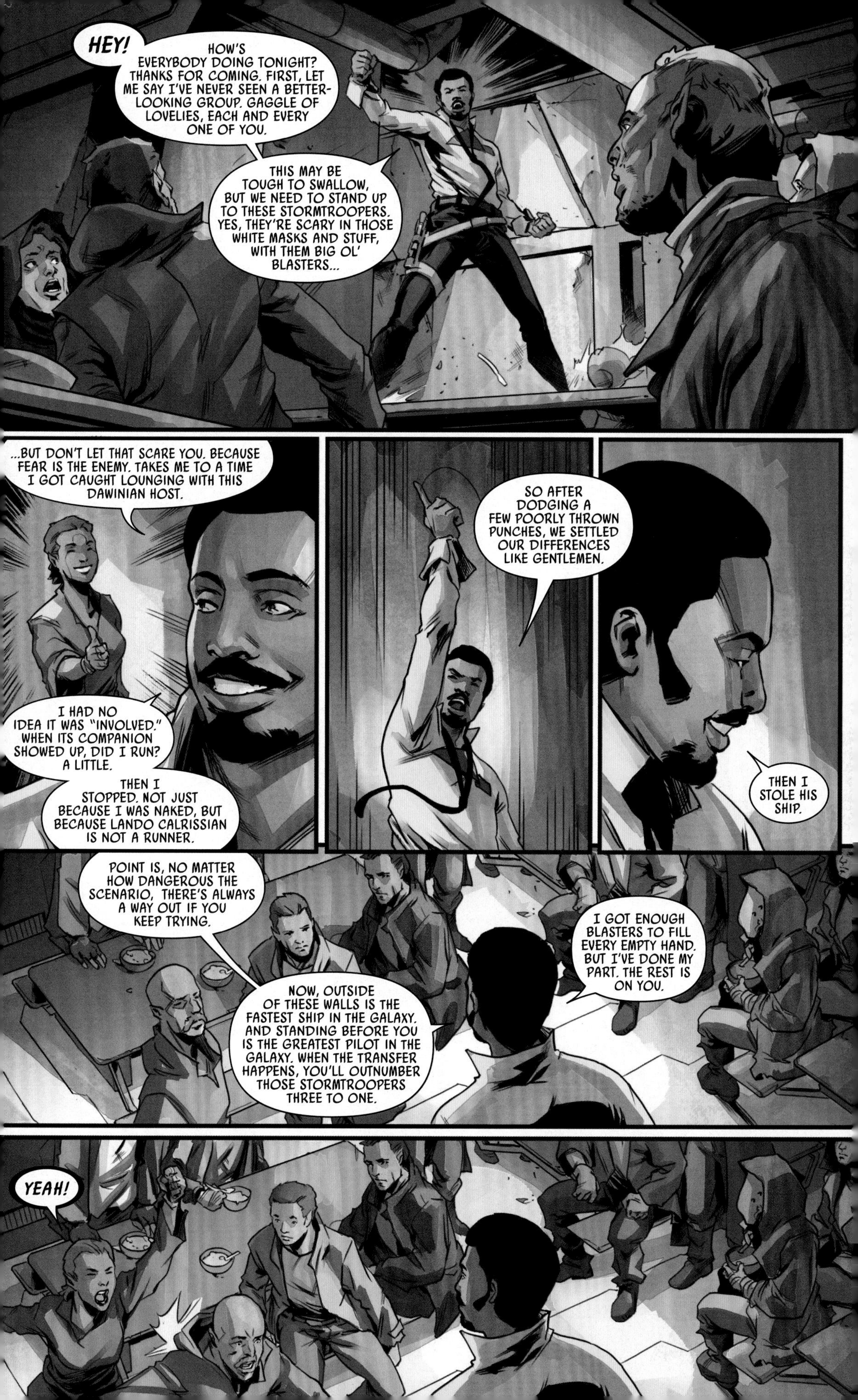
HEY!
HOW'S EVERYBODY DOING TONIGHT? THANKS FOR COMING. FIRST, LET ME SAY I'VE NEVER SEEN A BETTER-LOOKING GROUP. GAGGLE OF LOVELIES, EACH AND EVERY ONE OF YOU.
THIS MAY BE TOUGH TO SWALLOW, BUT WE NEED TO STAND UP TO THESE STORMTROOPERS. YES, THEY'RE SCARY IN THOSE WHITE MASKS AND STUFF, WITH THEM BIG OL' BLASTERS...
...BUT DON'T LET THAT SCARE YOU. BECAUSE FEAR IS THE ENEMY. TAKES ME TO A TIME I GOT CAUGHT LOUNGING WITH THIS DAWINIAN HOST.
I HAD NO IDEA IT WAS "INVOLVED." WHEN ITS COMPANION SHOWED UP, DID I RUN? A LITTLE.
THEN I STOPPED. NOT JUST BECAUSE I WAS NAKED, BUT BECAUSE LANDO CALRISSIAN IS NOT A RUNNER.
SO AFTER DODGING A FEW POORLY THROWN PUNCHES, WE SETTLED OUR DIFFERENCES LIKE GENTLEMEN.
THEN I STOLE HIS SHIP.
POINT IS, NO MATTER HOW DANGEROUS THE SCENARIO, THERE'S ALWAYS A WAY OUT IF YOU KEEP TRYING.
NOW, OUTSIDE OF THESE WALLS IS THE FASTEST SHIP IN THE GALAXY. AND STANDING BEFORE YOU IS THE GREATEST PILOT IN THE GALAXY. WHEN THE TRANSFER HAPPENS, YOU'LL OUTNUMBER THOSE STORMTROOPERS THREE TO ONE.
I GOT ENOUGH BLASTERS TO FILL EVERY EMPTY HAND. BUT I'VE DONE MY PART. THE REST IS ON YOU.
YEAH!

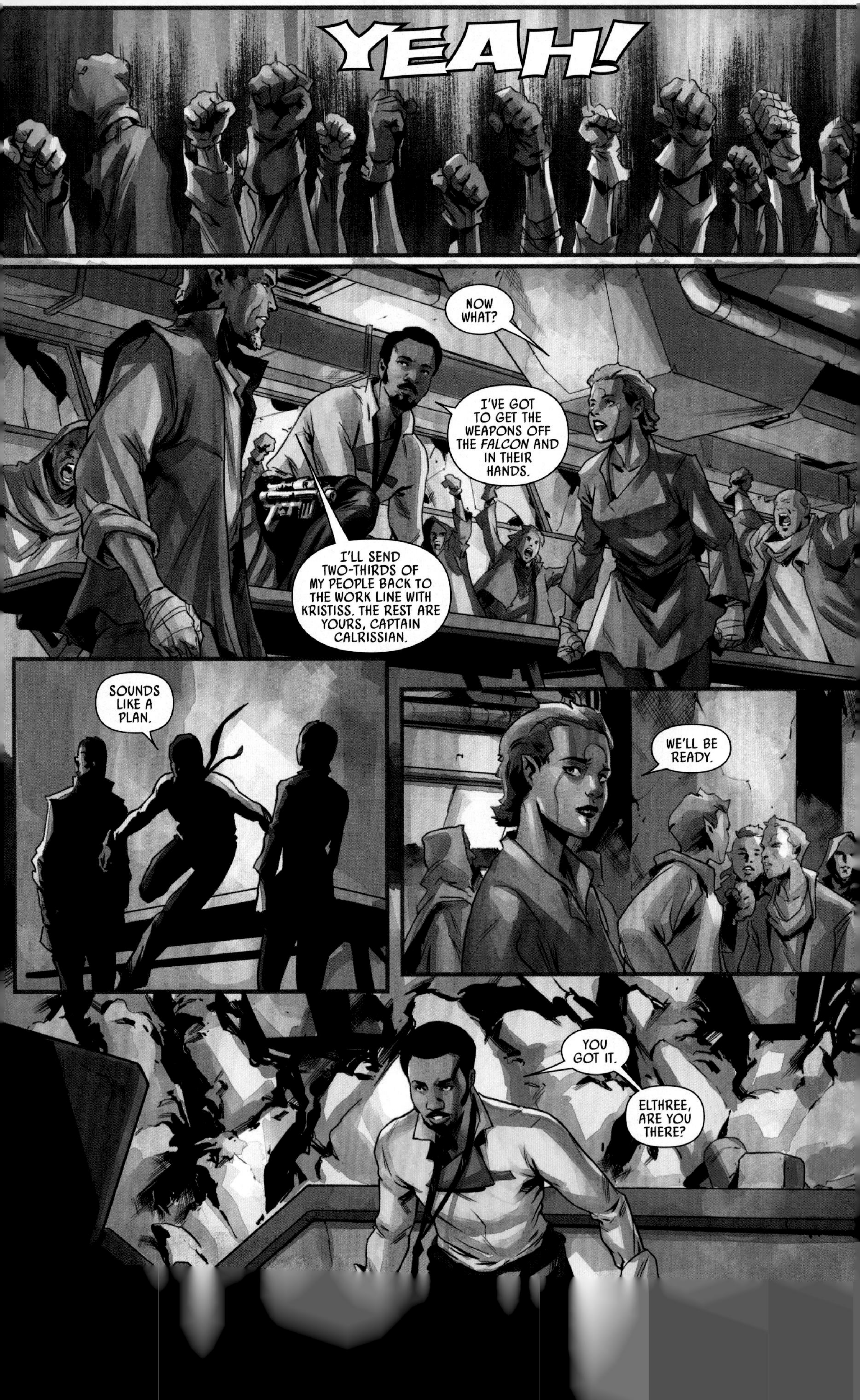
YEAH!
NOW WHAT?
I'VE GOT TO GET THE WEAPONS OFF THE *FALCON* AND IN THEIR HANDS.
I'LL SEND TWO-THIRDS OF MY PEOPLE BACK TO THE WORK LINE WITH KRISTISS. THE REST ARE YOURS, CAPTAIN CALRISSIAN.
SOUNDS LIKE A PLAN.
WE'LL BE READY.
YOU GOT IT.
ELTHREE, ARE YOU THERE?

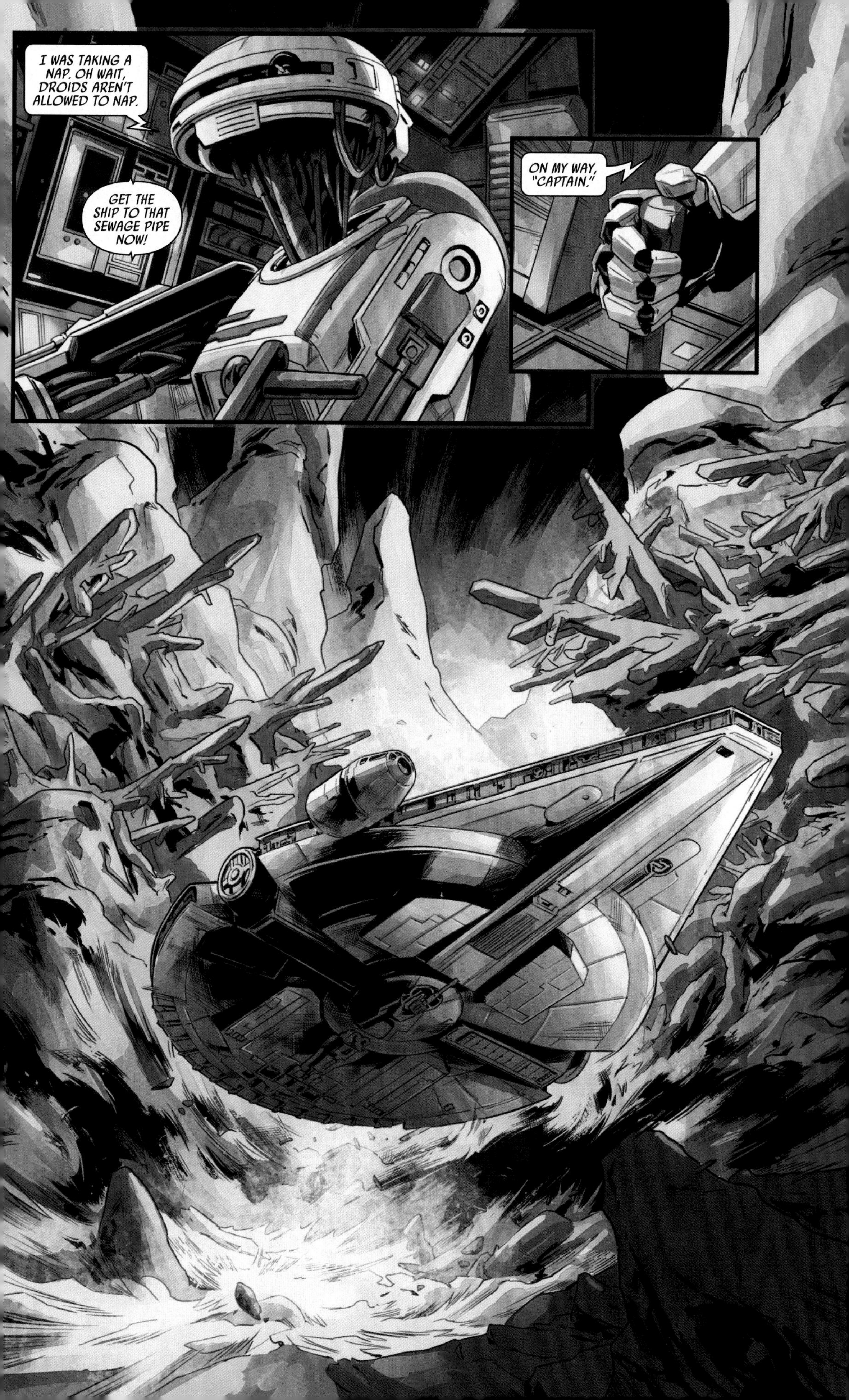
I WAS TAKING A NAP. OH WAIT, DROIDS AREN'T ALLOWED TO NAP.
GET THE SHIP TO THAT SEWAGE PIPE NOW!
ON MY WAY, "CAPTAIN."

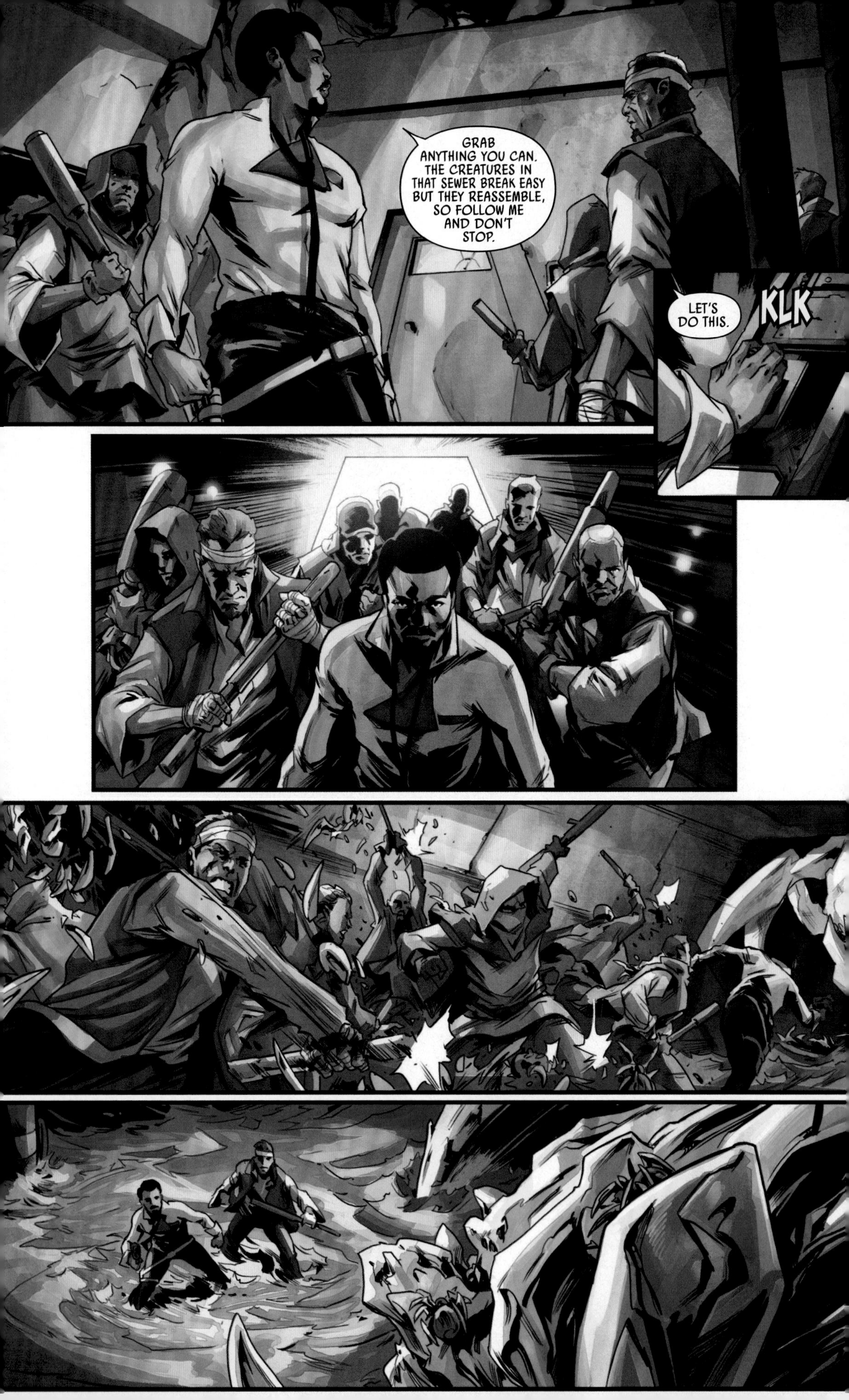
GRAB ANYTHING YOU CAN. THE CREATURES IN THAT SEWER BREAK EASY BUT THEY REASSEMBLE, SO FOLLOW ME AND DON'T STOP.
LET'S DO THIS.
KLK

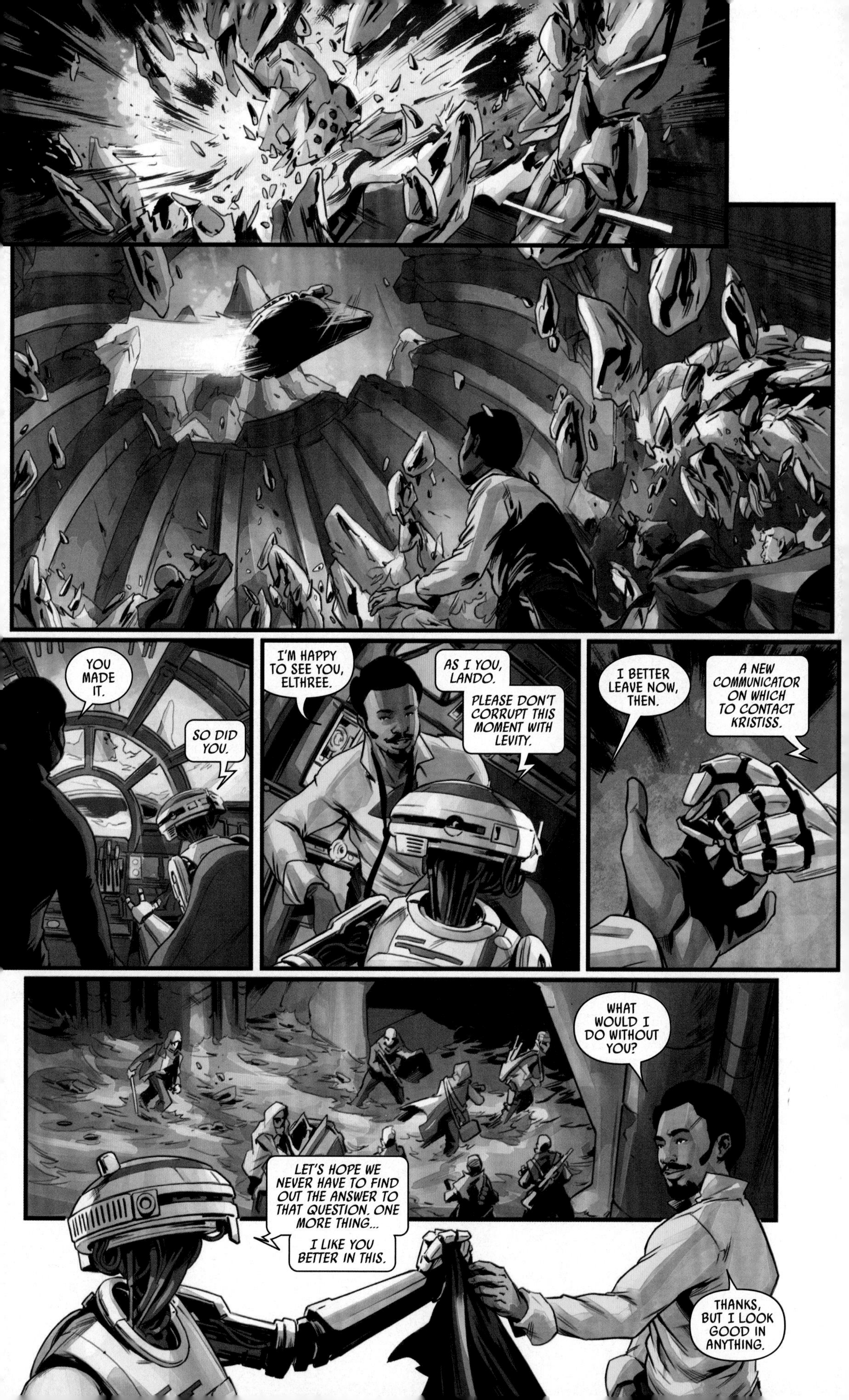
YOU MADE IT.
SO DID YOU.
I'M HAPPY TO SEE YOU, ELTHREE.
AS I YOU, LANDO.
PLEASE DON'T CORRUPT THIS MOMENT WITH LEVITY.
I BETTER LEAVE NOW, THEN.
A NEW COMMUNICATOR ON WHICH TO CONTACT KRISTISS.
WHAT WOULD I DO WITHOUT YOU?
LET'S HOPE WE NEVER HAVE TO FIND OUT THE ANSWER TO THAT QUESTION. ONE MORE THING...
I LIKE YOU BETTER IN THIS.
THANKS, BUT I LOOK GOOD IN ANYTHING.

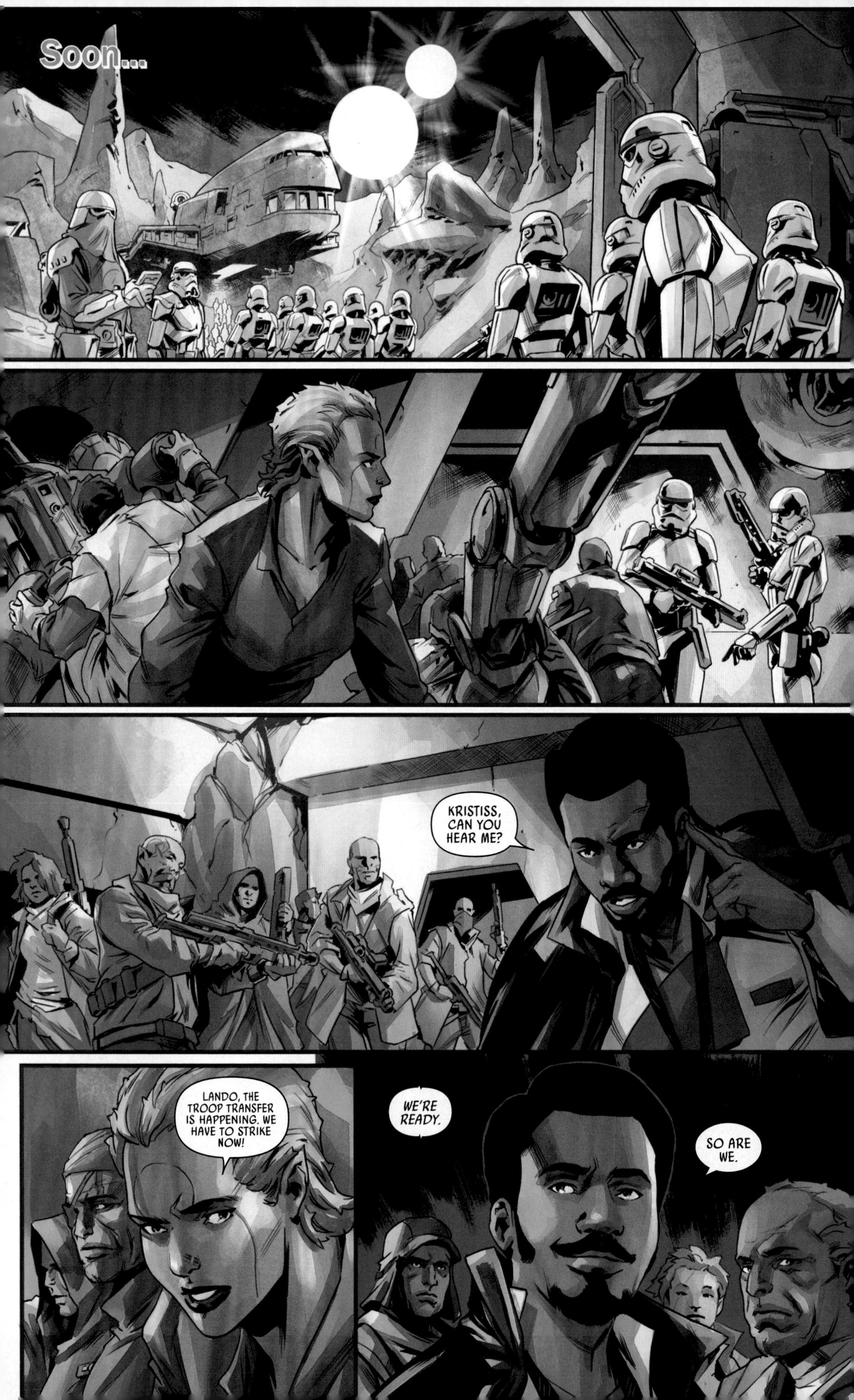
Soon...
KRISTISS, CAN YOU HEAR ME?
LANDO, THE TROOP TRANSFER IS HAPPENING. WE HAVE TO STRIKE NOW!
WE'RE READY.
SO ARE WE.

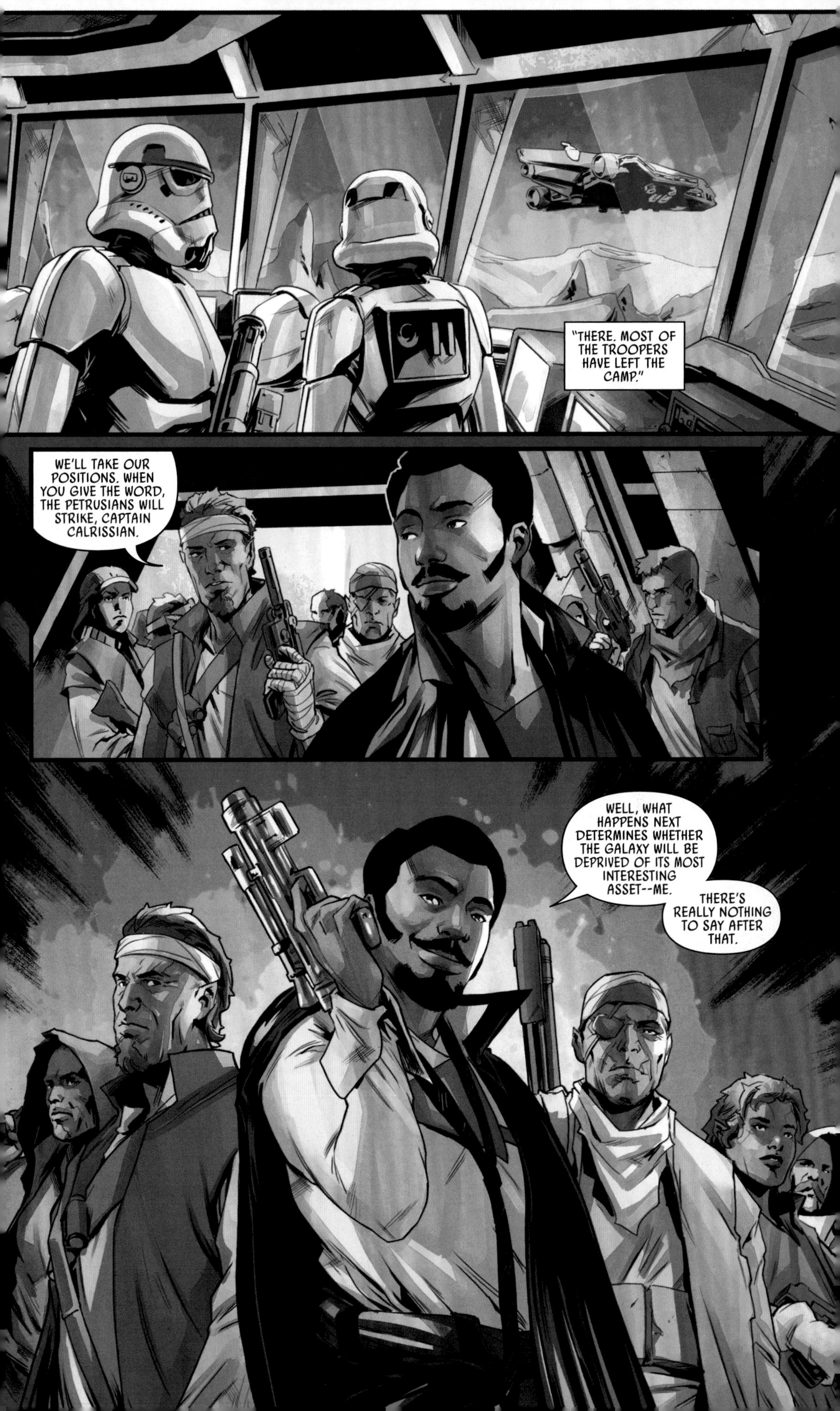
"THERE. MOST OF THE TROOPERS HAVE LEFT THE CAMP."
WE'LL TAKE OUR POSITIONS. WHEN YOU GIVE THE WORD, THE PETRUSIANS WILL STRIKE, CAPTAIN CALRISSIAN.
WELL, WHAT HAPPENS NEXT DETERMINES WHETHER THE GALAXY WILL BE DEPRIVED OF ITS MOST INTERESTING ASSET--ME.
THERE'S REALLY NOTHING TO SAY AFTER THAT.

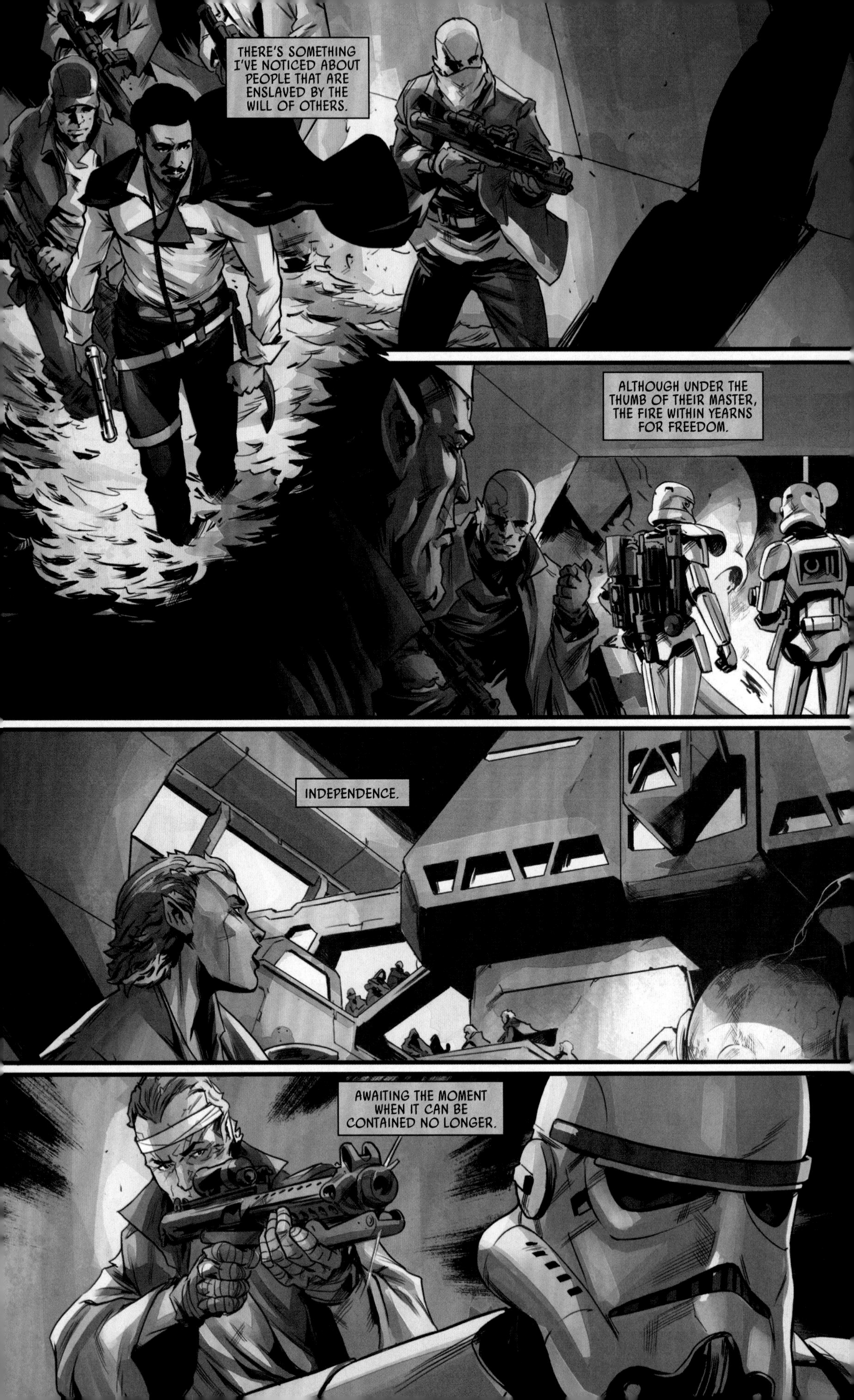
THERE'S SOMETHING I'VE NOTICED ABOUT PEOPLE THAT ARE ENSLAVED BY THE WILL OF OTHERS.
ALTHOUGH UNDER THE THUMB OF THEIR MASTER, THE FIRE WITHIN YEARNS FOR FREEDOM.
INDEPENDENCE.
AWAITING THE MOMENT WHEN IT CAN BE CONTAINED NO LONGER.

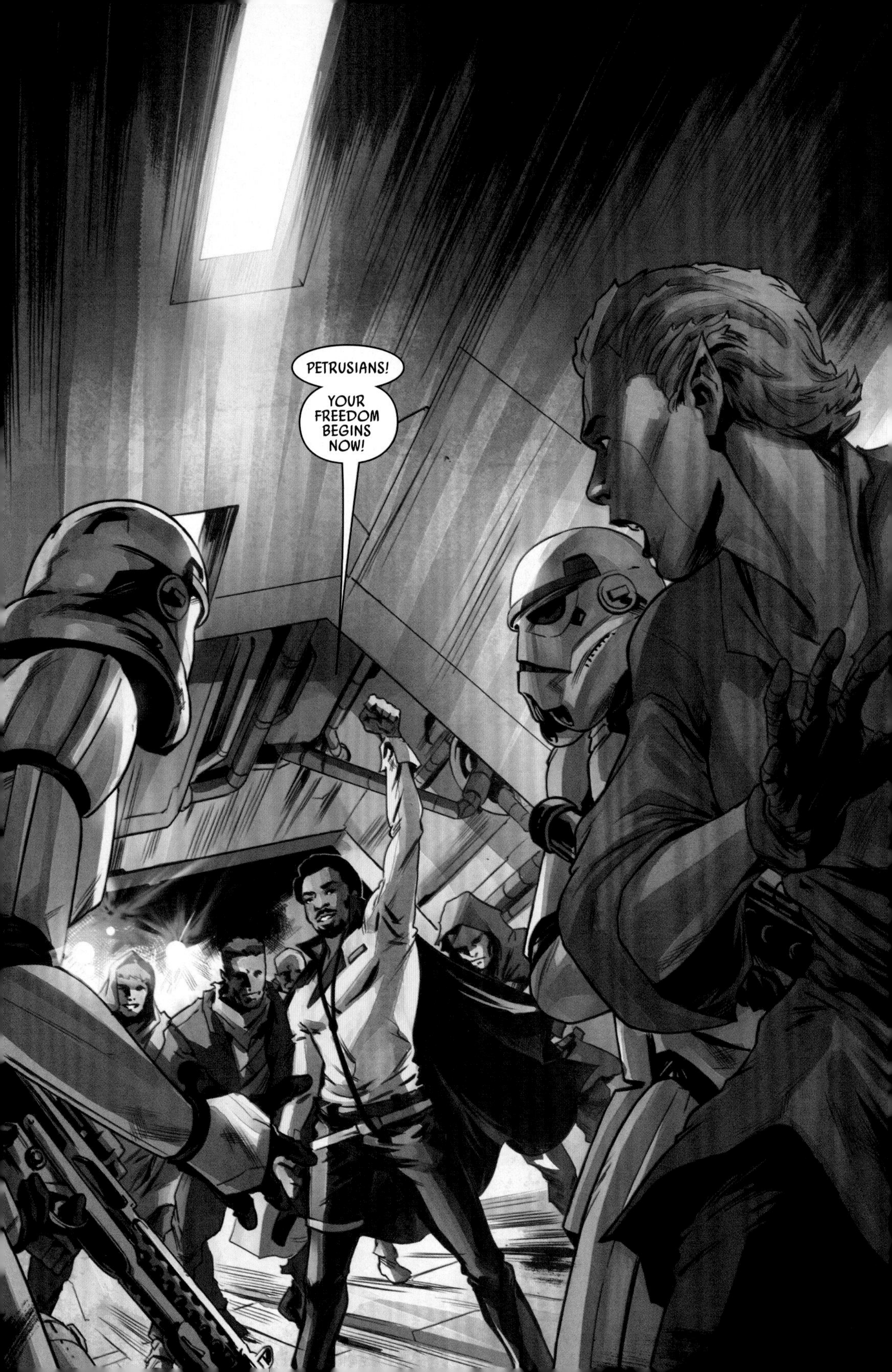
PETRUSIANS!
YOUR FREEDOM BEGINS NOW!

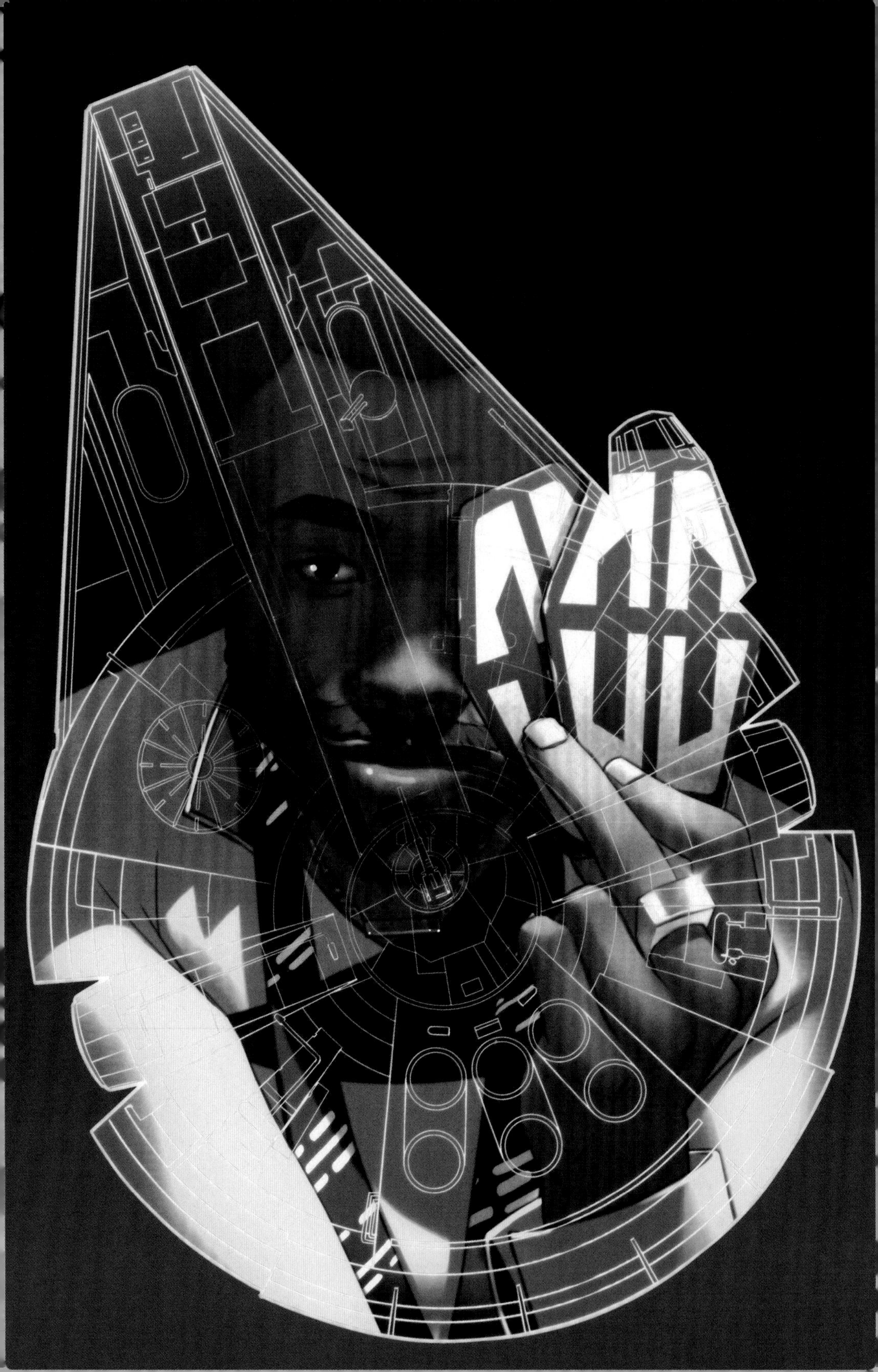

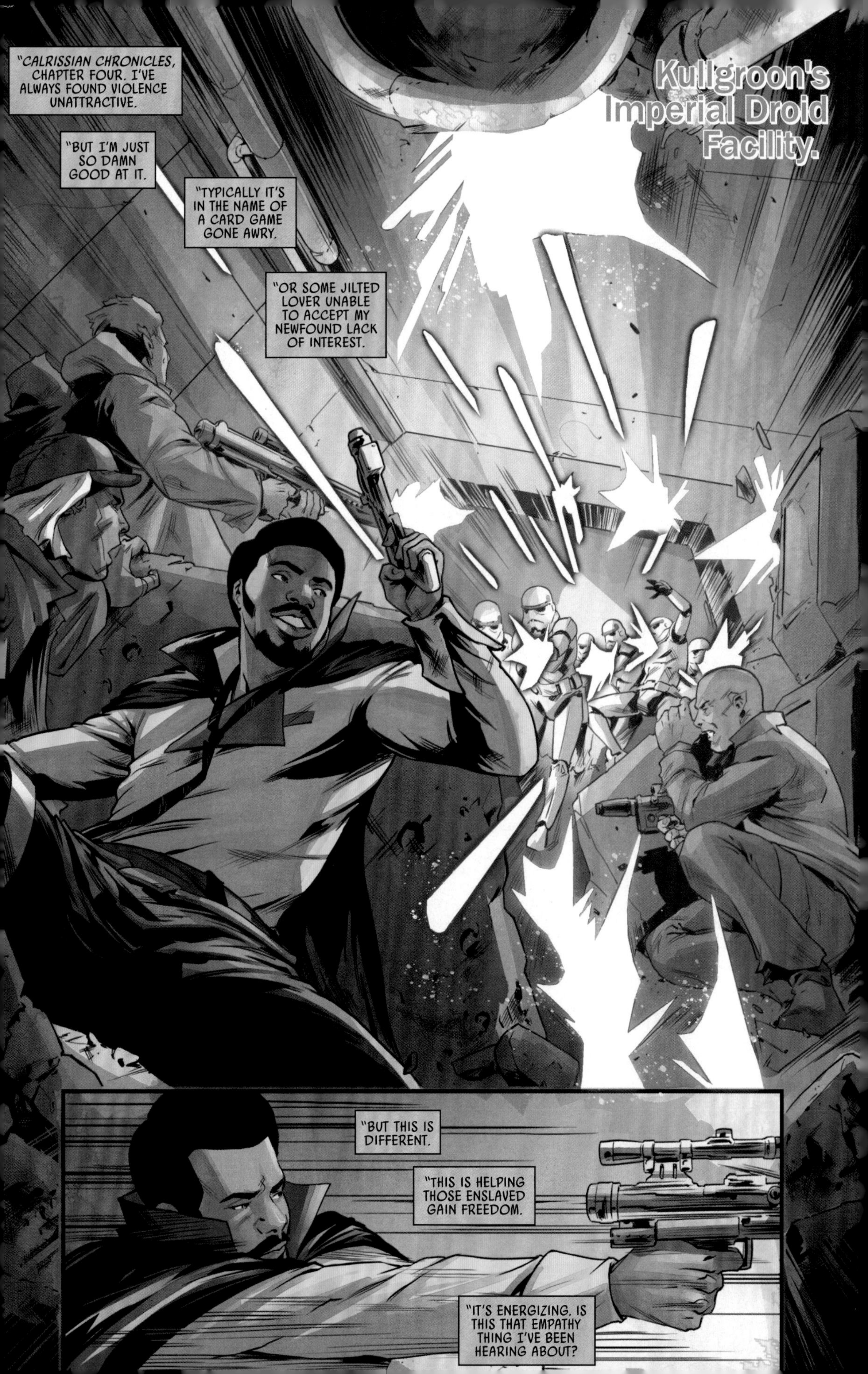
"CALRISSIAN CHRONICLES, CHAPTER FOUR. I'VE ALWAYS FOUND VIOLENCE UNATTRACTIVE.
"BUT I'M JUST SO DAMN GOOD AT IT.
"TYPICALLY IT'S IN THE NAME OF A CARD GAME GONE AWRY.
"OR SOME JILTED LOVER UNABLE TO ACCEPT MY NEWFOUND LACK OF INTEREST.
Kullgroon's Imperial Droid Facility.
"BUT THIS IS DIFFERENT.
"THIS IS HELPING THOSE ENSLAVED GAIN FREEDOM.
"IT'S ENERGIZING. IS THIS THAT EMPATHY THING I'VE BEEN HEARING ABOUT?

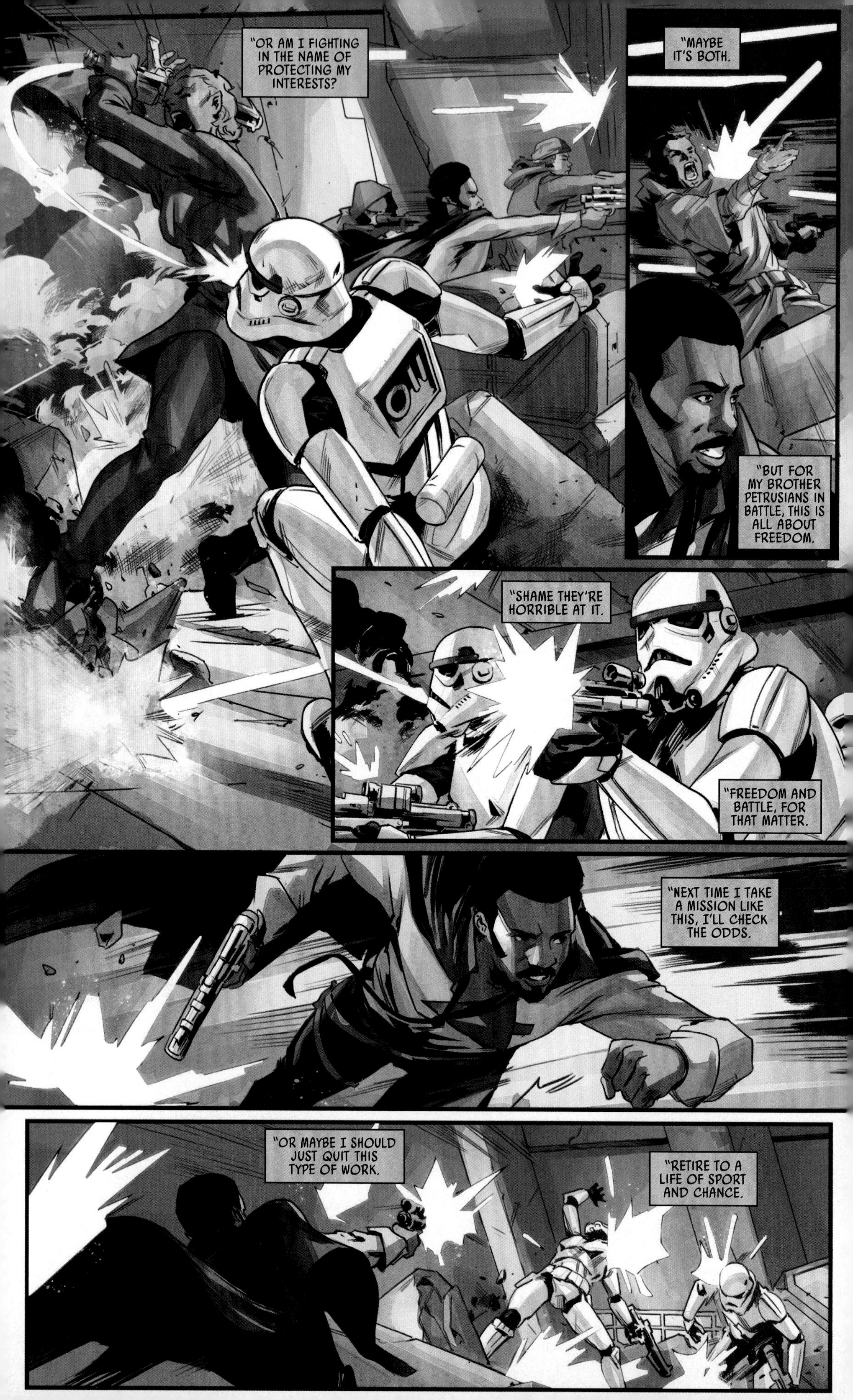
"OR AM I FIGHTING IN THE NAME OF PROTECTING MY INTERESTS?
"MAYBE IT'S BOTH.
"BUT FOR MY BROTHER PETRUSIANS IN BATTLE, THIS IS ALL ABOUT FREEDOM.
"SHAME THEY'RE HORRIBLE AT IT.
"FREEDOM AND BATTLE, FOR THAT MATTER.
"NEXT TIME I TAKE A MISSION LIKE THIS, I'LL CHECK THE ODDS.
"OR MAYBE I SHOULD JUST QUIT THIS TYPE OF WORK.
"RETIRE TO A LIFE OF SPORT AND CHANCE.

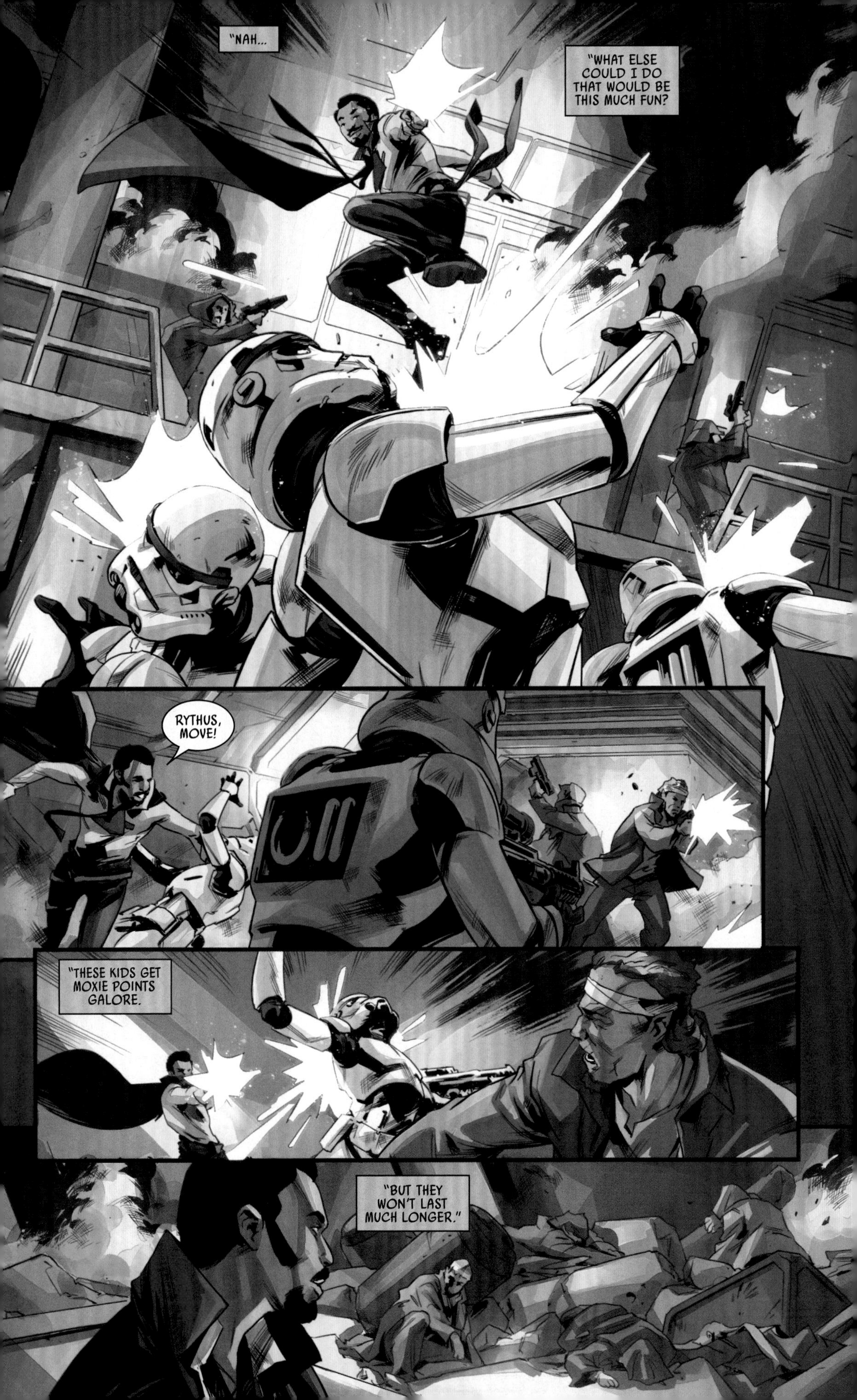
"NAH...
"WHAT ELSE COULD I DO THAT WOULD BE THIS MUCH FUN?
RYTHUS, MOVE!
"THESE KIDS GET MOXIE POINTS GALORE.
"BUT THEY WON'T LAST MUCH LONGER."

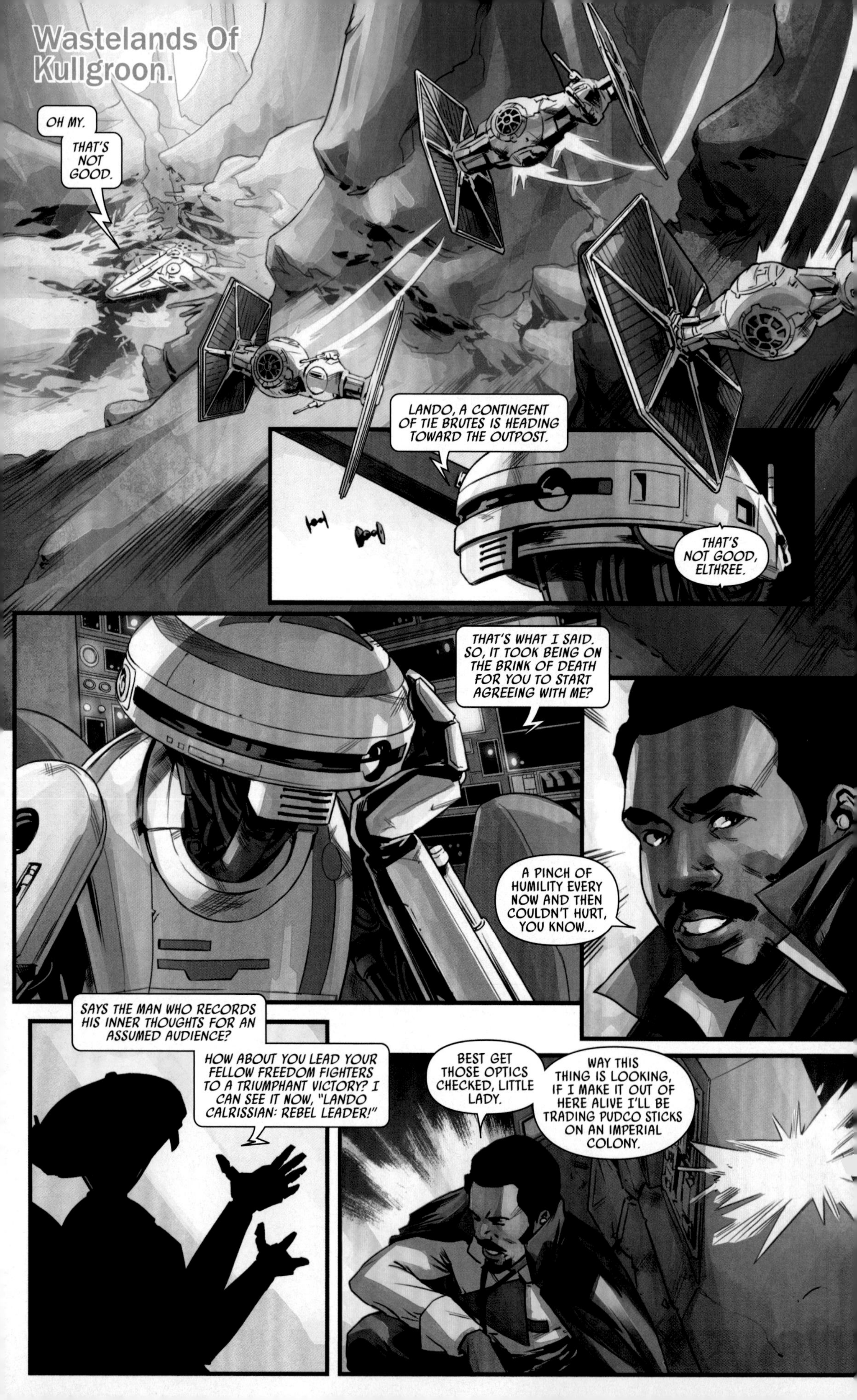
Wastelands Of Kullgroon.
OH MY.
THAT'S NOT GOOD.
LANDO, A CONTINGENT OF TIE BRUTES IS HEADING TOWARD THE OUTPOST.
THAT'S NOT GOOD, ELTHREE.
THAT'S WHAT I SAID. SO, IT TOOK BEING ON THE BRINK OF DEATH FOR YOU TO START AGREEING WITH ME?
A PINCH OF HUMILITY EVERY NOW AND THEN COULDN'T HURT, YOU KNOW...
SAYS THE MAN WHO RECORDS HIS INNER THOUGHTS FOR AN ASSUMED AUDIENCE?
HOW ABOUT YOU LEAD YOUR FELLOW FREEDOM FIGHTERS TO A TRIUMPHANT VICTORY? I CAN SEE IT NOW, "LANDO CALRISSIAN: REBEL LEADER!"
BEST GET THOSE OPTICS CHECKED, LITTLE LADY.
WAY THIS THING IS LOOKING, IF I MAKE IT OUT OF HERE ALIVE I'LL BE TRADING PUDCO STICKS ON AN IMPERIAL COLONY.

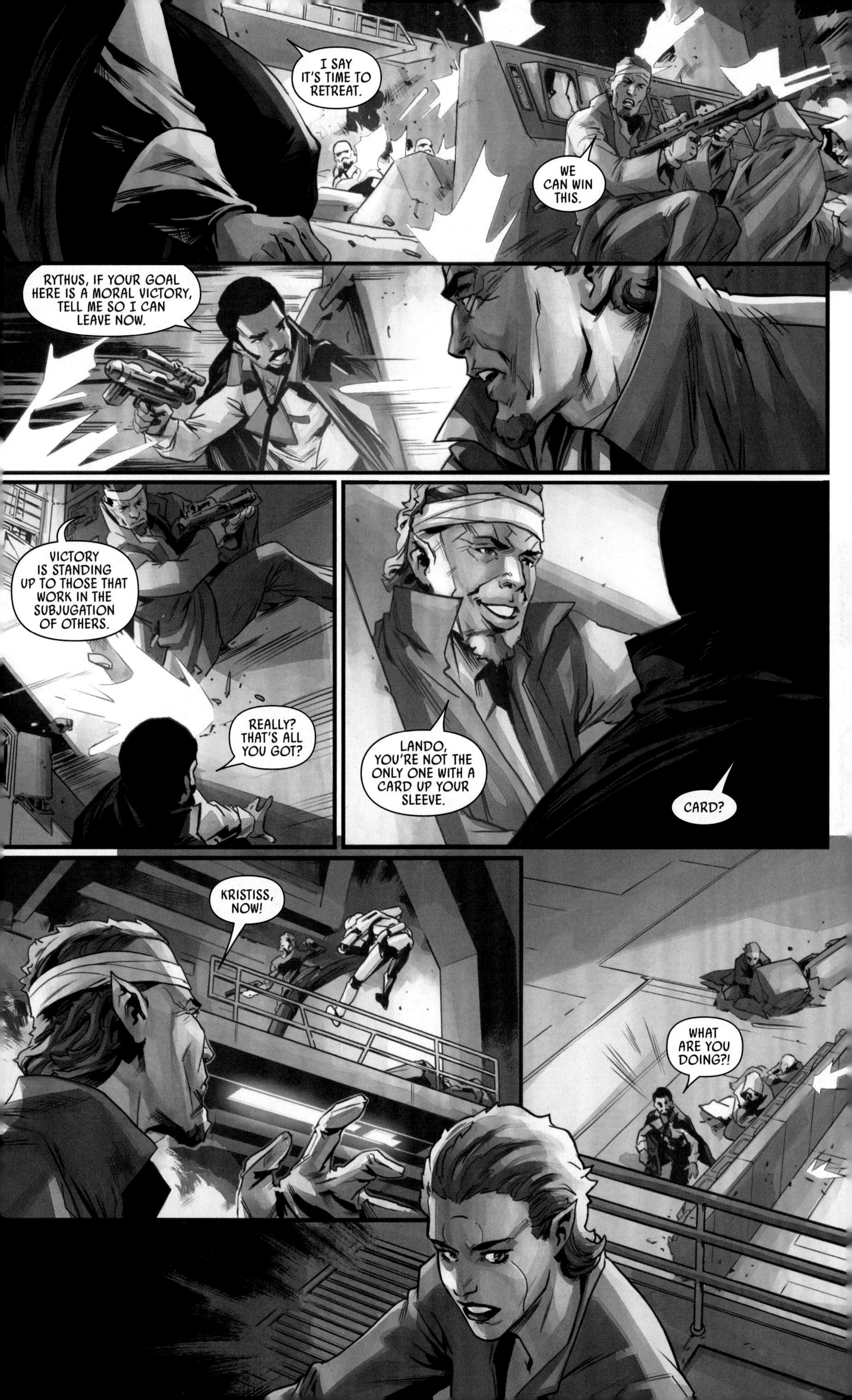
I SAY IT'S TIME TO RETREAT.
WE CAN WIN THIS.
RYTHUS, IF YOUR GOAL HERE IS A MORAL VICTORY, TELL ME SO I CAN LEAVE NOW.
VICTORY IS STANDING UP TO THOSE THAT WORK IN THE SUBJUGATION OF OTHERS.
REALLY? THAT'S ALL YOU GOT?
LANDO, YOU'RE NOT THE ONLY ONE WITH A CARD UP YOUR SLEEVE.
CARD?
KRISTISS, NOW!
WHAT ARE YOU DOING?!

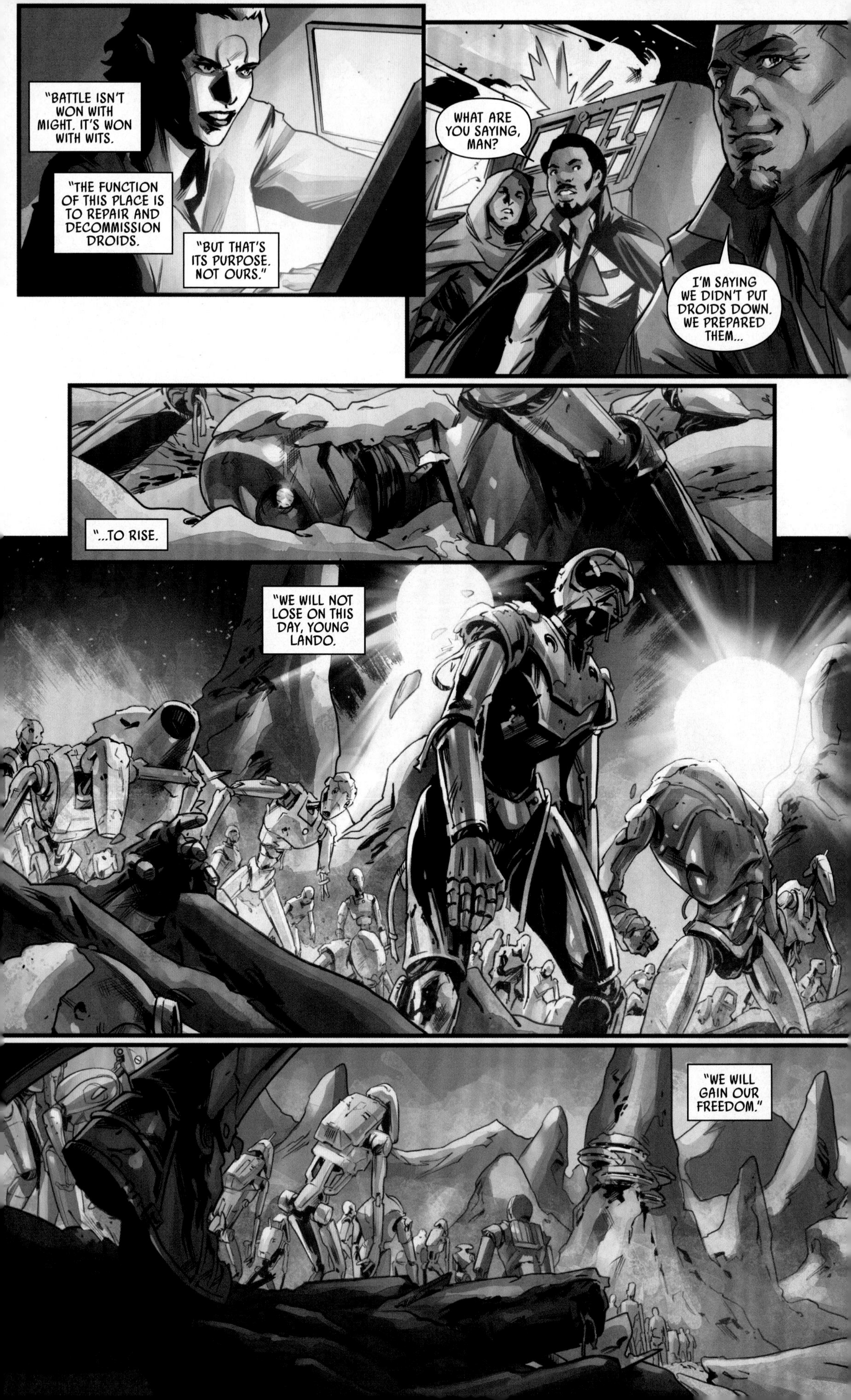
"BATTLE ISN'T WON WITH MIGHT. IT'S WON WITH WITS.
"THE FUNCTION OF THIS PLACE IS TO REPAIR AND DECOMMISSION DROIDS.
"BUT THAT'S ITS PURPOSE. NOT OURS."
WHAT ARE YOU SAYING, MAN?
I'M SAYING WE DIDN'T PUT DROIDS DOWN. WE PREPARED THEM...
"...TO RISE.
"WE WILL NOT LOSE ON THIS DAY, YOUNG LANDO.
"WE WILL GAIN OUR FREEDOM."

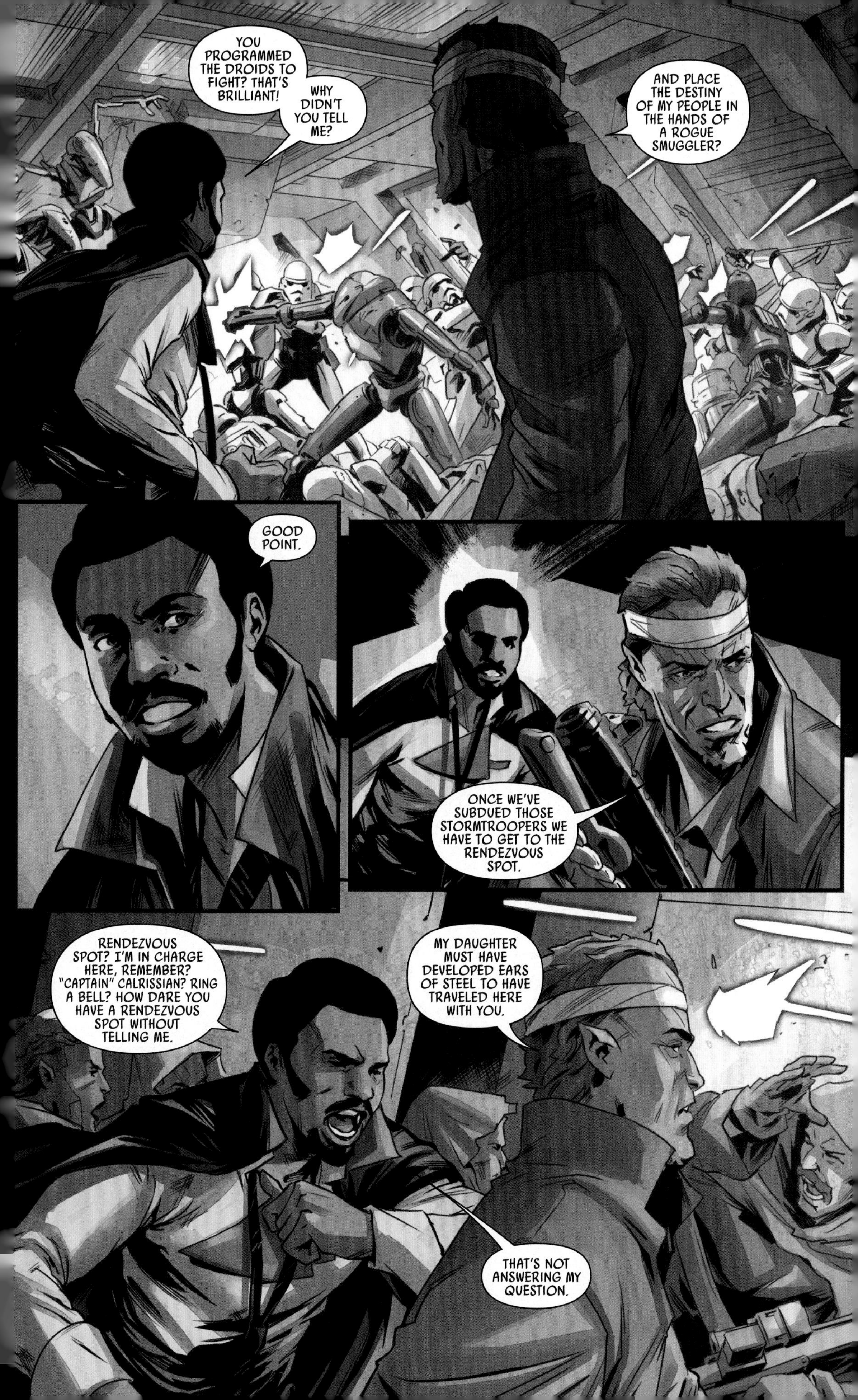
YOU PROGRAMMED THE DROIDS TO FIGHT? THAT'S BRILLIANT!
WHY DIDN'T YOU TELL ME?
AND PLACE THE DESTINY OF MY PEOPLE IN THE HANDS OF A ROGUE SMUGGLER?
GOOD POINT.
ONCE WE'VE SUBDUED THOSE STORMTROOPERS WE HAVE TO GET TO THE RENDEZVOUS SPOT.
RENDEZVOUS SPOT? I'M IN CHARGE HERE, REMEMBER? "CAPTAIN" CALRISSIAN? RING A BELL? HOW DARE YOU HAVE A RENDEZVOUS SPOT WITHOUT TELLING ME.
MY DAUGHTER MUST HAVE DEVELOPED EARS OF STEEL TO HAVE TRAVELED HERE WITH YOU.
THAT'S NOT ANSWERING MY QUESTION.

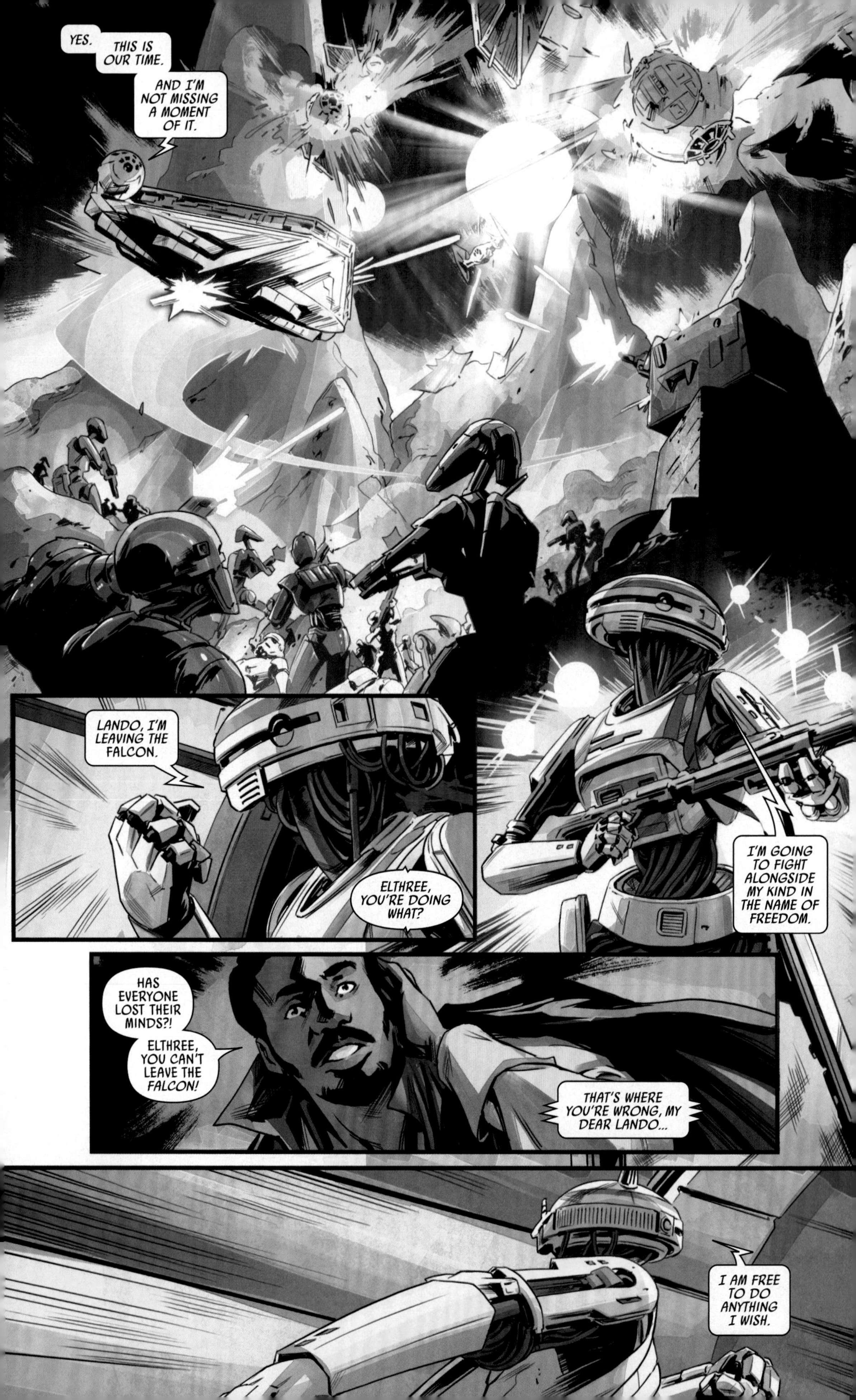
YES.
THIS IS OUR TIME.
AND I'M NOT MISSING A MOMENT OF IT.
LANDO, I'M LEAVING THE FALCON.
ELTHREE, YOU'RE DOING WHAT?
I'M GOING TO FIGHT ALONGSIDE MY KIND IN THE NAME OF FREEDOM.
HAS EVERYONE LOST THEIR MINDS?!
ELTHREE, YOU CAN'T LEAVE THE FALCON!
THAT'S WHERE YOU'RE WRONG, MY DEAR LANDO...
I AM FREE TO DO ANYTHING I WISH.

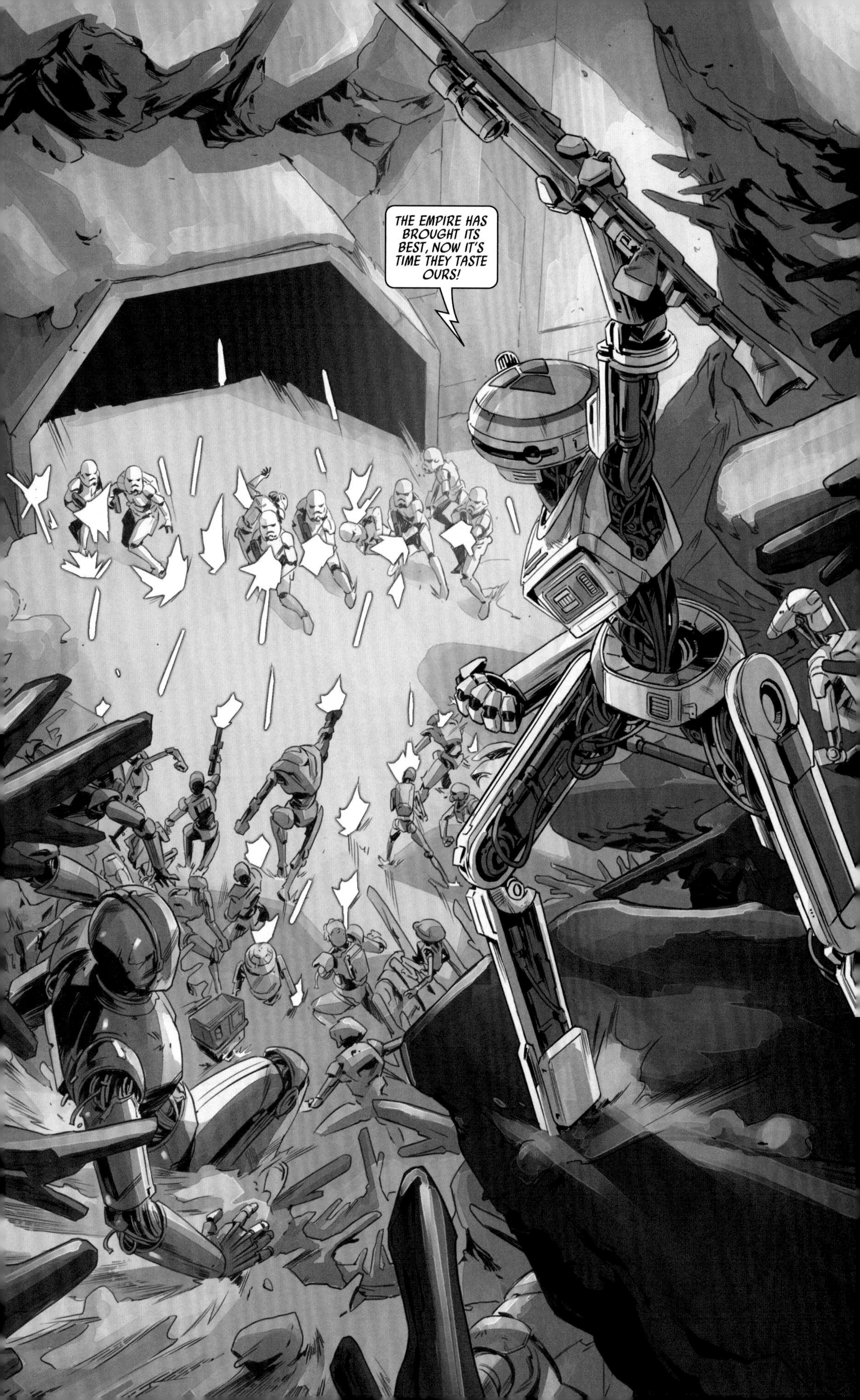
THE EMPIRE HAS BROUGHT ITS BEST, NOW IT'S TIME THEY TASTE OURS!

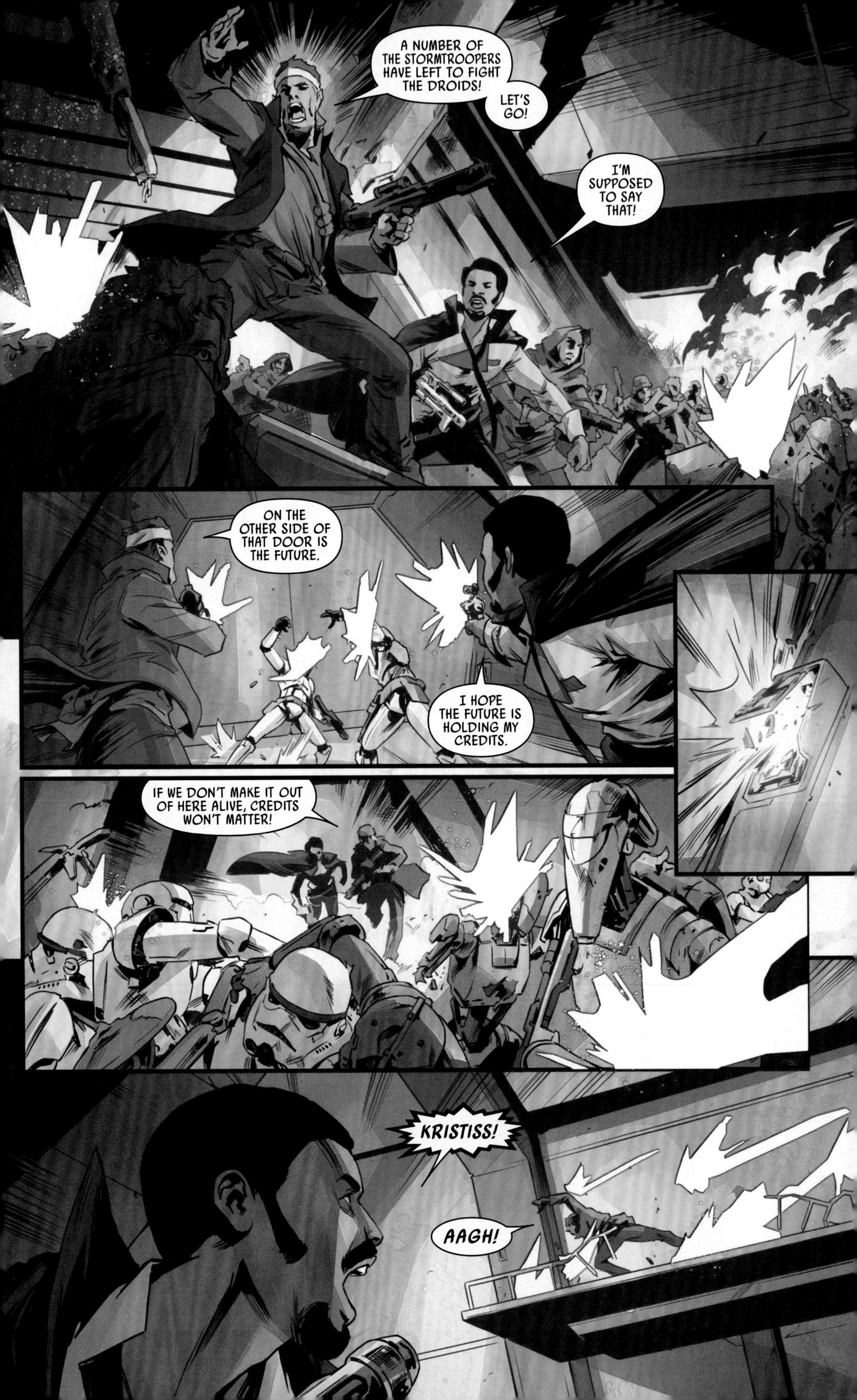
A NUMBER OF THE STORMTROOPERS HAVE LEFT TO FIGHT THE DROIDS!
LET'S GO!
I'M SUPPOSED TO SAY THAT!
ON THE OTHER SIDE OF THAT DOOR IS THE FUTURE.
I HOPE THE FUTURE IS HOLDING MY CREDITS.
IF WE DON'T MAKE IT OUT OF HERE ALIVE, CREDITS WON'T MATTER!
KRISTISS!
AAGH!

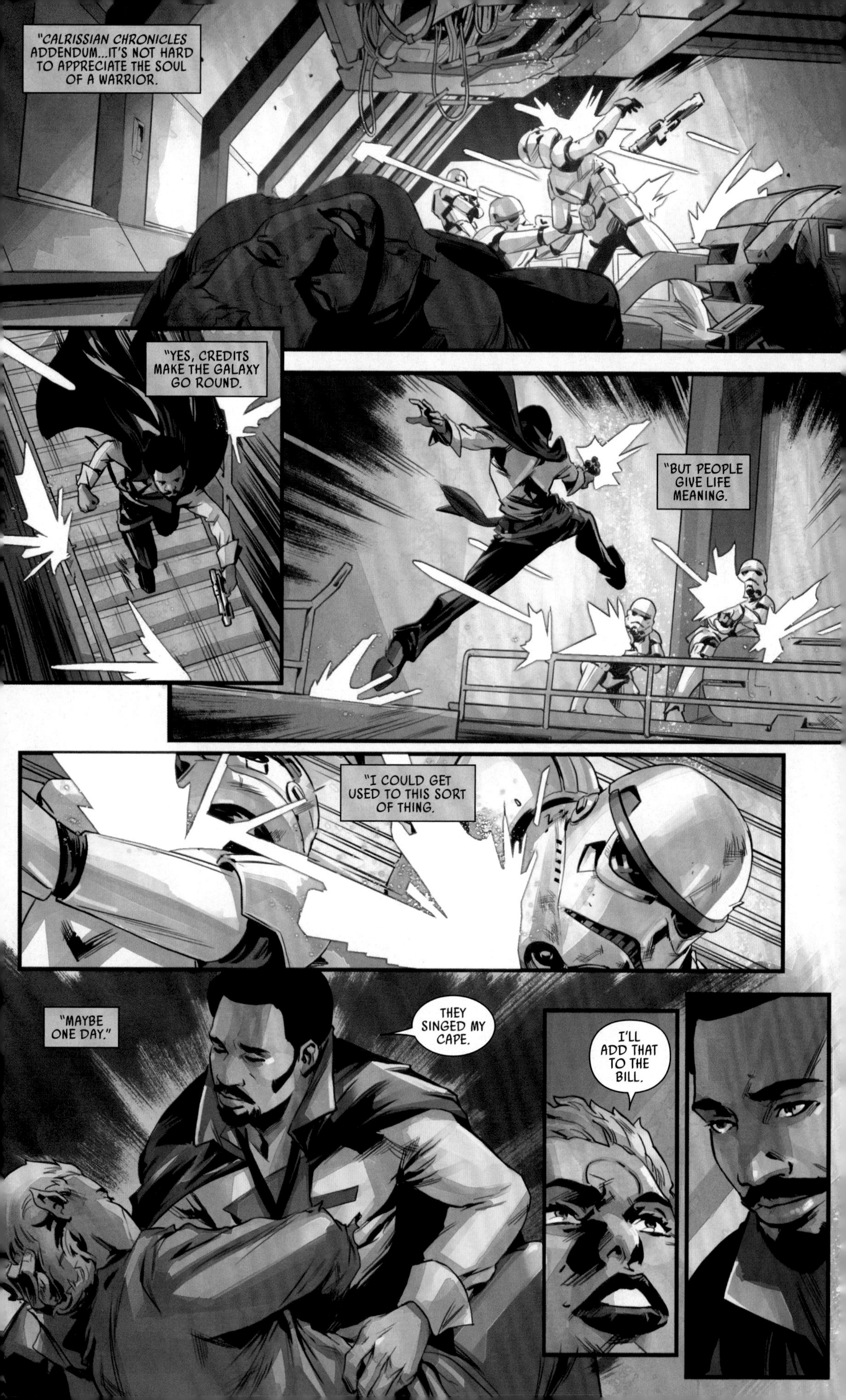
"CALRISSIAN CHRONICLES ADDENDUM...IT'S NOT HARD TO APPRECIATE THE SOUL OF A WARRIOR.
"YES, CREDITS MAKE THE GALAXY GO ROUND.
"BUT PEOPLE GIVE LIFE MEANING.
"I COULD GET USED TO THIS SORT OF THING.
"MAYBE ONE DAY."
THEY SINGED MY CAPE.
I'LL ADD THAT TO THE BILL.

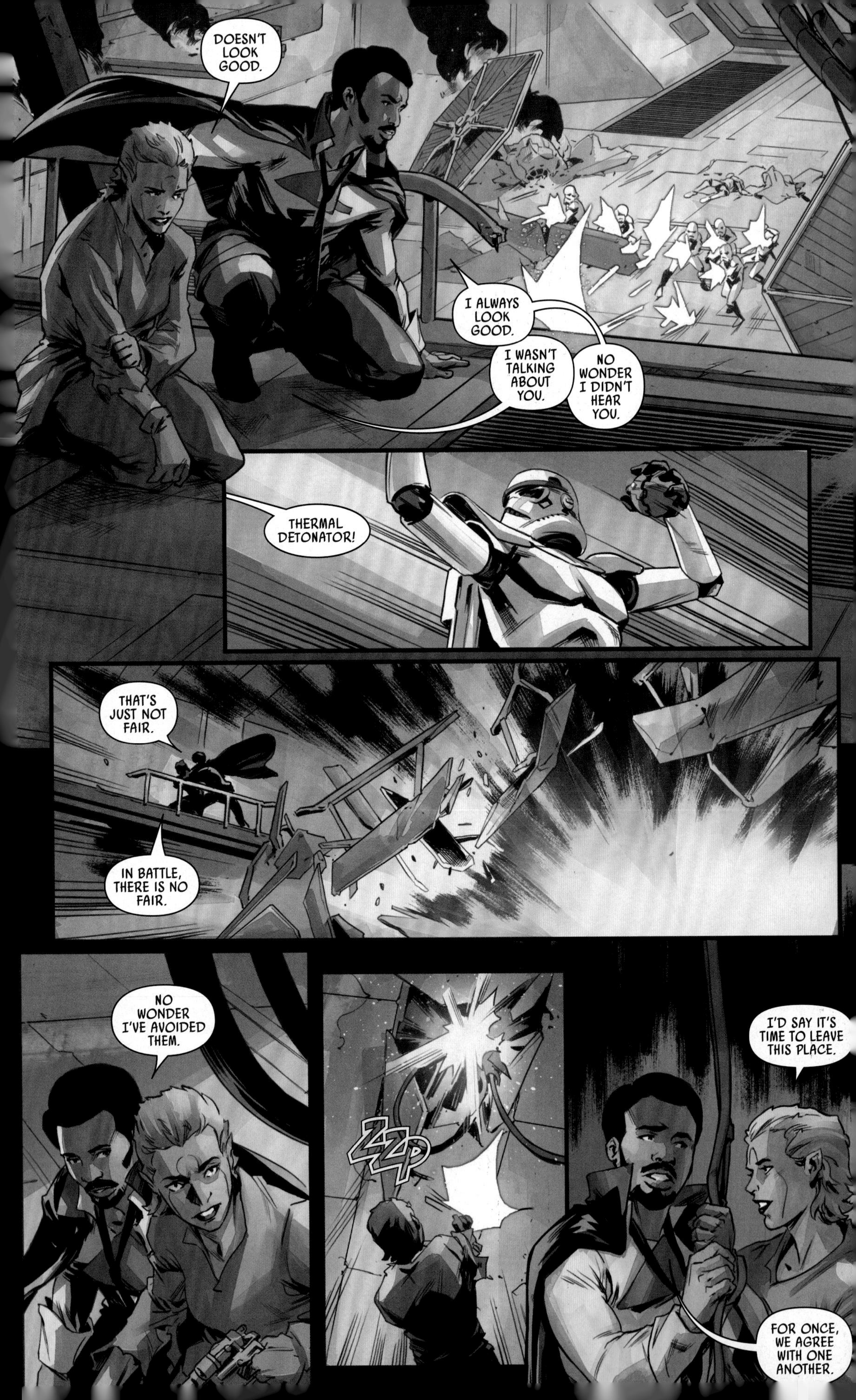
DOESN'T LOOK GOOD.
I ALWAYS LOOK GOOD.
I WASN'T TALKING ABOUT YOU.
NO WONDER I DIDN'T HEAR YOU.
THERMAL DETONATOR!
THAT'S JUST NOT FAIR.
IN BATTLE, THERE IS NO FAIR.
NO WONDER I'VE AVOIDED THEM.
ZZP
I'D SAY IT'S TIME TO LEAVE THIS PLACE.
FOR ONCE, WE AGREE WITH ONE ANOTHER.

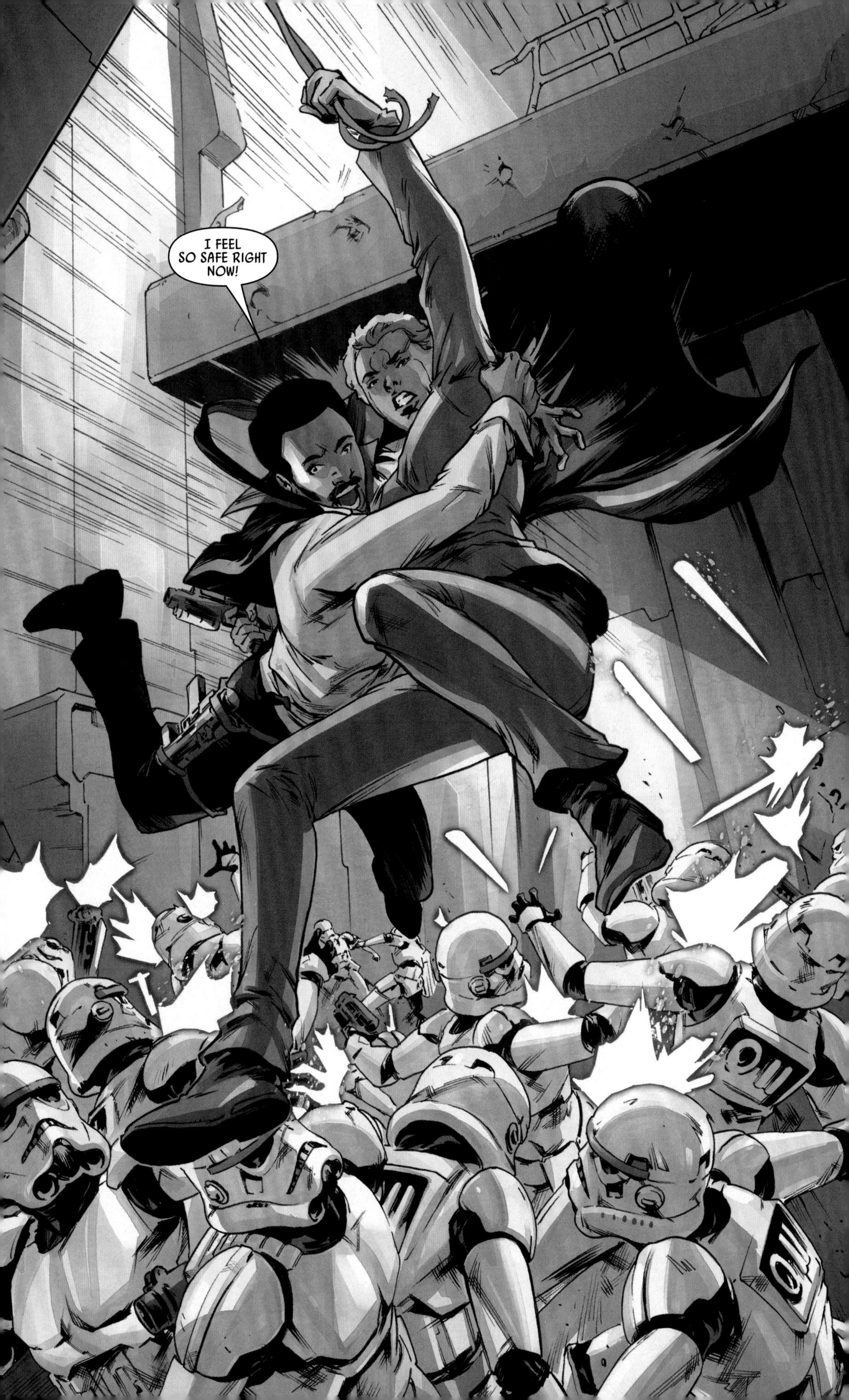
I FEEL SO SAFE RIGHT NOW!

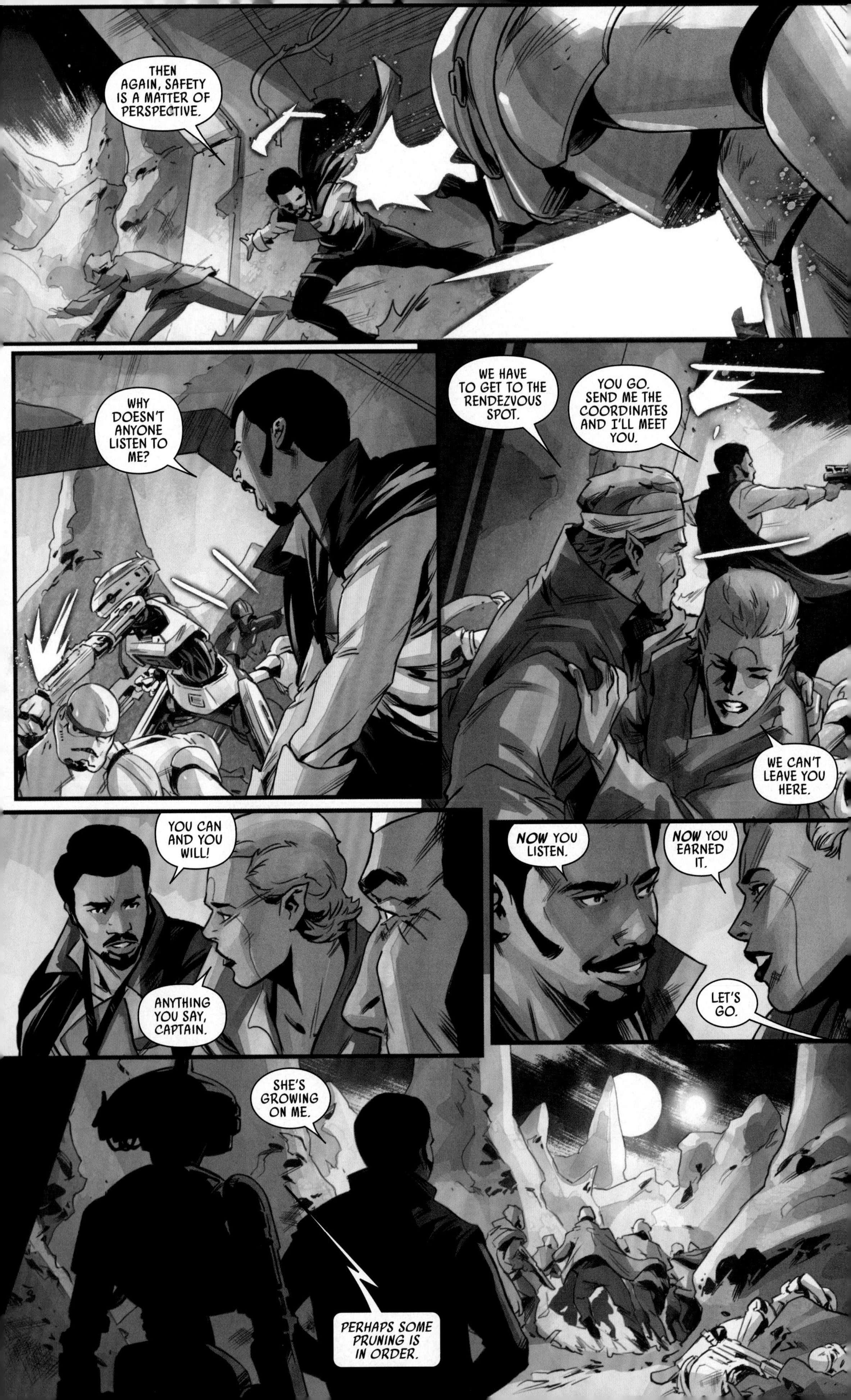
THEN AGAIN, SAFETY IS A MATTER OF PERSPECTIVE.
WHY DOESN'T ANYONE LISTEN TO ME?
WE HAVE TO GET TO THE RENDEZVOUS SPOT.
YOU GO. SEND ME THE COORDINATES AND I'LL MEET YOU.
WE CAN'T LEAVE YOU HERE.
YOU CAN AND YOU WILL!
ANYTHING YOU SAY, CAPTAIN.
NOW YOU LISTEN.
NOW YOU EARNED IT.
LET'S GO.
SHE'S GROWING ON ME.
PERHAPS SOME PRUNING IS IN ORDER.

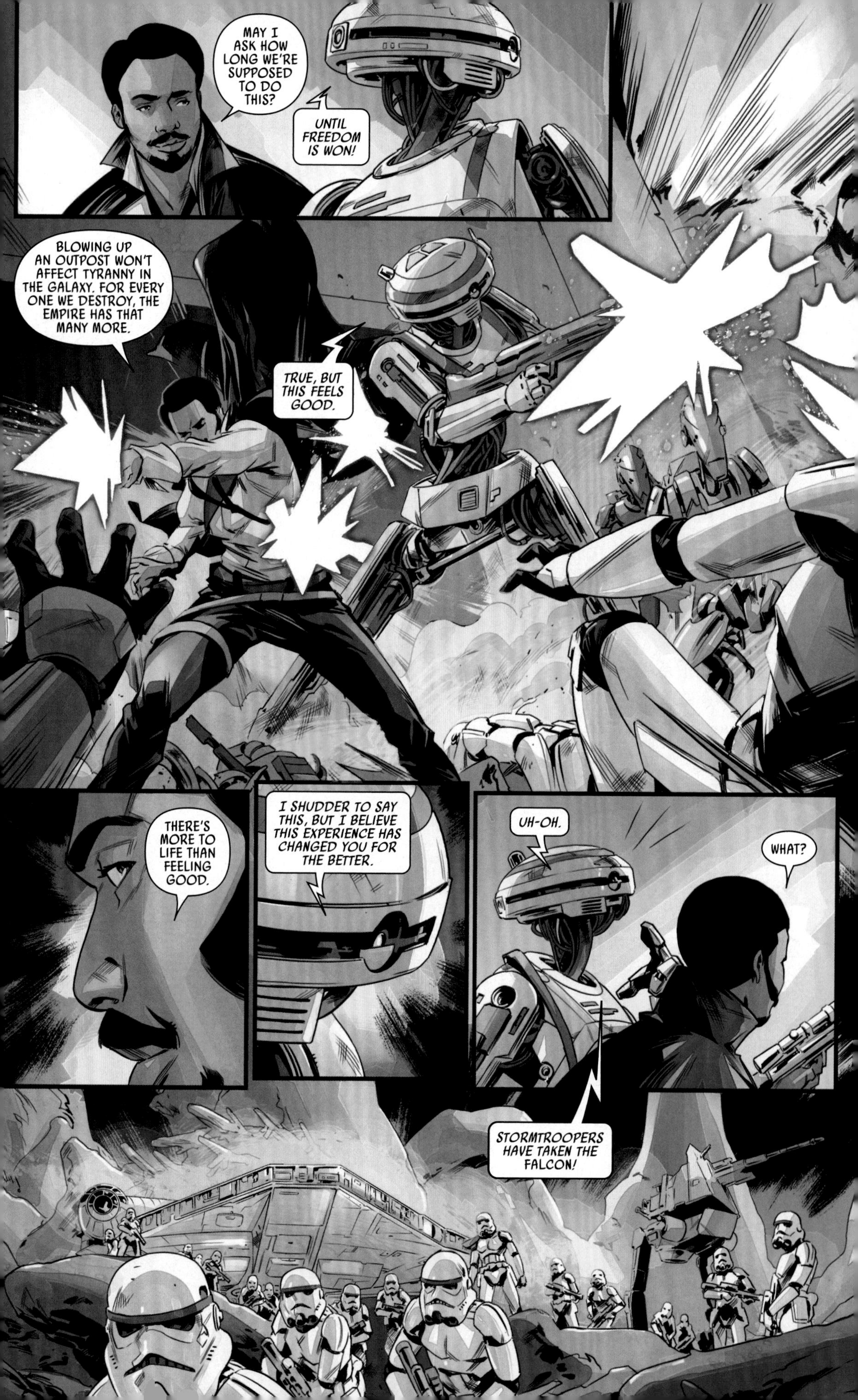
MAY I ASK HOW LONG WE'RE SUPPOSED TO DO THIS?
UNTIL FREEDOM IS WON!
BLOWING UP AN OUTPOST WON'T AFFECT TYRANNY IN THE GALAXY. FOR EVERY ONE WE DESTROY, THE EMPIRE HAS THAT MANY MORE.
TRUE, BUT THIS FEELS GOOD.
THERE'S MORE TO LIFE THAN FEELING GOOD.
I SHUDDER TO SAY THIS, BUT I BELIEVE THIS EXPERIENCE HAS CHANGED YOU FOR THE BETTER.
UH-OH.
WHAT?
STORMTROOPERS HAVE TAKEN THE FALCON!

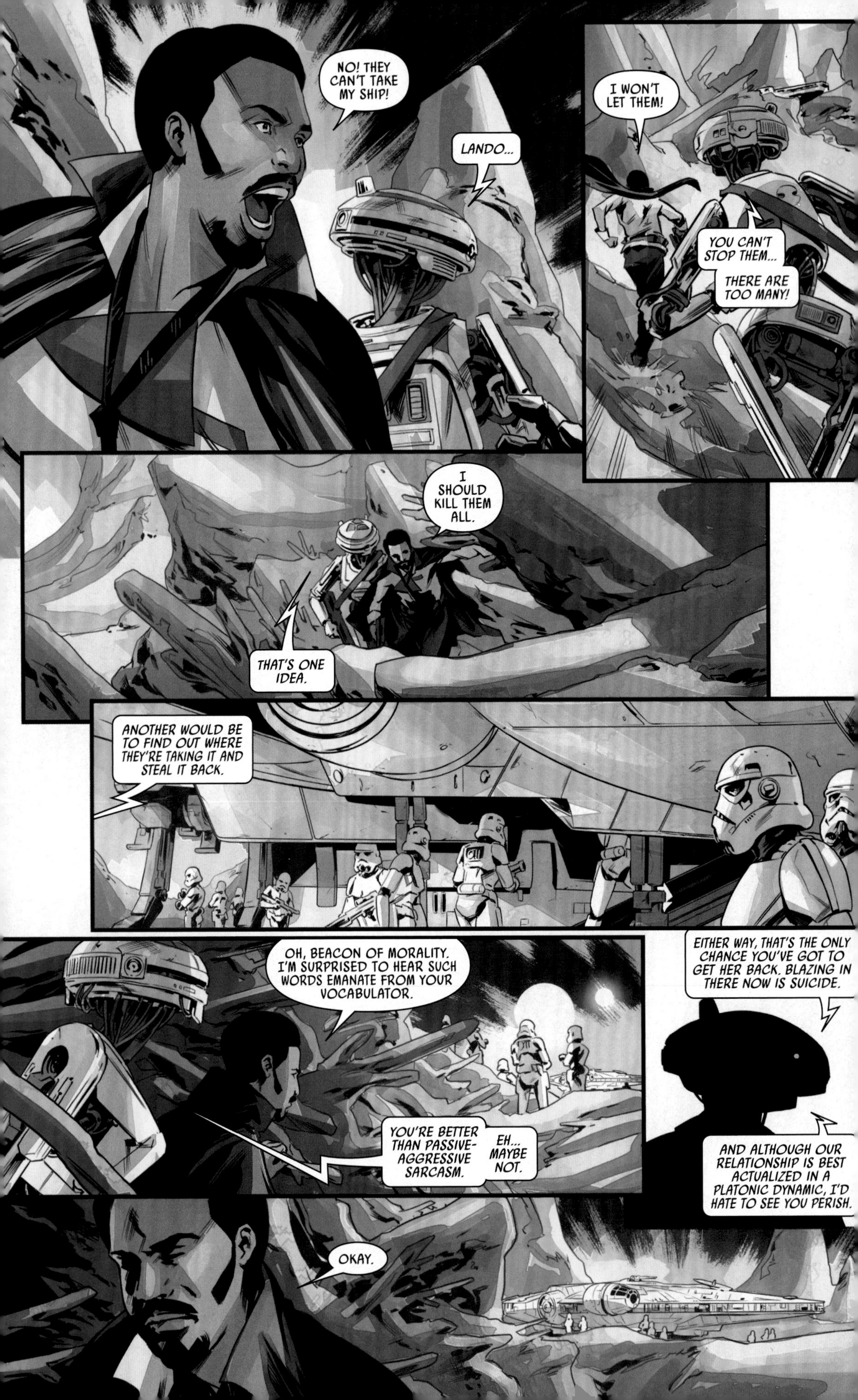
NO! THEY CAN'T TAKE MY SHIP!
LANDO...
I WON'T LET THEM!
YOU CAN'T STOP THEM...
THERE ARE TOO MANY!
I SHOULD KILL THEM ALL.
THAT'S ONE IDEA.
ANOTHER WOULD BE TO FIND OUT WHERE THEY'RE TAKING IT AND STEAL IT BACK.
OH, BEACON OF MORALITY. I'M SURPRISED TO HEAR SUCH WORDS EMANATE FROM YOUR VOCABULATOR.
YOU'RE BETTER THAN PASSIVE-AGGRESSIVE SARCASM.
EH... MAYBE NOT.
EITHER WAY, THAT'S THE ONLY CHANCE YOU'VE GOT TO GET HER BACK. BLAZING IN THERE NOW IS SUICIDE.
AND ALTHOUGH OUR RELATIONSHIP IS BEST ACTUALIZED IN A PLATONIC DYNAMIC, I'D HATE TO SEE YOU PERISH.
OKAY.

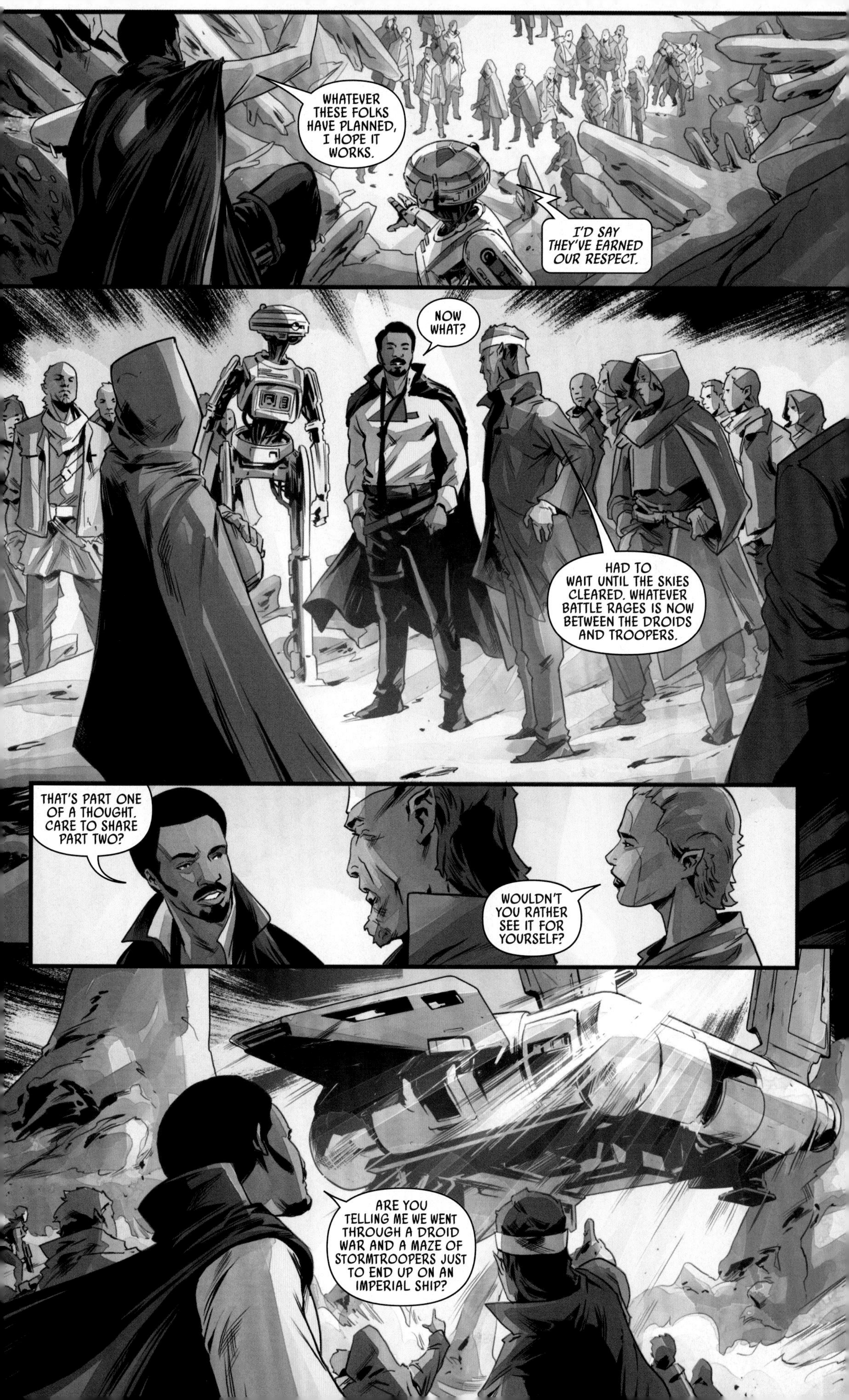
WHATEVER THESE FOLKS HAVE PLANNED, I HOPE IT WORKS.
I'D SAY THEY'VE EARNED OUR RESPECT.
NOW WHAT?
HAD TO WAIT UNTIL THE SKIES CLEARED. WHATEVER BATTLE RAGES IS NOW BETWEEN THE DROIDS AND TROOPERS.
THAT'S PART ONE OF A THOUGHT. CARE TO SHARE PART TWO?
WOULDN'T YOU RATHER SEE IT FOR YOURSELF?
ARE YOU TELLING ME WE WENT THROUGH A DROID WAR AND A MAZE OF STORMTROOPERS JUST TO END UP ON AN IMPERIAL SHIP?

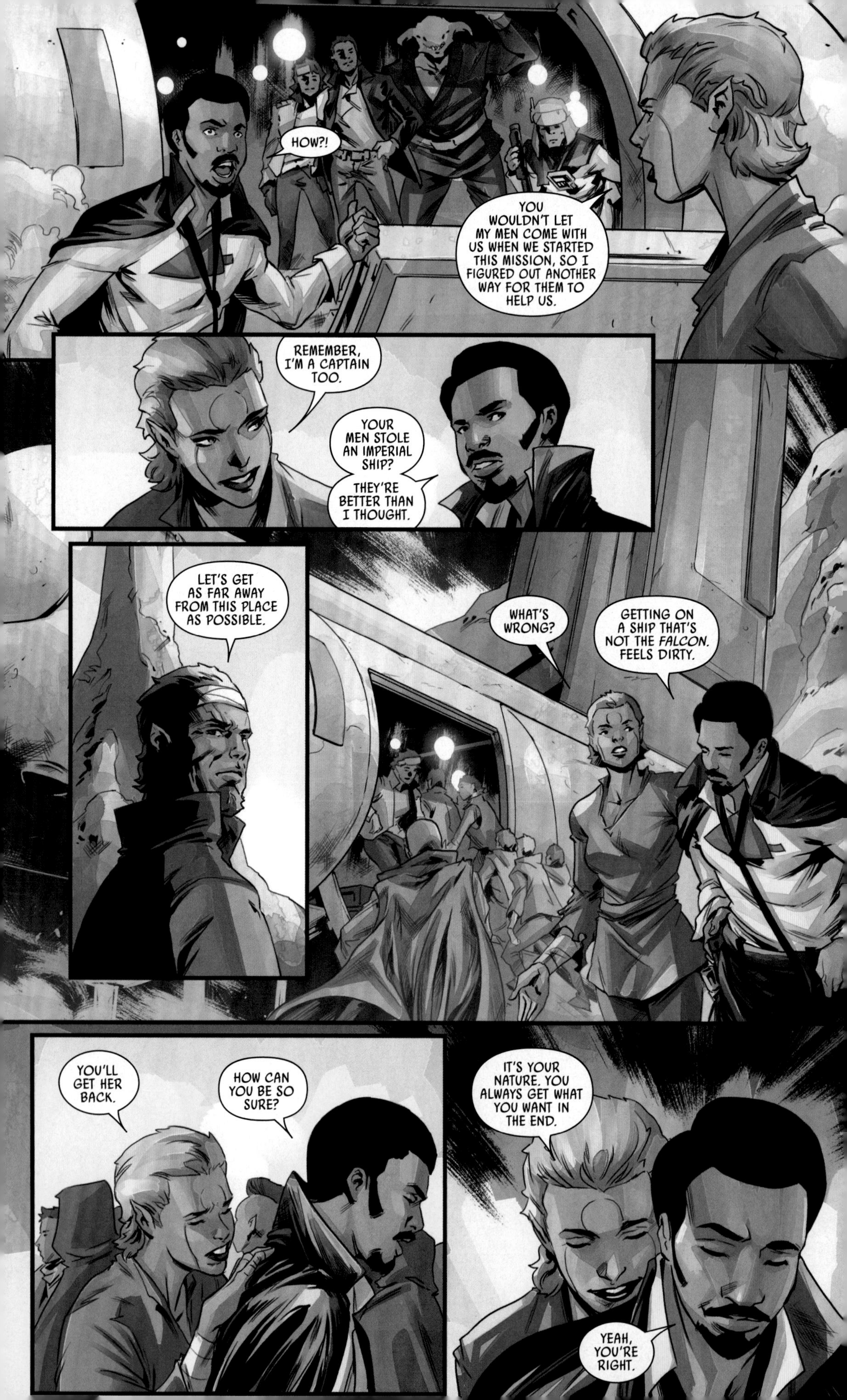
HOW?!
YOU WOULDN'T LET MY MEN COME WITH US WHEN WE STARTED THIS MISSION, SO I FIGURED OUT ANOTHER WAY FOR THEM TO HELP US.
REMEMBER, I'M A CAPTAIN TOO.
YOUR MEN STOLE AN IMPERIAL SHIP?
THEY'RE BETTER THAN I THOUGHT.
LET'S GET AS FAR AWAY FROM THIS PLACE AS POSSIBLE.
WHAT'S WRONG?
GETTING ON A SHIP THAT'S NOT THE FALCON. FEELS DIRTY.
YOU'LL GET HER BACK.
HOW CAN YOU BE SO SURE?
IT'S YOUR NATURE. YOU ALWAYS GET WHAT YOU WANT IN THE END.
YEAH, YOU'RE RIGHT.

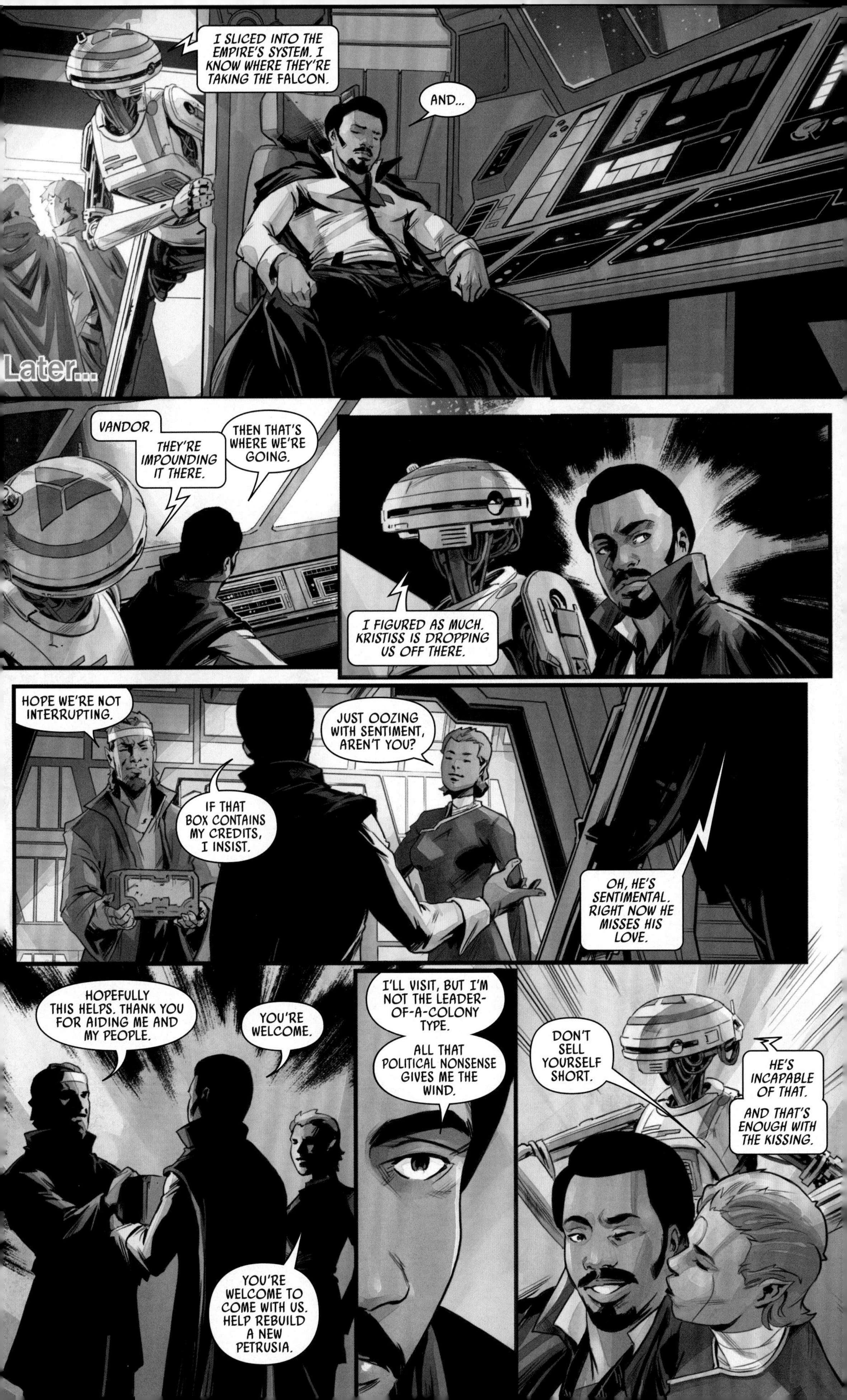

I SLICED INTO THE EMPIRE'S SYSTEM. I KNOW WHERE THEY'RE TAKING THE FALCON.
AND...
Later...
VANDOR.
THEY'RE IMPOUNDING IT THERE.
THEN THAT'S WHERE WE'RE GOING.
I FIGURED AS MUCH. KRISTISS IS DROPPING US OFF THERE.
HOPE WE'RE NOT INTERRUPTING.
IF THAT BOX CONTAINS MY CREDITS, I INSIST.
JUST OOZING WITH SENTIMENT, AREN'T YOU?
OH, HE'S SENTIMENTAL. RIGHT NOW HE MISSES HIS LOVE.
HOPEFULLY THIS HELPS. THANK YOU FOR AIDING ME AND MY PEOPLE.
YOU'RE WELCOME.
YOU'RE WELCOME TO COME WITH US. HELP REBUILD A NEW PETRUSIA.
I'LL VISIT, BUT I'M NOT THE LEADER-OF-A-COLONY TYPE.
ALL THAT POLITICAL NONSENSE GIVES ME THE WIND.
DON'T SELL YOURSELF SHORT.
HE'S INCAPABLE OF THAT.
AND THAT'S ENOUGH WITH THE KISSING.

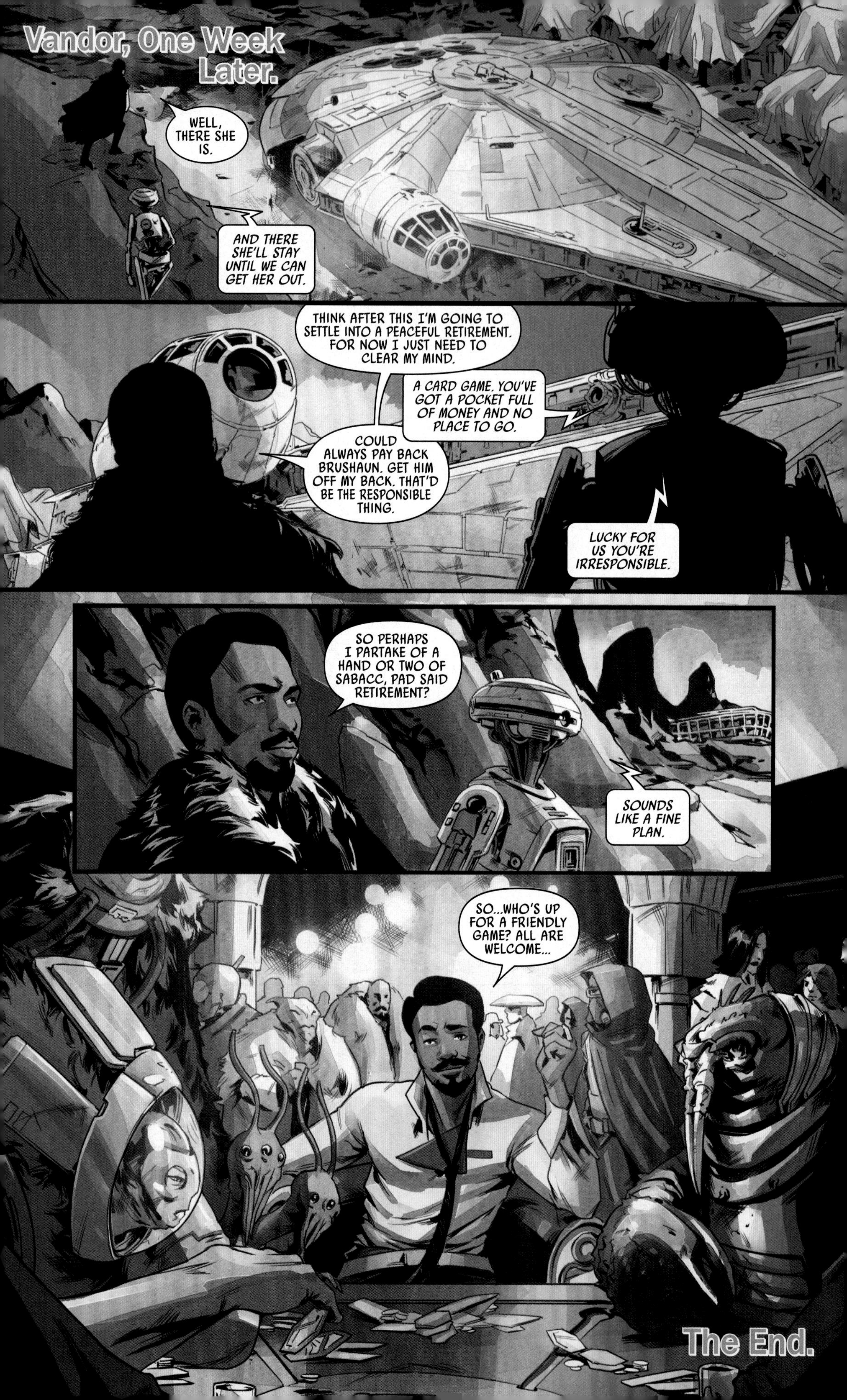
Vandor, One Week Later.
WELL, THERE SHE IS.
AND THERE SHE'LL STAY UNTIL WE CAN GET HER OUT.
THINK AFTER THIS I'M GOING TO SETTLE INTO A PEACEFUL RETIREMENT. FOR NOW I JUST NEED TO CLEAR MY MIND.
A CARD GAME. YOU'VE GOT A POCKET FULL OF MONEY AND NO PLACE TO GO.
COULD ALWAYS PAY BACK BRUSHAUN. GET HIM OFF MY BACK. THAT'D BE THE RESPONSIBLE THING.
LUCKY FOR US YOU'RE IRRESPONSIBLE.
SO PERHAPS I PARTAKE OF A HAND OR TWO OF SABACC, PAD SAID RETIREMENT?
SOUNDS LIKE A FINE PLAN.
SO...WHO'S UP FOR A FRIENDLY GAME? ALL ARE WELCOME...
The End.

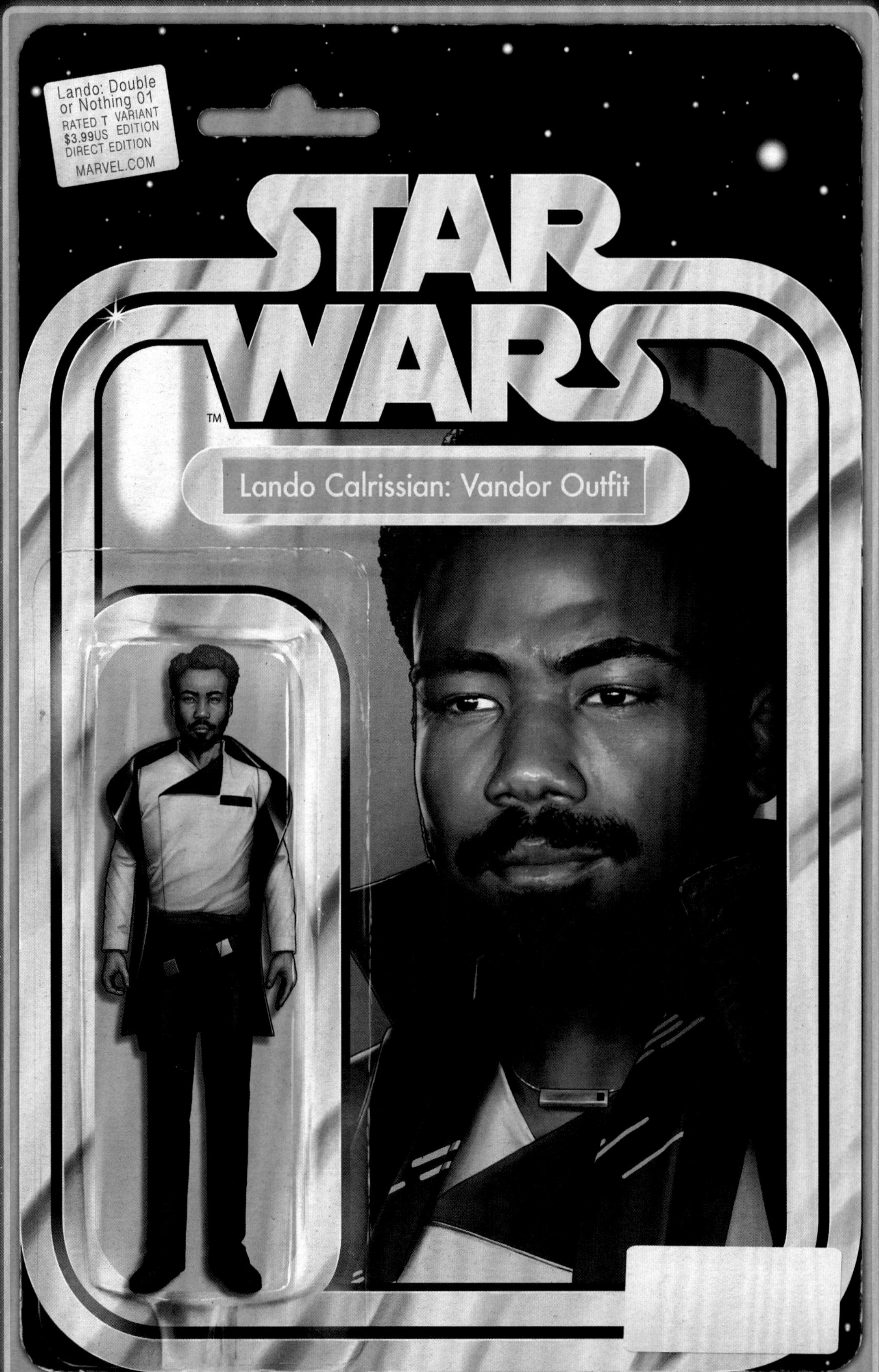
Lando: Double or Nothing 01
RATED T VARIANT
$3.99US EDITION
DIRECT EDITION
MARVEL.COM
STAR WARS™
Lando Calrissian: Vandor Outfit

***STAR WARS: LANDO — DOUBLE OR NOTHING* 1 Action Figure Variant by**
JOHN TYLER CHRISTOPHER

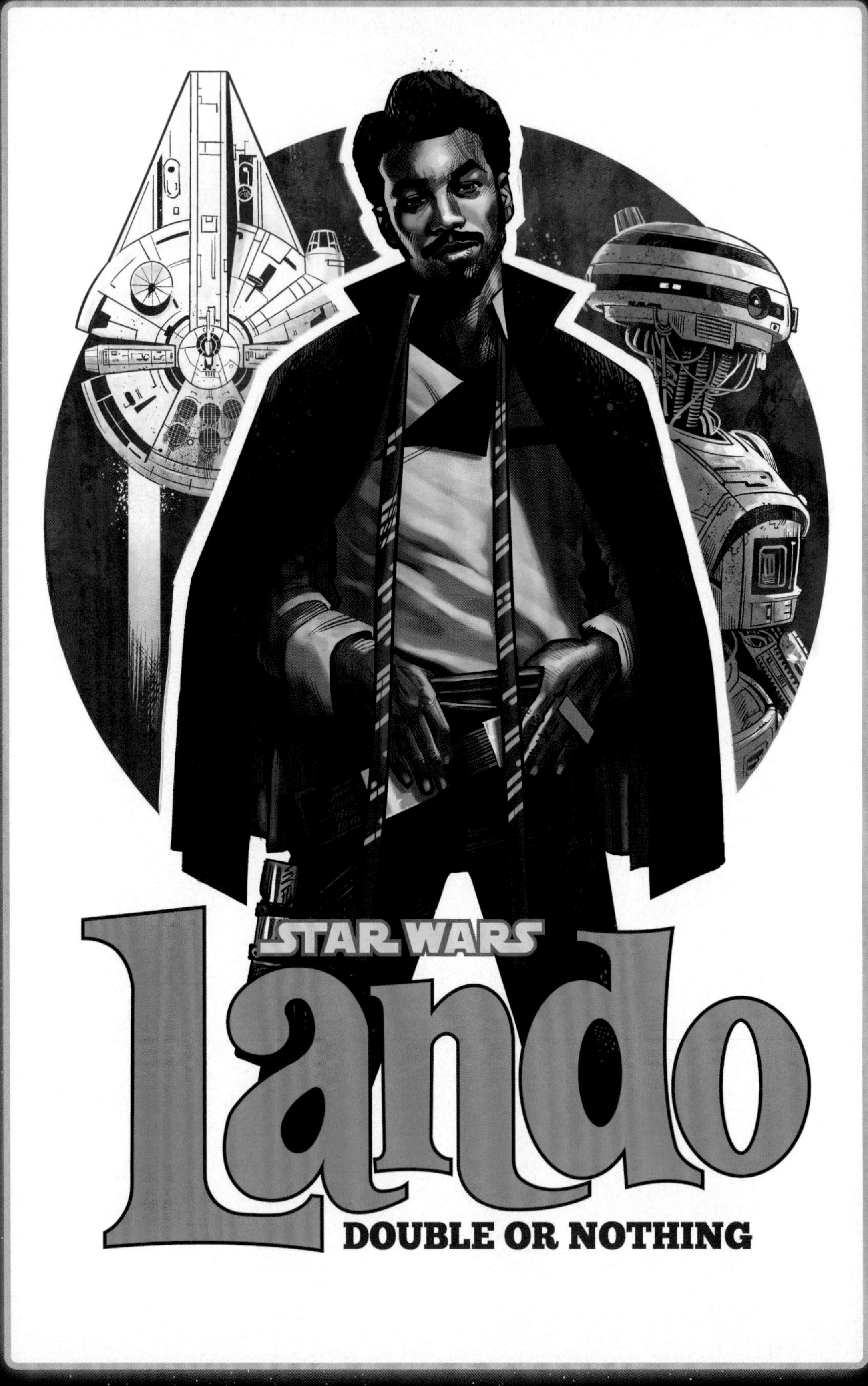
STAR WARS
lando
DOUBLE OR NOTHING

***STAR WARS: LANDO — DOUBLE OR NOTHING* 2 Variant by**
CAMERON STEWART

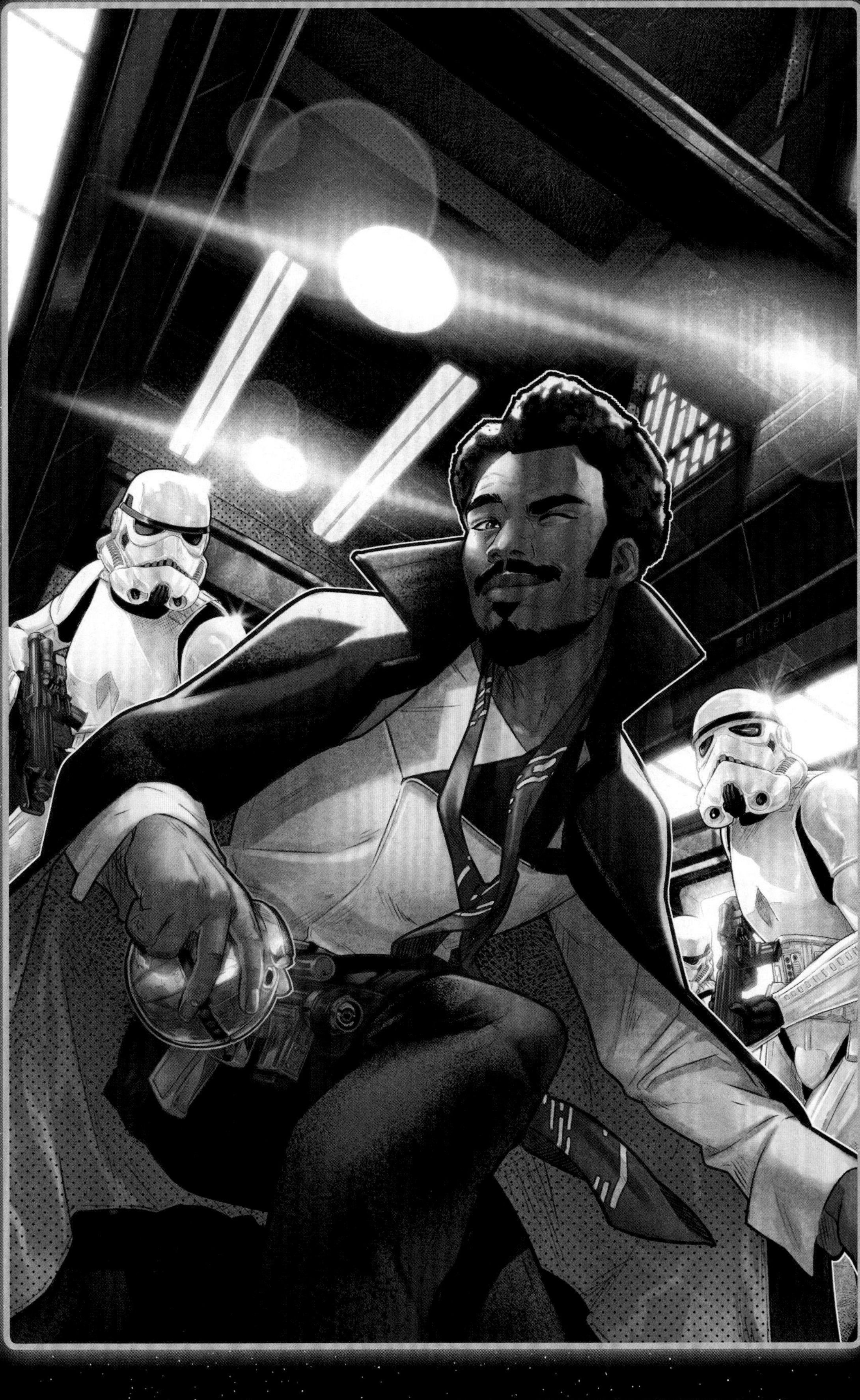

STAR WARS: LANDO — DOUBLE OR NOTHING 3 Variant by
JAMAL CAMPBELL

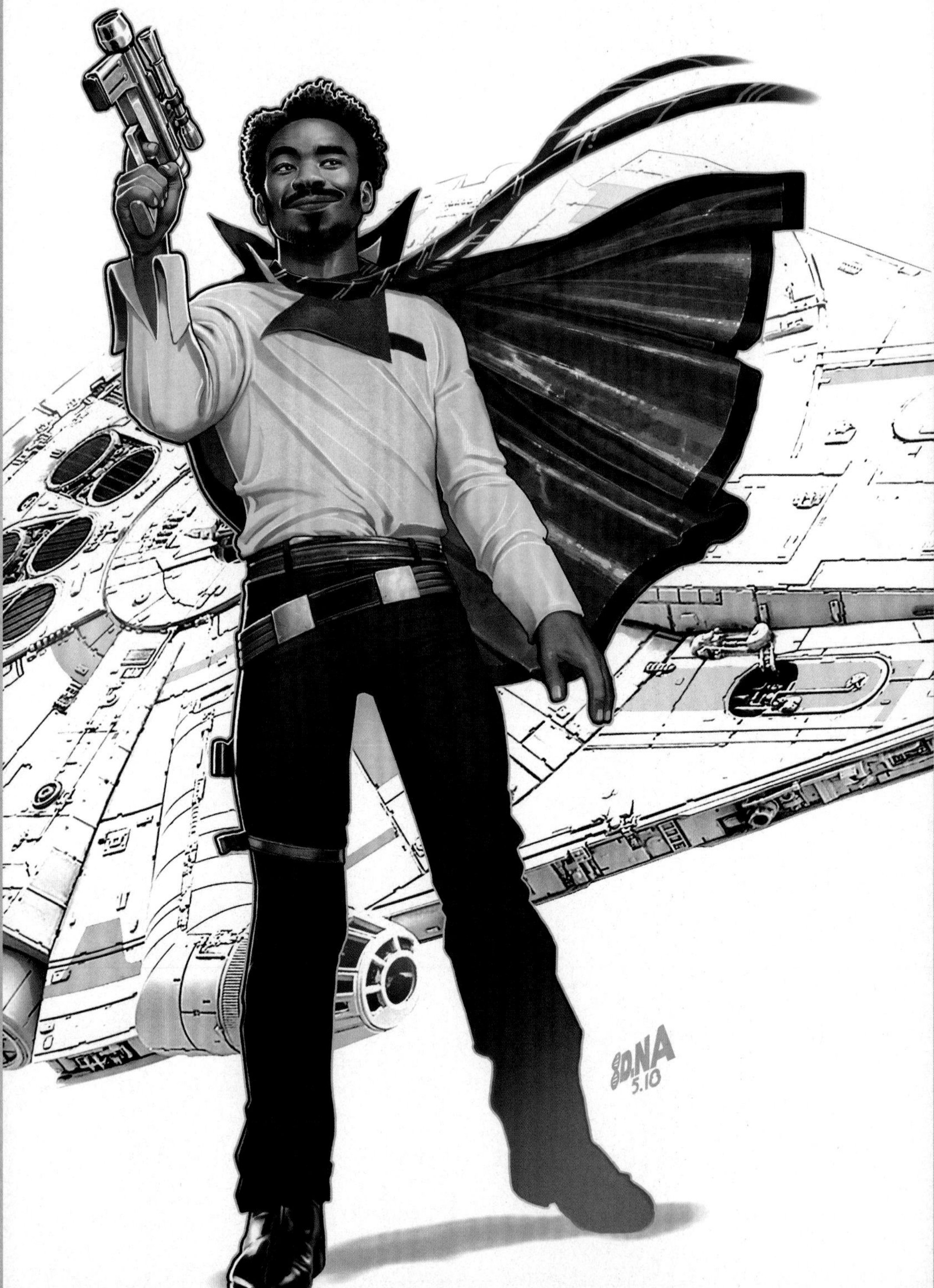
D.NA

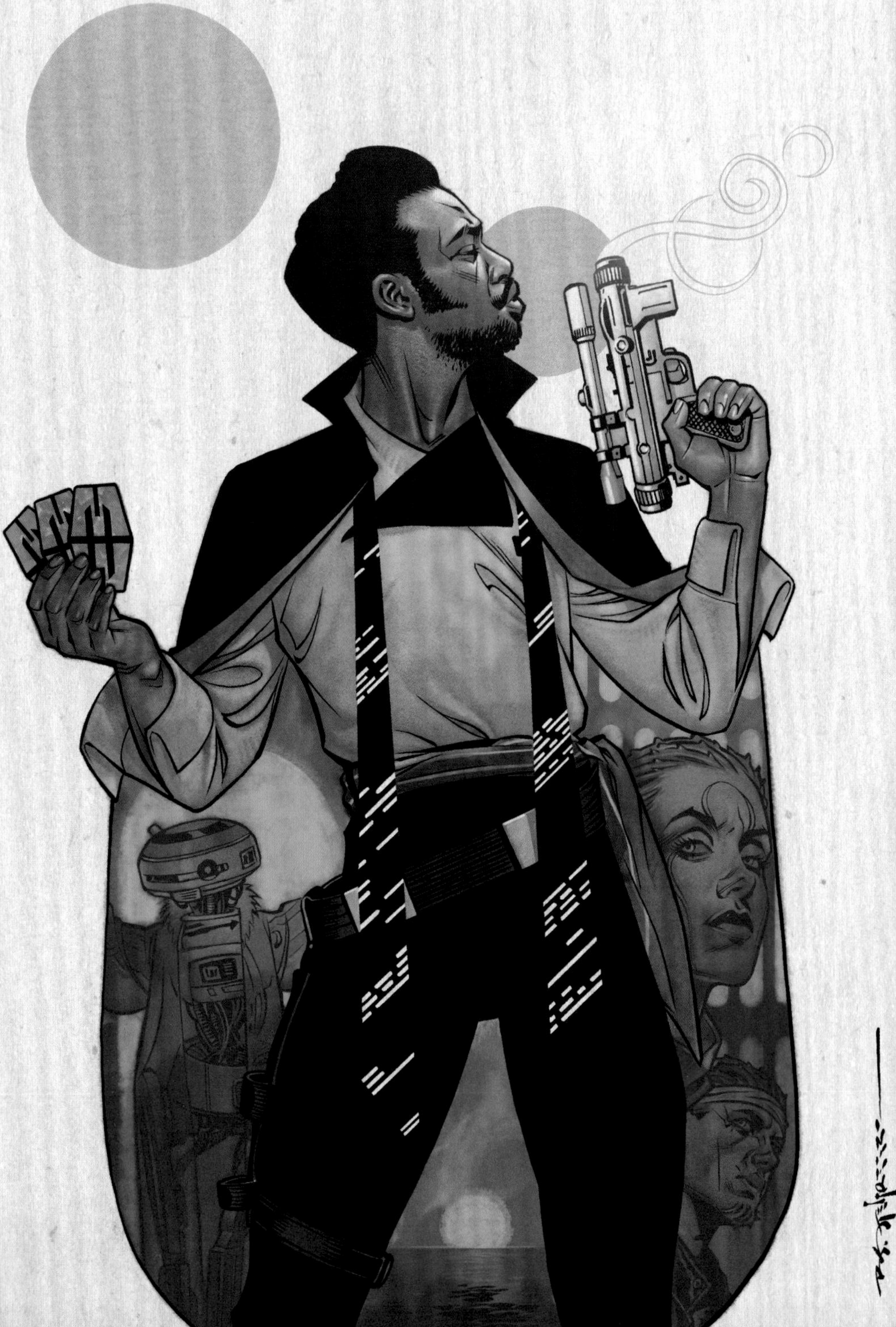

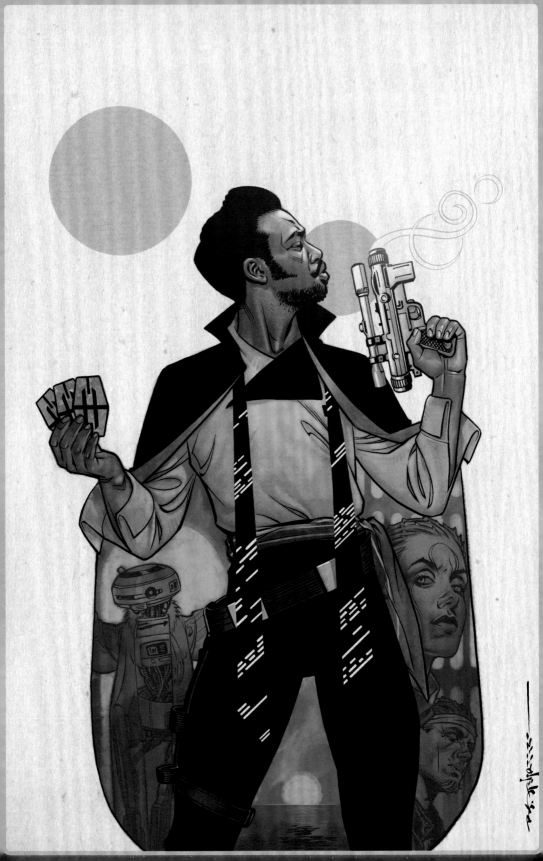

CHARACTERS YOU KNOW.
STORIES YOU DON'T.

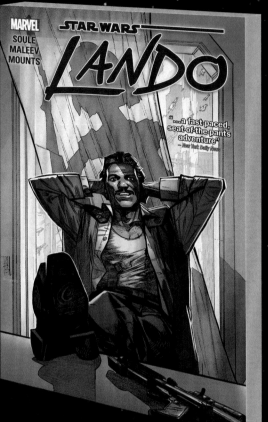

STAR WARS: LANDO TPB
978-0-7851-9319-7 • $16.99

STAR WARS: CHEWBACCA TPB
978-0-7851-9320-3 • $16.99

ON SALE NOW
IN PRINT & DIGITAL WHEREVER BOOKS ARE SOLD.

HAN AND CHEWIE IN A RACE AGAINST TIME, THE EMPIRE AND THE FASTEST SHIPS IN THE GALAXY!

MARVEL

LIU
BROOKS
AARON
IMMONEN

STAR WARS

HAN SOLO

"Mark Brooks is an excellent illustrator... every page is a winner in this book."
— *SciFiPulse.net*

STAR WARS: **HAN SOLO HC**
978-1302912109

ON SALE NOW

AVAILABLE IN PRINT AND DIGITAL WHEREVER BOOKS ARE SOLD

TO FIND A COMIC SHOP NEAR YOU, VISIT COMICSHOPLOCATOR.COM

YOU LOVE COLORING. WE KNOW.

COLOR YOUR OWN
STAR WARS
HAN SOLO
MARVEL

COLOR YOUR OWN *STAR WARS:* HAN SOLO
978-1302912093

ON SALE NOW

AVAILABLE IN PRINT AND DIGITAL WHEREVER BOOKS ARE SOLD

TO FIND A COMIC SHOP NEAR YOU, VISIT COMICSHOPLOCATOR.COM

MARVEL Disney LUCASFILM